Witchcraft
a Mystery
Tradition

About the Author

Raven Grimassi is a Neopagan scholar and award-winning author of over twelve books on Witchcraft, Wicca, and Neopaganism. He is a member of the American Folklore Society and is co-founder and co-director of the College of the Crossroads.

Raven's background includes training in the Rosicrucian Order as well as the study of the Kabbalah through the First Temple of Tifareth under Lady Sara Cunningham. His early magickal career began in the late 1960s and involved the study of works by Franz Bardon, Éliphas Lévi, William Barrett, Dion Fortune, William Gray, William Butler, and Israel Regardie.

Raven was the directing Elder of the tradition of Arician Witchcraft, and together with his wife, Stephanie Taylor, he developed a complete teaching system known as Ash, Birch, and Willow. This system was the culmination of over thirty-five years of study and practice in the magickal and spiritual traditions of the indigenous people of pre-Christian Europe.

Witchcraft
a Mystery
Tradition

Raven Grimassi

Chicago, Illinois

Paperback ISBN: 978-1-959883-59-3
Library of Congress Control Number on file.

Typesetting by Mads Oliver.
Editing by Becca Fleming.

Published by:
Crossed Crow Books, LLC
6934 N Glenwood Ave, Suite C
Chicago, IL 60626
www.crossedcrowbooks.com

Printed in the United States of America.
IBI

Contents

Preface

The material you are about to read is both ancient and new. It is ancient in the sense that it presents themes of great antiquity that are rooted in pre-Christian European concepts. It is new in the sense that the material is set within the template of popular modern Witchcraft. The motif is focused primarily upon a Celtic perspective, but the material also includes a comparison of Aegean/Mediterranean myths, concepts, and deities.

The modern presentation is not meant to indicate that the religion of Witchcraft, as presented in this book, is of an exclusive contemporary makeup. My purpose in providing the material is to demonstrate the opposite, that the core themes within Witchcraft (The Old Religion) are quite ancient and of authentic lineage. It is my personal belief and experience that Witchcraft is a religion that has evolved over countless centuries (as opposed to a modern construction). The Old Religion has naturally adapted and adopted new elements over the course of time. Its core essence, however, remains true to its distant origins.

Over the course of time, Witchcraft has absorbed various elements from a variety of sources. Magickal systems from the Middle Ages and Renaissance contributed various symbols and concepts. Witchcraft also adopted the terminology of Eastern Mysticism, and we now find such words as chakras, mudras, and so forth. However, the essential concepts represented in these elements are not foreign to Witchcraft as a magickal or mystical system. The modifications and adaptations we find in modern Witchcraft are simply footprints continuing in the sands of time.

The Mystery Tradition presented in this book contains the core elements that represent the commonality found in older forms of Witchcraft that predate Gardnerian Wicca or Witchcraft. Therefore, the Mysteries that are presented in the following chapters are applicable to any system or tradition of Witchcraft. This allows modern Witches to practice in accordance with the essential ways of their ancestors, which have withstood the test of time.

The material that is covered in this book is ideal for priests and priestesses of Witchcraft or Wicca as it provides a sound foundation rooted in the core themes of the Old Religion. These themes are revealed through myth and legend, for therein are contained the inner mechanisms that operate the Mysteries of Witchcraft. To further aid the priest and priestess, the book presents a cohesive and interconnected mythology of Witchcraft that defines the role of various deities and explains how they interact. This will aid in the formulation and construction of ritual themes as well as provide additional training material for students.

In considering the scope of this book, the needs of the isolated solitary Witch were of great importance to me. There are many solitary Witches who may not have the means of finding an experienced teacher or of becoming initiated. Their resources and alternatives to date have been very limited, relegated primarily to published materials.

The vast majority of modern published books on Witchcraft are either very basic or focused on modern systems, methods, and constructions. Because they are self-styled methods, they tend to disengage from the archetypal models, which are rooted in the collective consciousness and "soul memory." Therefore, they lack commonality, and thus, they promote a separated individuality. Where this becomes a problem is that what works well and uniquely for the individual tends to not meet the needs of the many. This makes it impossible for the solitary practitioner to grow in a guided method that reflects the core commonality that empowers the ways of Witchcraft.

One of the primary purposes of this book is to present material from deeper sources rooted in older ways. For it is the roots of a tree that nourish it and fix its place in time and purpose. The roots represent the commonality that has come together over the ages to form the essence and the foundation of Witchcraft. It is this root core that enlivens the Old Religion, and through it flows the life that is ever-ancient and ever-new.

This book is an attempt to connect the reader to the root sources. In so doing, I have included concepts, connections, and alignments here that have never before appeared in public writings. It is my hope that what is revealed in this book will guide the reader to new insights and additional signposts.

Introduction

When we think of Mysteries and things of a mystical nature, what image arises? It is not uncommon to imagine a magickal mist floating upon the water, or perhaps to think of soft whispers drifting amidst the trees of a strange forest. Things that are veiled, half seen or in shadow, speak of something hidden and yet known to some part of us that wishes to deny it.

It is perhaps for this reason that humankind turned to myths and legends in order to communicate a reality that is indiscernible to the conscious mind. Whether the problem of conscious acceptance is one of choice, or more related to the human condition, is a topic beyond the intended scope of this book.

The purpose of this book is to present what is shrouded in mist and veiled in secret. It is about the importance of myth and legend as a mystical function within the religious and spiritual tradition of Witchcraft. The function of the mythos within Witchcraft is to reconcile what the conscious mind cannot accept with what the subconscious mind cannot ignore.

It is an ancient Mystery Teaching that enlightenment is fifty percent of what is said and fifty percent of the context in which the words are spoken. A person could be presented with all the Mystery Teachings set before them at once and still not understand their significance. This is because the context is not there to make the connections.

The material in this book has been designed to provide both the teachings and the connections. However, the approach is not one of spoon-feeding the reader. Instead, the material is designed to intrigue the reader enough to draw them further down the path of exploration. It is self-discovery with a directed nudge.

There is an old saying that "no mystery is closed to an open mind." In order to understand the Mysteries, you must want to do so. The journey is not one of the intellect, it is instead a journey of the soul. The truths of the Mysteries are felt before they can be seen. They are seen before they can be discerned, and must then be discerned without rationalization.

In many faery legends, a mortal reaches for faery gold only to have it turn to dust. Herein resides the mystery, for you must not take from the Mysteries. You may only receive what comes to you for your efforts. Reach for it, and it will surely fade between your fingers. Then you will come away believing it was never there to begin with. But search for it with an open heart and a receptive mind, and it will be placed whole and lasting into your hands.

It is the way of the Mystery Teachings that you can only learn what it is you are prepared to know. This is why they have been preserved in myth and legend. In this way, you can revisit the mystical realms and characters of myth and legend in your studies. Each journey will reveal more of what was veiled, and so I encourage you to read back over the teachings from time to time. No matter how experienced you feel you may be, there is always something yet to be revealed. After over thirty years of practicing Witchcraft, this is something I realize every day.

I prepared and designed this book in the Mystery Tradition style, and one reading of it will not deliver all that it has to offer. If your approach to this material is feigned, then you will find nothing but a mirror where you will never see beyond yourself. If you enter the road to the Mysteries with respect and in earnest, then you will see with the eyes of the Spirit. Only such eyes can peer into the ancient mist and see through to the Otherworld.

When I began this project, I set a statue of the goddess Ceres above the monitor of my computer. Ceres is the Goddess of the Mysteries and she is my patroness on whose festival day I was born. Before writing each chapter of this book, I asked Ceres, "What shall be written today?" The result is this book you now have before you.

For my part, I wanted to open the way of the well-worn path that leads to the gateway of the Mysteries. I also wanted to leave a key under the mat and a map of what awaits beyond the threshold. There are no false trails and no dead ends on this map. When the road leads back upon itself, please know that it was intentional. When you wander off the path and into a faery thicket, please trust that the way out is part of the teaching.

The material in this book is drawn from very old sources rooted in pre-Christian beliefs and practices. It represents a long-standing tradition of European Witchcraft and occult concepts and tenets. However, in this book, I have used the common modern Craft structure (focused essentially on the Celtic theme) through which to convey the inner teachings of Witchcraft as a Mystery Tradition. Familiarity is an effective setting in which to communicate the uncommon or unknown.

In the forthcoming chapters of this book, you will find that some material is repeated here and there in other chapters. Please know that this is not "filler" material, nor is the material repeated verbatim. When conveying Mystery Teachings, it is necessary at times to repeat a concept in a different context. Sometimes it is also necessary to reaffirm various connections at key points for the reader.

The old axiom states: "Tell them what you're going to tell them, tell them, and then tell them what you've told them." It's not meant to be condescending nor dismissive of the intelligence of the reader. Instead, it is the extra effort a teacher applies in order to honor the time that a student invests toward learning.

Throughout the course of this book, I have carefully laid out the foundation of the Mystery Teachings and the primary elements around which they have been established. In order to help the reader understand the teachings and their connections, I have provided the cultural and mythical traditions in which the Mysteries are rooted. This involved looking at the oldest references in ancient literature to times that predate them and the authors.

The initial problem was that the modern Craft structure incorporates sabbat themes that do not (for the most part) belong to one singular cultural expression. This makes it difficult to present a cohesive and culturally linked mythos. One example is the inclusion of Ostara in a Celtic Wheel of the Year. The other problem is the naming of the autumn equinox after Mabon, a very minor character in Celtic legend. There is no cohesive mythos worthy of focusing an entire sabbat festival on this particularly obscure character.

The task became how to take the ancient core-rooted teachings of the old structure of Witchcraft and apply this to the new model of modern Witchcraft. The modern system has been largely modified over many decades in order to appeal to a contemporary audience. This made it difficult to simply overlay the old system atop the new one and then join the design together.

The fact that what we actually know about Celtic Pagan beliefs is fragmented and disjointed made it difficult to trust the modern reconstruction as a reliable model to work with. This was frustrating because the similarities and commonalities between old Witchcraft and new Witchcraft definitely spoke to an underlying authenticity of rootedness in the deep past. It was this that allowed me to trust that the two systems were first cousins if not direct siblings.

Examining the modern sabbats and the commonly associated deities, I found it puzzling that they appeared to lack a true cohesive interconnected storyline. Unlike the older system, the new seemed to lack a defined Goddess and God pair whose mythos carried them both individually and jointly through the sabbats, connecting to each other and the seasonal theme in general. In the modern model, the old Mystery themes were certainly discernable but the deities seemed to disappear here and there from the sabbat structure only to be curiously replaced by other characters in a "one-time appearance." At times, this seemed to be odd, if not wholly contrived.

I took hope that beneath the surface, the answers and old connections would be found and I began to dissect each modern sabbat in order to understand such things as why obscure deities held enough importance to have a sabbat named after them. I quickly discovered that the tangled threads of many introduced cultures would have to be untangled if a core mythos was to be recovered. Roman influence was of particular importance to me because many ancient Roman writings refer to Celtic deities and religious practices.

Next, I turned my attention to a comparison of Celtic and Aegean/ Mediterranean myths and legends. In particular, I focused on gods and goddesses that are associated with the sabbats in modern Witchcraft. From there, I began examining the lore surrounding each season. My goal was to construct, for a modern audience, a cohesive mythos using the popular Celtic pantheon normally appearing in modern writings. What I sought was a continuing thread running through each sabbat that clearly connected each deity and seasonal theme.

I found it useful to examine other cultural traditions of Witchcraft in an attempt to explore the commonality that exists at the core. A commonality, I felt, would provide a solid foundation and help retain the integrity of the work. Italian Witchcraft was particularly helpful due to its antiquity and the relatively minimal fragmentation of the tradition. I then began a careful comparison of Celtic myths and legends with those from the Aegean/Mediterranean region, focusing on seasonal themes, divisions of the year, and Underworld or Otherworld explorations.

Next, I focused on applying the preexisting Mystery themes of pre-Christian European Pagan cultures to the myths and legends of modern Witchcraft. This included examining the etymology of each deity and comparing this culture by culture. In addition, I used the comparison of specific Celtic deities with Roman and Greek deities that were originally equated or associated in classic literature. Here, I compared each myth, symbol, setting, and theme for confirmation of an authentic identification between one deity and another.

Once the jigsaw pieces of the puzzle appeared to indeed belong to the same picture, I began assembling and connecting them. In doing so, I believe I was successful in correcting some common errors that arose and became accepted within the Craft community, a process that began in the 1960s and accelerated in the 1980s. The result of this research and repair comprises a good portion of the book.

It is important to note, however, that this is only the body of the book. The soul of the book is what animates the teachings. This is not a spell book or a "how to" book of techniques and exercises. It is instead a book of journey and exploration. It is the experience within your spirit of what you are about to read that is the most important part of the book. What you choose to do with what you have learned will be the most important part of this spiritual journey.

It has been a sincere effort on my part to try and match the effort now required by you who wish to study the Inner Mysteries. In some regards, this is the most difficult and challenging book I've yet to write. It was an important work to undertake because there are many sincere seekers whose circumstances are such that they may never find a teacher or receive initiation. This is a theme that I see in my reader mail and find in people I meet across the country in my many travels as an author.

It is my sincere hope that the material in this book will serve your needs and enrich your understanding and practice of Witchcraft. May Ceres, the Goddess of the Mysteries, look with favor upon your quest.

CHAPTER ONE

Witchcraft & The
Old World

The concepts, beliefs, and practices of modern Witchcraft are rooted in ancient European Paganism. Witchcraft, as it exists today, is a religion and magickal system that has evolved over countless centuries. Although its basic foundational concepts appear in those of the Neolithic era, a variety of ideas and notions particular to the following periods have also influenced it. These influences include the Classical period, Middle Ages, Renaissance, nineteenth-century Romantic era, and the modern Wicca movement that arose in the mid-twentieth century.

To understand the core essence of Witchcraft, we must look to a time before the rise of Christianity, when the beliefs and practices of ancient Europe were unaltered by imported alien concepts. Despite the fact that European Pagans were diverse in their beliefs and practices, there is a core commonality that speaks of something older upon which all were based. Was there once a central primitive religion to explain the similarities, or are we simply looking at the ways humankind itself commonly conceives of religious and ritual elements?

When considering prehistoric beliefs, we are left with a great deal of speculation because we have no writings upon which to formulate our understanding of how prehistoric people perceived the items and images they left behind. Some commentators argue that in modern times, we reason with minds that are totally different from those of our prehistoric ancestors. This suggests that we cannot understand or view things in the same ways as our ancestors. However, such a view dismisses the core of our humanness and how we approach, analyze, and react to the unknown as a species. It also dismisses a key element of belief within Witchcraft, which is reincarnation. In this light, we still possess the collective soul experience, which means we were once our ancient ancestors. Therefore, as Witches, we can access the older understanding of the ancient beliefs and practices that are recorded as soul memories. See Chapter Eight for further information regarding such methods.

While we, as modern humans, like to think of ourselves as highly evolved beyond our prehistoric ancestors, we are, in fact, still just as subject to the primal or primitive part of our brains. History reveals that humans are still motivated by the same drives, goals, and ambitions today as they were thousands of years ago. Ancient Greek plays are as relevant today to human society and behavior as they were in their own time period. Is it then reasonable to assume that thousands of years before these ancient writings, humans were completely different? It is more likely that the ways in which our prehistoric ancestors thought and perceived were not as alien to us as a species as some commentators like to think.

We know that humans build upon existing ideas and concepts. One of the earliest writings in Western literature, the *Theogony*, demonstrates this fact. In this writing, the author Hesiod refers to an elder race of gods (the Titans) who existed before the rise of the gods of Olympus. Hesiod patterns the Olympic gods after the categories of the Titans, demonstrating an ongoing human tradition of passing along knowledge and information in an established format. To Hesiod, who wrote sometime around the seventh or eighth century BCE, the Titans were an almost forgotten race of gods from an earlier and half-remembered era. From where then did the earlier beliefs regarding the Titans originate in this misty past? Were they not based upon earlier prehistoric beliefs that came before them? It would seem reasonable to assume such to be the case and the commonality of the human experience to be the uniting factor.

In the remainder of this chapter, we will explore the primal concepts that evolved into religion in a manner that views everything as connected along a line of evolution. We will not view the things we examine as having no relationship or connection as generations passed through the ages. Instead, we will approach this as though humans passed on their religious concepts in the same manner as they passed on everything else related to their society and technology. It would seem odd to consider it in any other fashion. For even on a mundane level, the arrow that was once the spear is not unrelated to the tool, the concept, or the need. In a metaphorical sense, this applies as well to religious thought and conception.

The world of our ancestors was one filled with mystery and wonder. Imagine not knowing or even having any idea of what the Moon and the Sun were in the sky. What kept them there and how did they move about? Where did they go when they disappeared beneath the horizon? Who or what created them? Humans, being naturally curious beings, no doubt spent much time wondering about these and many other things.

In time, it became apparent that the mysterious world operated in patterns. The most noticeable ones presented themselves in the seasons and the migration of birds and animals. Later, when humans turned to farming (becoming less dependent upon the animals they hunted), the growing cycle of the crops was well noted. What appears to be apparent from ancient writings is a belief that a spirit or a deity was somehow involved in the cycles and processes of this mysterious world.

Images and statues were created to depict these unseen beings. A system of appropriate offerings was constructed, and a type of veneration or worship arose. These were all attempts at communication, supplication, and alliance-building. Some individuals within the early tribes seemed more attuned to the unseen world and its beings, and these people performed what might be called religious or spiritual tasks for the tribe. Various examples of this commonality in diverse human cultures are the European shaman, the American Indian Medicine Man or Woman, and the African Witch Doctor. But, for the purposes of this chapter, we are interested in the European Witch.

The earliest written references in Western culture to Witches can be found in ancient Greek literature. Here, such figures as Medea are priestesses of Hecate (a Titan) and are involved in themes related to magick, herbalism, and divination. They frequently live in rural settings away from developed towns and cities. From where did the concepts associated with Witchcraft in ancient times originate?

What were the origins of the ascribed beliefs and practices associated with these Witches? How did the Witches come to embrace them? The simplest answer is that such things were passed along from earlier periods of European Paganism and were eventually formed into a sect that came to be called *Witches.* But what were these earlier concepts and beliefs?

Prehistoric Religion

It is difficult to know precisely what prehistoric humans intended when they buried their dead with various objects or when they colored the body with red ocher. Some commentators suggest that such acts were designed to protect the living from the dead, while others believe that this indicated a belief in an afterlife where the departed would require their personal belongings. In either case, there appears to be a rooted belief that death does not exterminate the vitality of the departed individual.

The phenomena of dreaming may have caused early humans to believe in another world beyond this one, but similar in many ways. In the dream world, we encounter various situations in a realm similar to the waking world, but one in which magickal things happen. It is not uncommon in a dream for an object to turn into something different by itself. In dreams, we can fly, breathe underwater, and perform many tasks not possible in the waking world. What would primitive humans have made of this strange realm?

A person who is asleep looks very much like someone who is dead. This fact may also have established a connection between the absence of animation in this world and the reanimation in another. If one can appear dead (the dreamer) and yet experience another existence (the dream world), then perhaps actual death is much the same. In this light, it is not unreasonable to conclude that primitive humans believed in the survival of the individual who physically died in the waking world.

The creation of figurative art, evidenced as early as 30,000 BCE, demonstrates that humans of this period were conscious of symbolism and personification as a form of communication. Here also are signs of ritual process and the connection between desire and the manifestation of desire through the ritual expression of themes. This strongly suggests a belief that ritual/magickal actions can influence those forces that operate the natural world and its phenomena. Burial customs also suggest a belief that each world had some degree of influence upon the other. Here, we begin to see what modern humans might call *religion*, a word derived from the Latin *religare*, meaning "to tie together."

Primitive burial mounds featured a relatively small hole. The general view is that this hole allowed the spirit to come and go as it pleased. A more mystical view is that it allowed the light of the waking world to enter as well as the light of the dream world (the Moon). In any case, the burial mound would continue to carry Otherworld connotations throughout the passing centuries, eventually being viewed as faery mounds. A woodcut appearing in a pamphlet on Scottish Witchcraft, circa 1591, depicts a group of Witches standing over a mound. Inside the mound are three tiny adult characters feasting at a table, in front of which appears a full-size man laying on the floor (*Witchcraft in Early Modern Scotland*, Normand and Roberts). Some commentators view this as the depiction of a faery mound.

The placement of personal effects in the burial place of the dead can be viewed as an act of appeasement as well as preparation. In other words, it is an act designed to maintain the good favor of the deceased so that they wish no ill on the living. This basic concept appears in archaic Roman religion (itself derived from Etruscan religion) where we find spirits known as *Manes* (mah-nays). The Etruscans inherited the earlier Neolithic concepts, which then evolved into a more formalized and structured religion.

The Manes were essentially "good" spirits of the dead, often identified as ancestral spirits. In the earliest period, the Manes were believed to live in or around the burial site. In order to assure a good relationship, offerings were frequently given to the Manes. Neglecting to do so could evoke their ill will, which is a theme also seen later in faery lore.

The persistence of prehistoric traditions and primitive conceptions well into the Hellenistic and Roman period is noteworthy as we consider the foundation of Witchcraft as a Mystery Tradition. Writers of these periods were often astonished by the survival of prehistoric ritual customs reflected in grotto cults and the continued appearance of pictorial engravings. Here, survival themes readily appeared in the animistic concept of the supernatural, house-shaped tombs, the importance of divine signs, and a divinatory focus.

Another aspect of prehistoric religion is centered on what is called the *Cult of Bone*. Since bones are eventually all that survives the decomposition of a body, they held special significance. The skull, in particular, held much meaning for a variety of reasons and features prominently in ancient Celtic religion (explored in later chapters). The preservation of bones is widespread in cultures throughout the world. This Pagan practice was even adopted by Christianity and placed into the Cult of Saints, which featured the veneration of bones and other body relics.

The strong focus on the dead implies another relation to the afterlife. Prehistoric symbols associated with death include the vulture, owl, boar, and dog. These creatures continue to be associated with Underworld themes and deities well into the late Roman era and continue in folklore themes through the Middle Ages, Renaissance, and into modern times. The appearance of what many call the *White Lady* or *White Woman* in folklore seems rooted in these ancient concepts. The White Lady is said to shapeshift into an owl or a vulture and to be accompanied by a hound. The boar was a favored sacrificial animal to chthonic deities.

The White Lady is said to possess two aspects. She is the messenger of approaching death and the taker of life. In folklore, she appears three times in or near the home of one who is to die soon. Either the sound of an owl or the howling of a dog accompanies her appearance. This may be related to an ancient belief in the soul snatchers, which were supernatural birds that gathered to capture the soul as someone died.

Prehistoric images strongly suggest a belief in a female deity of death and regeneration. In time, a goddess known as Hecate (as we've seen, a Titan from prehistoric times) arises in connection with death, the souls of the dead, and roads that lead to the Underworld. In her first literary appearance (Hesiod's *Theogony*), she is a great goddess honored by Zeus. She presides over three realms: the sky, the earth, and the sea. Hesiod writes that Zeus did not take *"anything away of all that was her portion among the former Titan gods."* He goes on to say, *"...she holds, as the division was at the first from the beginning, privilege both in earth, and in heaven, and in sea."* This indicates that Hecate maintained her prehistoric attributes even into the literary period. In classical writings, Hecate is depicted as the Goddess of Witches, patroness of sorcerers and sorceresses, and guardian of the entrances into the Underworld.

The Ancient World

In the popular text now known as *The Charge of the Goddess* (which features the Goddess addressing her followers), we read *"I am the beauty of the green earth, and the white moon among the stars, and the mystery of the waters..."* Here we see a reference to three realms associated with the Goddess: earth, heavens, and waters (just as we saw in Hesiod's writings related to Hecate).

As noted earlier, the ancients believed in a cosmic structure consisting of three worlds. This appears in Southern European mythology as Ouranos (Overworld), Gaia (Middleworld), and Pontos (Underworld). In Northern Europe, it is depicted as Gwynvyd, Abred, and Annwn (or, by some accounts, Ceugant, Gwynvyd, and Abred).

Our ancestors believed that various deities possessed power over the Sun and Moon as well as the forces of nature, such as earthquakes. In prehistoric times, our ancestors believed that the phenomena itself was a god or a Goddess, evidenced by the primal attributes of the Titans. In order to appease the great deities, a system of appropriate offerings was designed. In the earliest of times, the offering of a human sacrifice was practiced. This was substituted in time by animal sacrifice, which itself was later replaced by plant sacrifice in the form of offering the "first fruits" and harvested grain.

Benevolent spirits as well as malevolent spirits were believed to roam the land. Sometimes these were spirits of the dead and other times they were the departed souls of the living. Offerings could be made to ensure good relations—or at least to keep peace in play. For even those beings that dwelled in the Otherworld could return among the living on certain occasions. As time passed, other realms of existence were conceived, and each had its unique concerns.

The highest world was that which contained the Sun, Moon, and the stars. This realm was called the *Overworld,* for it stretched above the Earth, covering it from horizon to horizon. Here dwelled the most powerful deities, who sometimes created kingdoms on top of the highest mountains of the Earth. However, it was among the distant stars that the true home of the high deities was set.

The Middleworld was the realm of mortal beings. Our ancestors believed that it floated in a great abyss, was carried on the back of a giant, or was held aloft from underneath by the branches of a great tree. Because this realm was situated between the Overworld and the

Underworld, it was visited by beings from both realms. Our ancestors believed that these beings possessed power over everything and everyone in the Middleworld.

The lowest world was deep in the earth or at the depths of the sea. Here dwelled the deities of the Underworld to whom the Sun, Moon, and the departed souls of the living returned. It was also from the Underworld that they all returned to the world of the living. In the West was the gate of entering, and in the East was the portal of return. As we shall see in later chapters, the Western quarter, the ocean, and water have strong ties to the Underworld.

Our ancestors associated divine power, and often some magickal properties, with various things that came into contact with the three realms. Thus, the Sun and Moon were held in high regard, as were the mountains that seemingly touched the sky. Clouds, lightning, wind, and other things connected to the sky were also given legendary or mythical attributes. Our ancestors believed that the deities of the Overworld sometimes communicated with humankind through signs in the sky, which were often meteors, solar ane lunar eclipses, or various weather phenomena. Because birds flew in the sky, they were frequently viewed as messengers of the Overworld deities.

The Middleworld, like the Overworld, also had its mystical connections. Trees, naturally rooted in the earth, were believed to possess special qualities, as were all plants in general (and herbs in particular). We know that many ancient people worshipped trees—the oak and ash in particular. The tree held special significance because it was rooted in the Underworld and its branches extended up toward the Overworld. Birds, the messengers of the gods, landed in trees and made their nests there, which further connected the tree to the Overworld. The roots of the tree extended into the Underworld, where they drew the secrets from this mysterious realm. Therefore, the tree knew the will of the gods on high, and the secrets of the gods below. In the Middleworld, it stood as a bridge (and in some tales, as a doorway) between the worlds.

The Underworld also had its connections to power and magick. Caves and crevices were believed to be doorways or entrances into the Underworld and were, therefore, magickal thresholds. Often within the cave were pools of water, and streams frequently issued forth from crevices. Lakes, oceans, and wells extended down into the earth, which also connected them to the Underworld. Oracle powers were associated with caves and crevices, being viewed as the "speaking mouth" of the Underworld. Supernatural beings were associated with wells, lakes, and oceans. In most cases, these entities were female in form, perhaps due to an association with the fluids of the female body. Some examples are the Lady of the Lake figure and nymphs like Egeria. The latter is associated with streams (and particularly in places where they flow directly into lakes).

It is not difficult to understand how the three great realms of the ancient view influenced Pagan beliefs over the centuries. As noted earlier, in ancient mythology, Hecate was given power over each of these three realms. In the earliest tales of Hecate, she grants special favor to herders, farmers, and fishermen. In later times, Hecate is maligned and transformed singularly into a dark goddess of the Underworld. By the classical era, Hecate was feared and dreaded instead of venerated, as in earlier times. Like the Witches who revered her, in the classical period, Hecate becomes an unwanted presence erroneously imagined to perform all sorts of ill deeds.

Witchcraft in Ancient Greece and Rome

As mentioned, the earliest records in Western culture to refer to Witches appear in ancient Greek and Roman writings. Witches certainly existed in other areas of Europe, but unfortunately, the regional inhabitants were illiterate during this era. Therefore, we have no written records through which we can examine Witches or Witchcraft outside of the Aegean/Mediterranean until much later in history.

By the time of the ancient Greeks, prehistoric concepts had evolved into a religion based upon nature in many ways. The forces of nature were personified into deities of fields, woods, rivers, springs, oceans, and the phenomena of nature itself. Spirits were believed to inhabit natural settings as well as objects.

By the classical era, the means of communicating with the animating forces of nature were more refined than in prehistoric times. The use of an oracle became a great focus and a means of communicating with the unseen realm that lie hidden from the waking world. Special individuals were selected to serve in the oracles, and they often bore the title of *priest* or *priestess*. Secret societies formed, such as those at Delphi and

Eleusis, and only initiates were allowed to partake in the Mysteries. It was in this world that the Witches first appear in recorded writings.

The names used to indicate a Witch in the early Greek and Latin writings are *pharmakis* and *saga*, respectively. *Pharmakis* refers to a person with knowledge of the pharmaceutical properties of plants (and in the case of Witches, such plants were largely herbs). *Saga* is a term used to indicate a person who practices divination. In other words, this is someone who can communicate with the Otherworld, a seer. Here we see the Witch as an herbalist and fortune teller.

To the Romans, the Witch figure was known as a *strix*, *striga*, or *venefica*. The first two words refer to a woman who could transform into a supernatural bird, which was, in most cases, a screech owl. We encountered the prehistoric roots of this figure earlier in the chapter. The last word (*venefica*) is a bit more complicated to understand. *Venefica* shares the same root word *vene* with such words as *venerate* (meaning "heartfelt") and *venereal* (meaning "love-making," or more plainly, an act of physical intimacy). *Vene* itself indicates a relationship to Venus, originally a goddess of cultivated gardens who became a goddess of love. Originally, *venefica* was a person who made love potions. Over the course of time, this became distorted to indicate someone who used poison potions. I refer the interested reader to my previous book, *The Witches' Craft,* for a more in-depth study of how and why this took place.

The Aegean/Mediterranean Witch lived in a world of magick, one in which the gods and goddesses wielded fantastic power. The Witch was an outcast of society, living in the herb-clad hills and remote areas away from the civilized areas. Unlike the city dwellers, the Witch worshipped the deities of field and forest, as well as the deities of night and the Underworld. Writers of this era tell us that Witches worshipped such goddesses as Hecate, Diana, and Proserpina.

Scholar Richard Gordon, in his article "Imagining Greek and Roman Magic" (Ankarloo and Clark, 1999) tells us that groups such as "wise women, herbalists, and smiths" were largely unaffected by the "processes of rationalization and moralization" that came with the development of state religion. All these classes were associated with magick, including the smith. In Greek mythology, a race of smiths known as the *Telchines* were shapeshifters who imparted useful arts to humankind. In Chapter Two, we will encounter the smith as an aspect of the Witches' God.

The writers on classical Witchcraft depict Witches using cauldrons, olive wood wands, spinning tops or wheels, a variety of plants, and invocations to the Moon, stars, and various goddesses. The list of goddesses includes Hebe, Tellus/Gaia, Venus, Diana, Hecate, and Proserpina. Witches of this era were also believed to possess the power to draw the Moon down from the night sky.

The ancient writers Horace, Lucan, and Ovid refer to drawing the Moon down as a ritual magickal act. Horace, in his classic work titled *The Epodes*, states that this is accomplished by chanting specific words from a book. Aristophanes made fun of this art and apparently believed it was a charlatan trick of some sort. He was an academic who was cynical of the beliefs of the common people of his period regarding the popular view of Witches and Witchcraft (among other things). We have the same type of academic personalities in our modern era. This demonstrates that the disbelief of scholars is indeed as ancient as the very things they disbelieve.

In the book *Magic, Witchcraft and Ghosts in the Greek and Roman Worlds*, by Daniel Ogden (2002), the author mentions Sophocles' reference to Witches and nudity. Sophocles, in his work *Rhizotomoi,* describes a Witch reaping herbs in the nude. Ogden also notes Ovid's reference to the Witch Medea (in his *Metamorphoses*) performing magick in an "open dress." Historian Ruth Martin, in her book *Witchcraft and the Inquisition in Venice 1550-1650* (1989), states that it was common during the Renaissance period for Italian Witches to recite their conjurations in the nude with their hair loose around their shoulders. We also have the Witch trial of Gabrina Alberti in 1375 who confessed to going out at night, removing her clothing, and worshipping the brightest star in the sky. Could this all be the continuation of a longstanding ancient tradition?

Ovid, in his work titled *Fasti*, notes the ancient practice of ritual nudity by the worshippers of the god Faunus. Faunus (in the tale told by Ovid) demands that his followers gather nude at his festivals. Ovid also notes that the ancient Cult of the Luperci regularly performed nude rituals at the festival of Lupercus. Modern scholar Ronald Hutton states that *"No known cult in the ancient world was carried on by devotees who all worshipped regularly in the nude like the Witches portrayed by Leland and inspired by Gardner"* (1991). However, the references we've seen in this chapter seem to suggest otherwise.

Another feature of Aegean/Mediterranean Witchcraft is the importance of the crossroads. In ancient times, a crossroad was where three roads met and formed a "Y" figure. A pole was set where the roads intersected and three masks were hung upon it to represent the goddess Hecate. Each mask faced one of the paths. From this practice arose a sort of nickname for Hecate, which was *Trivia* (meaning "of the three ways").

The crossroads were traditionally places where magick was performed to chthonic deities and spirits of the night. It was also believed that the souls of people who died unjustly or unavenged haunted the crossroads. They could be called upon to assist sorcerers and sorceresses against their own enemies because the souls were of a vengeful nature themselves. This type of magick has come to be viewed as "black" or "dark magick."

Another interesting aspect of Witchcraft in the Aegean/Mediterranean is the Witches' preference for bronze over iron or steel. Even well into the late Roman period, writers describe Witches cutting herbs with bronze sickles, and iron is considered taboo. The aversion to iron in association with magick is widespread throughout most of continental Europe and the British Isles.

Witchcraft and the World of Northern Europe

Due to the lack of written records, it is difficult to describe or establish what Witchcraft was like in Northern Europe before the arrival of the Romans. However, we can look for clues about the religious and magickal practices of Northern European tribes in the written accounts of various Greek and Roman writers. We can also look at the unique elements found in Northern Europe and apply the principle of "transmitted generational teachings" from which we can work backward to reconstruct a reasonable model.

As in Southern Europe, the world known to the Witches of the North was one of magick. The inherent powers and forces residing in nature directed the course of things for better or worse. Spirits controlled or greatly influenced various events, and certain people possessed the ability to work in partnership with them. These people came to be known as *Witches*.

The Roman historian Tacitus wrote that the Germanic tribes were divided into two main cults. One formed around the theme of symbolic atonement and the other was more of a shamanic nature. According to Tacitus, the Germanic people regarded women as predisposed to prophetic powers, and priestesses held significance in the tribal structure. Divination was performed using strips of wood cut from nut-bearing trees. Symbols or sigils were marked on the strips, and over the course of time, these evolved into the runic symbols we know today (*The Encyclopedia of Magic & Witchcraft*, Greenwood, 2001).

Tacitus describes the English tribes in the same way as the Germanic. He also adds that they worship an Earth Mother Goddess who he names *Nerthus*. The Nordic tribes are depicted as more sophisticated and possess a cosmic view of nine worlds that include the realm of the gods known as *Asgard*. Asgard is connected to the other worlds by a rainbow bridge.

Among the Anglo-Saxons, we find the mystical principle known as *Wyrd*. This is an all-powerful force of destiny. The word itself can be used to indicate not only destiny but also raw energy and prophetic knowledge. Wyrd is, in the Mystery Tradition of Witchcraft, the essential and magickal property that interconnects all things. This is the world that the Witches of Northern Europe arise within and inherit the evolved Neolithic concepts of their distant ancestors.

The Witch is an interesting figure, particularly in England. Traditions regarding Witches are rooted deep in antiquity. In Kent, England, there is a megalithic chamber tomb called *Kit's Coty*. For centuries, it has been held that Witches raised the tomb. Another legend is associated with the Rollright Stones of Oxfordshire, England. The tale is told that a king rode with his knights to reach Long Compton. Were he to reach this place, the king would control all of England. A Witch appeared and directed him to a nearby hill, but before he could reach it, the king and his men were transformed into standing stones. Whether the Witch in this tale was a villain or a hero who saved England is a matter of perspective.

According to historian Jeffrey Russell (*A History of Witchcraft*, 1980), the earliest reference to a Witch in England appears in a ninth-century trial, and here the word *wicca* is first recorded. *Wicca* is the root origin of the word *Witch* in the English language. In the context of the trial, the reference is to the user of magick, which is not surprising, because Witchcraft is also a magickal system. Russell argues for the separation of words used to denote a Witch and a magick user, saying the two are distinct but were confused with one another. Historians and archaeologists spend a great deal of time and energy trying to separate magick and sorcery from Witchcraft as well as other things that the Witch as a practitioner knows to be inseparable.

In the British Isles, Celtic culture influenced the beliefs and practices of Witches living in these lands. One of the most long-lasting influences came from the ancient Faery Faith. The Witch inherited a world that bordered the mystical realms of the Elven and Fae races. Doorways and mystical mists that appeared and then vanished called to the woodland Witch. In the deep wooded places, the Witch learned the music of the *sidhe,* an ancient race of immortal Faeries, which could suspend or accelerate time itself.

The realm in which the Elven and Fae races dwell is often called the *Otherworld.* In Celtic lore, it was a place where some mortals could go, sometimes during life and after death as well. In some ways, this offered mortals an alternative to the Underworld formed by human concepts. The attraction of the Otherworld, and its mystical call, persisted well into Christian times and appears in the tales of King Arthur. Perhaps this is, in part, something that author T.W. Rolleston wrote of:

"The Otherworld was not a place of gloom and suffering, but of light and liberation. The Sun was as much the god of that world as he was of this" (*Myths and Legends of the Celtic Race,* 1911).

It is noteworthy also that the concept of an Underworld depicted as dark, lifeless, and menacing does not appear until the late Bronze Age (*Myth of the Goddess,* Baring and Cashford, 1991).

The Witches' World

Within Witchcraft, we find a sacred oral tradition reflective of our history from the perspective of us who have lived it. This is often in opposition to the view of many historians who essentially believe that what is not documented never existed. Witches, on the other hand, tend to view things in a less rigid manner.

According to the oral tradition of Witches, we were once the priests and priestesses of a peasant Pagan religion. Members of this secret sect met at night beneath the Full Moon, for these were the "misfits" and "outcasts" who did not fit into mainstream society. Little has changed over the centuries, and the Witchcraft community still embraces individuals frequently rejected in mainstream society. These include LGBTQIA+ folks and other people with the courage to live their lives authentically in accord with who they are inside their hearts, minds, and spirits.

Historian Albert Grenier wrote on a similar topic in his book *The Roman Spirit in Religion, Thought, and Art* (1926). Here, Grenier spoke of a quasi-order of social misfits and outcasts in ancient times. Grenier states that gods of the streets, fields, roads, and crossroads take such people under their protection, and of these deities, Grenier writes:

"About their altars on the crossroads they collect all the vagabonds, all those who have no family, no hearth, no worship of their own. Their humble devotees combine to celebrate their feasts as best they can, forming Colleges of the Crossroads, collegia compitalicia."

In ancient Witchcraft, the teachings were passed to apprentices from those masters who learned from the first Witches. Nature and the spirits and deities of nature taught these first masters. They were educated and trained in the deep wooded places. Their instructors were the hills, rocks, ancient forests, and other entities that arose when the Earth itself was young. Here, amidst the scent of primeval forests moist beneath the Full Moon, the Old Ones called to the Witches from a distant age.

Ancient Witches favored the rural places where the deities of field and forest, Sun and Moon, were still venerated. Hesiod, in his *Theogony*, wrote that he was not "of the oak and stone" when he tried to depict himself as more sophisticated and inspired directly by the Muses sent to him by the gods of Olympus. Here, we see a distinct division between the rustics of the country and the refined city dwellers. The cities had succumbed to "official" religion, sanctioned and influenced by those who held political power. This offered little, if anything, of interest to the Witch. Witches have always danced to an older and different tune, and so it continues to this very day.

The Witches' world was one of nature veneration, and of honoring the Horned God of the forests and his consort, the Moon Goddess. The stag antlers of the Lord of the Woods were shaped with crescent-formed branches, denoting his betrothal to *she who wore the crescent on her brow*. As a sign of her love, the Goddess brought the Full Moon over the forest to shed its light upon the branches. There, backlit by the soft light of the Moon, the tree branches took on the appearance of antlers, a token of honor to the Horned God of the woods from *she who moved above in the night sky*. Here in the dark woods, the God and Goddess kept their ancient covenant.

The Horned God and the Crescent-Browed Lady taught magick to their Witches. He taught of stone, fire, drum, and flute. She taught of torchlight, misty smoke, starry night, and cauldron. Together, they led their Witches through doorways that entered other realms beyond the imagination of those whose world was of the Sun's light.

In the Otherworld, there was no realm of punishment or dread, for such concepts arose from those whose religions grew in the cities. The Witch saw neither "evil" nor "good" in nature, but instead, they perceived an intelligence that restored and maintained order and the repetition of endless cycles. To the Witch, forces both seen and unseen participated in this magickal process. Just as this world had its magickal people (the Witches), so too did the Otherworld (the Elven or Fae). Together, they worked between the worlds for a common cause, and many believed that the Elven, Fae, and Witch were of a similar race. It is interesting to note that even well into the Renaissance, Witches were believed to interact with elemental spirits of Earth, Air, Fire, and Water (among others). Francesco Guazzo mentions this in his book *Compendium Maleficarum*, published in 1609.

Examining the things associated with Witches that appear in Western literature for well over 2,500 years, we find some interesting connections to ancient themes. The classical creatures associated with Witches are the frog, toad, snake, and owl. These creatures appear in cave art, Neolithic pottery, and iconography in conjunction with lunar symbolism. In later times, the cat, bat, and mouse become associated with Witches. All of these creatures are active at night and largely move about unseen, which gave them an air of mystery.

The concept of the Witch's familiar spirit is rooted in the animal spirit of Neolithic religion. The tribal totem animal or animal guide is an earlier reflection of the relationship between the Witch and their spirit ally. In many Witch trials, particularly those of the British

Isles, the records indicate a belief among those accused of Witchcraft that the familiar is passed down from Witch to Witch. The records indicate that typically, this occurred within family lines. I refer the interested reader to my previous book, *The Witch's Familiar* (Llewellyn, 2003).

In this chapter, we have looked briefly at the prehistoric influences on European Paganism. We have seen glimpses of the subsequent influence of European Pagan concepts regarding the beliefs and practices of pre-Christian Witchcraft. Now we must turn to a deeper examination of the Mystery Teachings that are the core essence of Witchcraft as a religion and spirituality. Therefore, let us now turn to the next chapter, where we will encounter the foundation of the Mystery Tradition of Witchcraft.

CHAPTER TWO

ᚷhe ꟽystery ᚷradition in ꟽodern ᚹitchcraft

In this chapter, we will explore what a Mystery Tradition is, why it's important, and how it operates in Witchcraft. The focus of this chapter is on how the Mysteries formed from the concepts and notions that early humans held regarding the world around them. Here, we will explore the various aspect of Witchcraft that developed as tools that could be used to communicate with nature and the Otherworld. The reader is advised that a portion of this related material appeared in my previous book *Spirit of the Witch*, and is reintroduced here in modified form due to its relevance to this current chapter's theme.

The Mystery Tradition in modern Witchcraft is rooted in the concepts of ancient pre-Christian European Paganism, which we noted in Chapter One. The Mysteries contain elements of ancestral views concerning nature, spirits, the gods and goddesses, magick, and various mystical realms of existence. The Mystery Tradition, like the religion of Witchcraft itself, has evolved over the centuries. While its core teachings have remained unchanged, many subsequent elements have been integrated and modified over time in order to serve the needs and understandings of each generation into whose hands it has passed.

The teachings of any Mystery Tradition are designed to convey concepts that can only be understood and integrated through story and imagery. In Witchcraft, this is often referred to as the *mythos*.

This mythos permeates the foundation of each seasonal rite and its associated deity. The mythos also emerges in the basic and essential tenets of theology within Witchcraft.

In modern Witchcraft, each seasonal ritual (sabbat) personifies the energy flowing within the seasonal tides of nature. Each tide marks agricultural events as well as the migratory movements of animals and their seasonal responses. Such things were of foremost importance to our ancestors who created rituals and magickal systems to correspond with each prevailing tide.

In addition to the cycles of nature, the practitioners of a Mystery Tradition also hold the view of Otherworld influences at work within the Material Realm. The Material Realm is considered to be a lower (and somewhat distorted) reflection of what is actually taking place on a higher level within another dimension. The seasonal sabbats mark the points at which the energy of both realms meet and interface during the course of a year.

The most powerful points were marked by the equinox or solstice period, which brought dramatic changes in weather conditions. The periods that fell midpoint between the solstice and equinox were called the *cross-quarters*. These marked magickal periods connected to the Otherworld, which manifested in relation to beliefs about the birth, power, decline, and rebirth of the Sun.

Our Pagan ancestors considered the three days prior to any equinox or solstice as a time when the energy could be magickally influenced. This period of time was called the *Ember Days*. Rituals and magickal rites were performed to safeguard against any negative contamination. Historian Carlo Ginzburg writes briefly on this topic in his book *Ecstasies: Deciphering the Witches' Sabbat*. In his book *The Night Battles: Witchcraft and Agrarian Cults in the Sixteenth and Seventeenth Centuries,* Ginzburg goes into greater depth.

According to Ginzburg, ritual battles took place between opposing forces of "good" and "bad," known respectively as the *benandanti* and *malandanti*. The outcome of such battles indicated whether or not the crops and herds of the seasons would flourish or diminish. Ginzburg presents material suggesting that such rites or beliefs continued well into the seventeenth century. Allegations of Witchcraft and heresy brought the attention of the Church to these matters, which later appear in the interrogation records of the Inquisition at Cumo, Italy.

Older indications of a connection between this world and the next are found in such things as the ancient standing stones, stone altars, decorated cave entrances, and the sacredness of fire. These items also strongly suggest a perceived "meeting point" between the worlds. This is covered later in the chapter. To understand the Mystery Tradition within Witchcraft, we must first understand the mystical view of the Otherworld and the Underworld as well as that of the "spirit within the land" of the material world.

The Otherworld

In the Mystery Tradition, the Otherworld is part of a larger realm known as the *Underworld*. Although they merge and blend at various points, it is important, for the purpose of this book, to keep them somewhat distinct from one another. This is no easy task, for in both realms, beings of a non-material nature can reside as well as the souls of those who have departed from physical existence.

Old European legends depict Faeries and other beings living beneath the earth in hollow mounds. In Celtic legend, a mythical race known as the *Tuatha de Danann* withdraws from humankind and resides beneath the earth. Some commentators suggest that this story is the root source of the Faery Faith in Celtic lore. In old Celtic faery lore, the *sidhe* (Faery Folk) are immortals living in ancient barrows and cairns.

The Tuatha de Danann are associated with several Otherworld realms including *Mag Mell* (the Pleasant Plain), *Emain Ablach* (the Fortress of Apples), and *Tir na nOg* (the Land of Youth). These realms are associated with Otherworld lands such as Avalon in the Arthurian mythos. The concept of Avalon, also known as the *Isle of Apples,* is rooted in ancient faery lore. Here we find the "Silver Bough" that allowed a living mortal to enter and withdraw from the Otherworld. According to legend, the Faery Queen sometimes offered the branch to "worthy" mortals. It granted safe passage and provided food during the stay in the Otherworld (for to eat any other food offered there prevented one from ever leaving).

The theme of a secret and hidden island associated with the Otherworld has persisted for countless generations. One of the oldest forms is a mystical green island that drifts on the western sea. Although the living can catch a glimpse of it, when approached, the island slips beneath the water and disappears. In early imagery, the island appeared with several mountain peaks, and in later times, this evolved into the image of a castle with four towers. For those who possess the sight, the green isle can be seen from a distance amidst the clouds on the western horizon for a brief moment just as the Sun sinks beneath the sea.

Water is a common connection to the Otherworld, and many European myths and legends feature a Faery woman at the core. One such example is the figure known as the *Lady of the Lake*. Other tales present a spring or a well that is a sacred place to faeries. The goddess Diana who bore the title *Queen of the Fairies* was worshipped at Lake Nemi in a ritual performed when the Full Moon could be seen reflected upon the surface of the water.

The water connections permeate both the Otherworld and the Underworld mythos. Two primary elements are featured in Underworld themes. These elements are the pool (or lake) and the river. The placement of such bodies of water within the Underworld indicates a mystical nature and primal power.

Historian Walter Otto states that to the ancients, water was the element in which the primal Mysteries of all life dwelled. Intertwined in the essence of water were the principles of birth, life, and death, which joined in the "dance" of past, present, and future. Everything began in water, and as Otto suggests, *"Where the sources of Becoming are, there too is prophecy"* (*Dionysus, Myth and Cult,* 161). To better understand all of this on a deeper level, we must first comprehend the Underworld itself.

The Underworld

Among the Celts, the Underworld was known by different names according to the region in which the theme resided. The Welsh Underworld was known as *Annwn*. This realm featured a magickal cauldron of regeneration. As noted earlier, the Irish Underworld was known as *Tir na nOg* and also featured a magickal cauldron, which supplied an ever-renewed source of food. The Irish Underworld was depicted as an idealized mirror image of earthly life.

The modern concept of the "Summerland," found in contemporary Witchcraft, reflects the Irish theme of the endless summer, bounty, peace, and beauty associated with Tir na nOg, the Land of Eternal

Youth. By contrast, the Welsh view of the Underworld included certain dangers, which was particularly true for a living person who entered the realm of Annwn. The Aegean/Mediterranean concept depicted the Underworld as divided into realms both horrifying and delightful (such as Tartarus and the Elysian Fields).

The writings of Homer (*The Odyssey*) contain the earliest recorded depictions of the Underworld in Western literature. In Homer's tale, Circe tells Odysseus that in order to reach the "House of Hades," he must sail north and traverse the waters of Oceanus and reach the "fertile shore of Persephone's country." Circe describes it as containing groves of poplar and willow trees, which "shed their fruit" out of normal season.

Circe instructs Odysseus to seek out the dark abode of Hades, which lies near the place where the rivers Pyriphlegethon and Cocytus (a branch of Styx) flow into Acheron. Homer's description of the Underworld includes a section known as the "Meadow of Asphodel" which later came to be known as the *Elysian Fields*. Other Underworld areas are called "the Gates of the Sun" and the "Land of Dreams." In Celtic legend, the Underworld realm known as Annwn is often called the *Kingdom of Shades*. Like the Aegean/Mediterranean concept of the Underworld, Annwn is divided into zones presided over by the gods and the other beings. The Celtic Underworld also features different mountain ranges, rivers, and impassable chasms. The Cave of Cruachain was one of the most commonly known entrances to the Otherworld in Celtic lore.

The ancient writer Pausanias, in Book Ten of his accounts of traveling through Greece, refers to a painting of Hades at Delphi. Pausanias describes the painting as featuring water like a river with reeds growing in it. The forms of fishes appear dim like shadows rather than fish. On the river is a boat with the ferryman at the oars. The people on the boat are not distinguishable. In Celtic lore, a river flows to the Underworld castle in which the figure known as Mabon has been imprisoned. A salmon leads Mabon's rescuers to discover and retrieve Mabon.

The theme of the fish or some sea creature in Underworld lore appears in many pre-Christian European cultures. Proserpina, an Underworld goddess among the ancient Romans, is often depicted riding a dolphin that escorts souls into the netherworld. The Celtic goddess Nehalennia is also associated with the dolphin and the sea.

She is likewise depicted as a goddess who guides or escorts across the sea. Nehalennia, like Proserpina, is intimately linked with the hound.

Dogs feature prominently in both Celtic and Aegean/Mediterranean Underworld themes. In Celtic lore, the Underworld dog is described as white with red ears, or as a speckled, grayish-red. In Aegean/Mediterranean lore, the three-headed dog is the most common depiction. In ancient lore, the dog is often associated with chthonic deities and Underworld themes of guardianship. Guardians of the Underworld serve two purposes, which are to block the way in or out for anyone lacking the entitlement to pass.

Celtic and Aegean/Mediterranean myths and legends contain tales of heroic adventures into the Underworld. There are two basic and essential themes attached to such tales. The first theme involves the retrieval of an object or a person, and the other theme centers on the retrieval of information. In the latter case, this is related to either seeking out specific souls or deities.

In Aegean/Mediterranean tales, the hero is frequently guided into the Underworld by a deity (such as Hermes in Book Twenty-Four of *The Odyssey*) or is accompanied by a mystical figure known as a Sibyl (as in the case of Aeneas in Virgil's *Aeneid*). However, in Book Eleven of *The Odyssey*, the Greek hero Odysseus journeys without a direct guide, and he is accompanied only by a small band of fellow warriors. The hero in Celtic tales typically sets off on his own as well but is ultimately directed through encounters with various animals and spirits along the way.

In Virgil's ancient tale (*The Aeneid*), the hero Aeneas journeys through the Underworld and discovers a countless number of souls gathered on the banks of the river known as Lethe. Aeneas is told that these are the souls of those who will be reborn into a new physical body. Aeneas is informed that these souls drink first from the waters of Lethe, which abolishes their troubles and removes their conscious memories. The absence of memory then causes a desire to "reenter bodily life" and the soul is then returned to the world of the living. This general theme appears in the Celtic view of the realm known as *Gwynvyd*. Here, the soul also passes into a state of forgetfulness in which the recollection of the past life is removed.

Since ancient times, water has been perceived as both a creator and destroyer of life. Ancient Pagan lore maintains strong connections between water and the Underworld, particularly in the form of wells, springs, ponds, lakes, and rivers. The Judeo-Christian notion of baptizing in a river in order to be "born again" may be rooted in the Pagan Underworld concepts depicted in Virgil's *Aeneid*. In any case, water both delivered and took back life. Here, it became a type of transportation between the worlds for spirits and souls.

Water flowed from beneath the earth and across the land. It gathered into pools, ponds, and lakes. Water could also be drawn up from wells. It was cleansing and provided the essential drink as well as food in the form of various creatures that lived within it. Just as water contained physical beings, it also contained spiritual ones. Nymphs, undines, mermaids, and Lady of the Lake figures are just a few examples. Here, once again, water was connected to something in a "supernatural" sense. This mystical connection allowed communication to take place to and from the Underworld. Because of this, oracle properties were often associated with water, and the art of scrying in the dark liquid of a cauldron is but one example.

In the Mystery Tradition of Old Witchcraft, the cauldron becomes a tool for harnessing the mystical properties of water for use in magick. The cauldron is a magickal vessel that transforms anything placed into the water it contains. The full, round shape of the cauldron filled with liquid was much like the pregnant belly of a woman, from whom water bursts forth and ushers in the birth of an infant. This is one of the reasons why it became a symbol of the Women's Inner Mystery Tradition. Here, the cauldron is viewed as the Vessel of Transformation. Erich Neumann wrote of this general theme in his book *The Great Mother:*

"The vessel of Transformation viewed as magickal can only be effected by the woman because she herself, in her body that corresponds to the Great Goddess, is the cauldron of incarnation, birth, and rebirth. And that is why the magickal cauldron or pot is always in the hands of the female mana figure, the priestess and later the witch."

The Women's Mystery Tradition in Witchcraft is primarily focused on the theme of transformation. The fire and the vessels that transformed raw food into cooked food were some early symbols. Primitive pottery ovens appear shaped like pregnant bellies. Vessels for carrying water also appear in this womb-like configuration (many of which are painted with stripes that resemble the so-called "stretchmarks" associated with pregnancy). Here, we see the connection between material substance and water, and the womb that transforms substance into a child that is born in the spilling of water.

Historian Diane Purkiss, in her book *The Witch in History* (1996), notes that the cauldron is not only a cooking pot but also a womb symbol from which metaphorical children are born. This is the Witches' magick, the birthing of the unseen into the material world, and the opening of doorways into the spirit realm.

The "Cauldron of Rebirth" is featured in both Welsh and Irish myths. In many legends, the magickal cauldron possesses the power to heal and restore. In the Welsh tale of Branwen, a magickal cauldron appears with the ability to restore dead warriors to life by cooking them overnight. This basic concept also appears in the ancient classical tale of Jason and the Argonauts. In this story, the Witch Medea uses a cauldron to restore life to the dead placed within it. Medea dips burning twigs into the mixture and stirs the potion with a dry branch from an olive tree.

Among many pre-Christian European people, trees were important symbols of rebirth. Deciduous trees lost their foliage in the winter and appeared like the skeletons of the dead. In the spring season, new life appeared on the old branches as the trees took on their previous form. The tree also became a symbol of the bridge between the realms of the Overworld, Middleworld, and Underworld. To better understand this important connection, we must turn our attention now to the sacred tree of Pagan religions.

Teachings of the Sacred Tree

Our ancient ancestors knew that a seed must be buried in the earth in order for a plant to grow. If the seed were kept in a pouch, it produced nothing. Therefore, to the primitive mind, the power to create a plant did not dwell in the seed, but in the earth. There was seemingly something beneath the ground that generated life.

For our ancestors, the Underworld was a place of great mystery. Life sprang forth from beneath the ground in a variety of forms. To the primitive mind, it must have also appeared that something beneath the ground produced such creatures as the snake, weasel, badger, and other animals that live in burrows.

The Sun and Moon appeared to arise from beneath the ground and return each day or night. This perspective added to the belief that deep in the ground, another world existed, and so this mysterious realm came to be called *the Underworld*. Trees, with their massive roots extending deep into the ground, were thought to penetrate the dark kingdom below. Therefore, the tree itself must know the Mysteries hidden deep within the netherworld.

As noted earlier, it is common knowledge that our European ancestors once worshipped or highly venerated trees. Some trees were believed to house various deities and spirits. Tales of holy trees abound in European lore. The oak, ash, and hawthorn trees feature prominently in such lore. Other sacred trees include the rowan, birch, elder, willow, walnut, and many others. Throughout Europe, sacred groves were established and dedicated to various gods and goddesses.

We noted in Chapter One that trees were not only rooted in the Underworld, but their branches extended into the Overworld. Birds (messengers of the gods in ancient belief) descended and landed on tree branches. Some of the earliest carvings of deities were bird figures, and these later evolved into bird-headed humanoid figures. This prehistoric theme survived among the Egyptian deity forms, many of which possessed the head of a bird. Horus the hawk-headed and Thoth the ibis-headed are but two clear examples.

Just as the tree reached down into the Underworld and upward to touch the Overworld, it also stood firmly in the Middleworld of humankind. In this world was its trunk, and in many folktales, a hollow at the base of the tree was a doorway into the faery realm or the Otherworld. In European lore, trees stood as both doorways to hidden realms and as guardians to the entrance. Their roots granted access to the Underworld as a pathway, just as the branches allowed spiritual access to the Overworld. Traditionally, the hawthorn tree was said to guard access to the portal pillar trees, which were the ash and oak. Together, they formed the triple imagery symbolism of the woodland Mysteries.

Tree branches were considered magickal and were taken from the trees as staves. In later times, wands were carved from the branches for ritual and magickal service. Trees were once intimately connected to specific deities represented by a sacred tree. To carry a sacred branch was to declare oneself as an intermediary of the deity or to be in some type of service to a specific god or goddess. The latter implied that one was also under the protection of their deity. As we shall see in other chapters, such a figure arises as the Divine King.

As noted earlier, in Aegean/Mediterranean lore, the "Golden Bough" allowed safe passage into the Underworld, and in Northern European lore, the "Silver Bough" allowed access to the Faery Realm. The mythical Odin hung on a tree and obtained enlightenment as well as the ability to foretell the future through a system of runic symbols. In European legend, Slain God figures were bound to trees in a willing sacrifice. Even the sacrificial figure known as Jesus Christ technically died on a tree as well.

Slain gods are intimately connected to the Earth and the Underworld. Slain gods are typically buried in the soil or a cave so as to return their power and fertility to the land. In this sense, they enter the Underworld and bring a renewed spirit back into the world of the living with the approach of spring. Standing stones or rings of stones frequently mark the sacred grounds associated with the Slain God mythos.

As mentioned at the beginning of this chapter, such things as ancient standing stones, stone altars, decorated cave entrances, and the sacredness of fire indicate older connections between this world and the next. As such, they form a unified symbolism as the meeting point between the worlds. To better understand this connection, we must now turn to the hidden meaning of stone, wood, and fire.

Fire and Stone (The Hearth Teachings)

In the Mystery Tradition of Witchcraft, fire and stone share an intimate relationship. This relationship may well be rooted in the ancient memory of the cave and fire, which gave shelter and protection to our ancestors. Both the cave and fire were to have mystical connections that would influence religious and magickal beliefs far into the future. The imprint on the human psyche of the ancient cave would later invoke memories of ancestors transformed by time into spirits dwelling in the dark Underworld. The ancient memory of fire would recall a realm of flitting shadows in a world that was neither day nor night.

To our ancestors, fire was a great Mystery, and it became one of the earliest forms to represent divinity. For primitive humans, fire came from beneath the earth in the form of lava, and fell from the sky as lightning. Fire provided warmth, cooked meals, produced light, protected against wild animals, and transformed raw materials (clay into pottery, wood into ashes, and so forth).

In ancient times, humans produced fire by using the heat of friction to ignite wood. Later, glass was used to focus the Sun's light onto wood or kindling in order to ignite it. An ancient belief held that the fire actually resided within the wood and had to be coaxed out in the manners described. This concept would later merge with concepts associated with tree worship. Here, fire would become the indwelling spirit of a god or goddess within the tree and its wood. Some of the earliest deities were worshipped or venerated in or near caves and grottos. Sacred fires were kept in such places as a symbol of the presence of a deity.

In ancient times, Moon goddesses were worshipped in a grotto where water issued forth from between rocky crevices. Her priestesses had to take special care of the magickal water from the Underworld, and a sacred fire in the grotto represented the light of the Moon (which flickers like fire on the surface of the water). A grotto located in a grove where there was a lake or a spring was considered especially sacred. Here, the Moon Goddess was the light of the fire itself, and as noted earlier, it was believed that fire lay hidden within wood.

In early times, the security of the divine fire required an ample supply of sacred wood that was dried and readily available in the grove or grotto of the Moon Goddess. Later in history, lamps replaced the wood, but the earlier symbolism was still intact as the lamp's fuel was often olive oil. This connected the fire back to the wood, which in this case, was an olive tree.

There is an interesting legend in which the goddess Diana is smuggled out of Greece inside a bundle of branches and delivered to Lake Nemi in Italy. Thus, Diana was the latent flame within the wood, awaiting rebirth in her new grove. The bundle of branches in which she arrived was the first supply of her torches. Stone altars were erected to the deities of our ancestors, and the sacred setting was often demarcated with large stones. Before the elaborate temples of the Aegean/Mediterranean regions were built, megaliths, menhirs, or dolmens formed primitive temples and sacred sites. Archaeological findings confirm the use of firepits at such sites. Many of the more complex formations appear to be oriented to the Sun and its journey throughout the year. Frequently, a particular stone is set so that the Sun appears to sit on its apex or to shine through a hole cut in the rock. Here, we find a spiritual fire associated with the stone.

Over the long course of countless centuries, fire eventually became domesticated and was brought into the home where it burned in the hearth. In the Aegean/Mediterranean region, the Hearth Goddess was known as Hestia/Vesta. She symbolized the purity of the divine flame, and thus its natural state (untainted by civilized human development) was preserved in the same form previously known to our ancestors. In the fire and stone of the hearth existed the unchanged link that maintained the primal connection to the ancestral spirit of our forebears.

In Celtic lore, the goddess Brighid was associated with fire. Many commentators believe that St. Brigid absorbed many elements of the Pagan goddess. One example is the keeping of a perpetual fire by nuns in the convent at Kildare. Men were not allowed entry into the area where the fire was kept. It is interesting to note that men were also not allowed in the temple of Vesta/Hestia.

Brighid, as a triple goddess, extended her nature to the three elements associated with fire in Celtic lore. Here, fire was related to the smithcraft, the mystical fire that burned beneath the Cauldron of Inspiration, and to the household hearth. The relighting of the hearth with the needfire in Celtic lore suggests the power of transformation ascribed to fire. A needfire was produced in times of great distress, and its purpose was to remove the contaminating factor and replace it with the purity of a new fire. Thus, all hearth fires in the land were extinguished and then relighted by a torch bearing the flame taken from the needfire, which typically burned as a bonfire on a nearby hill. James Frazer, in *The Golden Bough*, comments that the Church denounced such practices as heathen in origin, noting that they continued into the first half of the nineteenth century.

It is noteworthy that the ancient symbols of fire, sacred wood, caves, and stone all come together in one place as the hearth. The classic hearth was made of piled and mortared stone. The cave-like opening of the hearth housed the wood and fire. Across the top of the hearth was laid a mantle stone slab. Here, women tended the sacred fire of hearth and home, a domesticated version of the old Vesta fire. In ancient Rome, ancestral shrines were placed above the hearth as a living connection to those family members who dwelled in the Underworld. Here again, we see the cave symbolism in the hearth as an entrance to the Underworld.

On the fireplace hung the symbols of the woman, the keeper of the hearth fire. The female symbols associated with Witchcraft were the cauldron and the broom. At the hearth, the female Witch stands as a priestess of pure flame, and in this, she is the keeper of the ancient sacred flame. The mystical connection of the divine spirit of the Goddess dwelling within the wood of her grove arises in the Witch and her broom. The cauldron in Witchcraft is one of the most potent symbols of the Women's Inner Mystery Tradition. As noted earlier, this is the vessel of transformation, which Erich Neumann associates with the Great Goddess as a symbol of incarnation, birth, and rebirth (*The Great Mother,* 1972).

According to Neumann, the tending of fire was at the center of the Women's Mysteries. In the ancient "roundhouse" of primitive human culture, women created tools and vessels. The so-called roundhouse was typical of Neolithic dwellings, and the only entrance or exit was a hole in the center of the roof with the tended fire directly beneath it. This symbolism was later incorporated into the structure of the temple of the goddess Vesta. Neumann (*The Great Mother*) writes of this:

> *"But at the center of the mysteries over which the female group presided stood the guarding and tending of the fire. As in the house round about, female domination is symbolized in its center, the fireplace, the seat of warmth and food preparation, the 'hearth,' which is also the original altar. In ancient Rome this basic matriarchal element was most conspicuously preserved in the cult of Vesta and its round temple. This is the old round house or tent with a fireplace in the middle. Models of these prehistoric houses were found in the form of cinerary urns in the Roman period."*

Since the cauldron has been associated with magick since ancient times, it is no surprise to find it in the hands of the Witch figure. Standing before her hearth, where Vesta's flame dances upon the sacred log that guards the entrance to the Underworld, the Witch oversees the cauldron of transformation.

Historian Diane Purkiss, in her book *The Witch in History* (1996), speaks of the cauldron as a symbol of women's control over food production, which could be seen as a potential threat to the men of the community. Purkiss notes that the cauldron is not only a cooking pot but also a womb symbol from which metaphorical children are born. This is the Witches' magick, the birthing of the unseen into the material world and the opening of doorways into the spirit realm.

It is only natural that the bubbling cauldron should come to represent the transformational powers of the woman. The legendary potions brewed in the Witches' cauldron are reflections of the woman's bodily fluids, which to primitive minds must have seemed magickal. For example, to observe blood flowing from a woman for days (menstruation) without causing death or physical decline. Another Mystery was the production of milk from the breast, transforming one life-giving substance (blood) into another.

Neumann theorizes that to early humans, "a universal symbolic formula" existed: woman = body = vessel = world. Through this concept, nature is viewed as the Great Mother and women as microcosmic representations of this Goddess (her principles having been seen through metaphors associated with the body and bodily functions of women in general). In this view, the womb is reflected in the cauldron (where transformation takes place) and the breasts become the chalice (where nourishment is consumed in the fullness of the residing liquid substance).

The assignment of the Witch as a priestess, her traditional tools associated with the ancient Women's Mysteries, and the connection with the hearth strongly suggest the deep roots of the Witch figure in the antiquity of religious and spiritual concepts.

As noted earlier, the broom is a magickal tool associated with the hearth and the Witch. The Witches' broom symbolizes the branch of the sacred tree that was once considered to be a god or goddess. It is the tree rooted in the Underworld and stretching into the starry night. Traditionally, the Witches' broom was made from the branch of an ash tree. The sweep was made from small dried birch twigs, which were fastened to the base of the handle with strips of willow bark.

In ancient lore, the ash tree is associated with the waters of life and with the sea. The birch was said to have power over spirits, which, in ancient times, were believed to dwell in the air. The willow, with its branches turned back toward the ground, was believed to bind things to the earth. Therefore, the Witches' broom was linked to Earth, Water, and Air.

When considering the broom to be reflective of the sacred tree that housed a deity, we must consider what deity ancient Witches worshipped. The earliest literary mention of a goddess associated with Witches is Hecate. In Chapter One, we encountered her as a goddess ruling "a portion of the earth, sea, and the starry heavens." It is noteworthy here to recall the broom's link to Earth, Water, and Air. These images and connections depict the Witch intimately linked to Hecate, sharing with the goddess a portion of those things allotted to her by Zeus. The broom is, in some regards, a key to the three realms and allows the Witch the gift of spiritual flight to the starry heavens where the Moon silently awaits.

The ancient writers Horace and Lucan depict Witches as worshipping Hecate, Diana, and Proserpina. Horace also writes that Witches sing incantations from a book and thereby draw down the Moon from the heavens. The Moon has long been associated with Witches and with the Women's Mysteries in general. Neumann notes:

"...the favored spiritual symbol of the matriarchal sphere is the moon in its relation to the night and the Great Mother of the night sky. The moon, as the luminous aspect of the night, belongs to her; it is her fruit, her sublimation as light, as [an] expression of her essential spirit" (The Great Mother, 1972).

As we have seen within the symbolism detailed in this chapter, the Witch is connected to some of the most primary and essential aspects of sacredness and divinity as viewed by our ancient ancestors. The tools associated with Witchcraft are rooted in hearth and home, and field and forest. They additionally share connections with nature and are associated with primitive religious themes. Likewise, they are the symbols of feminine power and influence, both in secrecy and in open communities.

The Mythos

As noted in the book *Roman and European Mythologies*, compiled by Yves Bonnefoy (1992), the myths of the ancient gods survived well into the Middle Ages on several levels. Bonnefoy notes that its primary conveyor was folklore and that among the Pagans living in rural areas, polytheism "tenaciously persisted" despite the rise to power of Christianity. He adds that even though the followers of Christianity annihilated the sacred Pagan temples, the "cult of sylvans and nymphs" continued to thrive.

Bonnefoy describes how during the sixth century, Christian youth were educated in the ancient fables and were taught to read using a list of ancient Pagan deity names. In the twelfth century, during the so-called Carolingian Renaissance, the study of classical Greek and Roman writings flourished. Bonnefoy notes that these periods of focus on pre-Christian literature were accompanied by a continual rise in Neopaganism (*Roman and European Mythologies,* 1992).

Jean Seznec, in his book *The Survival of the Pagan Gods* (1953), presents a great deal of compelling evidence regarding the preservation of Pagan concepts and deity forms in Christian culture. Seznec points not only to the continued study of classical literature as a contributing factor, but also to the Pagan themes that were popular in art and architecture even in the late periods of the Renaissance era.

Elements of Paganism survived not only in popular culture but also in a less diluted form among the rural people who had no access to formal education. They lived much as their Pagan ancestors had lived and had little time or need for philosophical pursuits. Nature, and the forces of nature (whether called a saint, deity, or spirit), dictated the lives of the farmer and country dweller. Here also lived the Witch as they had for countless generations.

The myths and legends we find in the religion of Witchcraft are, not surprisingly, those that relate to the seasons of nature. Equally unsurprising is the appearance of ancient gods and goddesses related to the seasonal rites, along with Pagan themes of great antiquity. Together, these all combine within the rituals of Witchcraft to reflect the Inner Mystery Teachings, which convey the spiritual essence of the Old Religion.

The mythos within Witchcraft consists of multiple layers with several storylines running simultaneously. There are three primary sagas that form the foundation upon which the rituals are designed. Each of these contains a mini-saga, complete with various characters that symbolize the forces at work. The first saga centers on the Wheel of the Year, consisting of eight sabbats, and relates a tale of the courtship, mating, and marriage of the God and Goddess.

In the second saga appears the death of the God, who is shortly followed into the Underworld by the Goddess. She enters the Underworld in order to retrieve the God, and is challenged at the seven gates. Eventually, she encounters the Lord of the Shadowed Realm (unrecognized as her transformed mate) and falls in love with him. Together, they bear a child who is the new Sun God born at Yule. Within the second saga is a related theme concerning the Harvest Lord or Slain God, who is sometimes referred to as *the Divine King*.

The third saga presents the year as divided into two primary aspects, which are the waxing and waning forces that mark the period of growth and the period of decline within nature. Depending upon the cultural expression, the personifications of these forces are depicted as either the Holly and Oak King or the Stag and Wolf figure.

The mythos within the Mystery Tradition of Witchcraft expresses through metaphor what can only be interpreted and truly understood by the spirit within. One of the Mystery Teachings centers on the concept that, within each of us, there is a meeting point where our consciousness interfaces with the Divine Source from which we were created. This is sometimes referred to as the *stillpoint* or the *inner sacred space* where we meet with Divinity.

In *The Charge of the Goddess* (one of the popular texts of the Witchcraft community), there is a section that directs the seeker on an inward journey. It states that if we seek enlightenment in the external world, it will remain elusive, for enlightenment arises when we meet with the divine center at the core of our own being. What we seek outside we can find within, for the doorway has always been unlocked deep within the soul.

In part, the mythos presents a Mystery play in which we find ourselves in the cast of characters. Through this identification of ourselves with the hero, we become aligned with the principle itself. Once aligned with this, we are brought directly into the energy stream that empowers and delivers the hero in their quest. The process, once initiated, is automatic and leads the seeker deep into the labyrinth where all holy or sacred quests await on the other side. The key is receptivity and the map is found in the footprints of those who have walked the path long before us.

The Mystery View

In the Mystery Tradition, the view is held that humankind, as the self-appointed master of nature, severed its primal link with the natural world. This separation isolated humankind from the balance of spirit and matter. This resulted in a loss of natural community, and humankind solidified the situation by creating its own environment with its own laws and principles. Nature then became something outside of the cities, a wilderness in which humankind was but a visitor or traveler.

The Mystery Teachings are designed to bring humankind back into its original relationship with nature. In order to accomplish this, the Mystery Teachings reintroduce seekers to the spirit of the land. This requires, in part, a mystical interpretation of the secrets that reside in nature. In addition, the seeker rediscovers their inner connections to the balance of matter and spirit. In the process, a transformation takes place, guided by the Mystery Teachings of transformation itself. Here, they are divided into categories known as the Fermentation Mysteries and the Cauldron Mysteries. I refer the interested reader to my previous book *The Wiccan Mysteries* for more details on this aspect of Mystery Teachings.

Through a study of the Mystery Teachings, a series of memory-chain associations are created in the mind. These serve as conduits for the flow of ancestral knowledge and wisdom. Once established in the psyche of the student, the memory-chain associations draw out the metaphors contained within the rituals, myths, and legends of Witchcraft. Initiation, in the metaphysical sense, is the passing on and receiving of the key memory-chain associations.

The process of initiation, traditionally performed in a ritual setting, is a spiritual experience. Here, the mundane personality (the persona associated with the body the soul inhabits) is bypassed, and the consciousness of the indwelling soul is brought into alignment with the essence of the soul's individuality (its true nature when not incarnated in a body). This is what some people might call the *higher self.* Once true initiation takes place, the individual no longer lives day-to-day in the mindset of a common incarnate being. Instead, they live and experience life as an evolutionary process.

Once the higher consciousness can operate freely and directly in the physical body without resistance or interference by the personality, then the initiate can perceive things that would remain hidden from ordinary view. In this elevated view, the initiate can see deeply into the realm of causes. This allows the initiate to perceive events as they form in the astral substance from which all material forms and events are derived. To some, this is called *the gift of divination or prophecy.*

The alignment to the higher self establishes the consciousness actively on a higher plane of existence. Here, the will of the initiate functions directly (and with full consciousness) in the planes that oversee and influence the realms that cause manifestation to occur. This allows changes to occur in conformity with the will of the initiate. Such ability has resulted in the initiate being regarded as one who possesses magickal powers.

In the Mystery Tradition of Witchcraft, the initiate can discern the inner mechanism of nature. This theme refers to the metaphysical principles that operate behind the forms that manifest in the Material Realm. Therefore, a study and understanding of nature is an important component of discernment.

Nature as the Blueprint

The theme of the spirit of the artist within the artwork is one we shall encounter many times throughout this book. By examining the way nature operates, we can learn something about the way the minds of the creators operate. This, in turn, gives us clues about the nature of the creators themselves and some insights (limited though they may be) into the inner workings of divinity.

In the Mystery Tradition, physical forms within the material dimension are regarded as concrete energy patterns generated from the Elemental Plane. The Elemental Plane receives the image that becomes the form from a higher plane (this is covered further in Chapters Five and Eight).

As already noted, the consciousness of the initiate works directly in those planes that serve to bring about the manifestation of personal will.

The principle at work within the appearance of forms that are generated in non-material realms is summed up in the axiom "as above, so below." This refers to the principle that whatever appears in any dimension is actually a lesser reflection of the original concept or image of it that exists on a higher dimension. Therefore, the saying goes that "what is below is like that which is above." However, we must note that it does not say they are the same thing, but instead, that they are *like* one another.

Physical forms are energy patterns that vibrate at such a low frequency that they become very dense. This makes them appear and behave as though they are solid objects. However, we know that physical objects are comprised of molecules and atoms joined together in a cohesive pattern. These particles, which make up a material object, have space between them and thus, the material object is not truly solid. This is because none of the particles actually meet in a physical sense. Instead, they meet and are joined together in cohesive energy fields. Here, we see that energy forms what we call objects, and this is the very principle we are talking about. When one can attract, condense, and form energy, then one can create anything that is envisioned by personal will. Here is another level of what we might refer to as a *meeting point*.

The initiate also looks at mythology as a blueprint for how divine energy operates and the way it can react when it interfaces with human consciousness. In this sense, the deities can be viewed, in part, as energy patterns that operate in the Material Dimension but are generated from a higher dimension. In the case of the latter, we are referring to the Divine Dimension.

Myths can serve as the blueprints for not only understanding our relationship with the Divine but also for learning to construct new ways of interfacing and interacting with the Divine Source. A study of the mythos is therefore essential in order to align the consciousness of the initiate. Such an alignment brings a greater depth of understanding to ritual, magick, and our relationship with other entities and deities.

Let us now turn to the next chapter, where we will encounter the God as perceived in the Mystery Tradition of Witchcraft. Following that chapter, we shall meet the Witches' Goddess, and thereby deepen our understanding of divinity as expressed and understood within the religion of Witchcraft.

CHAPTER THREE

The God of the Witches

In this chapter, we will examine that aspect of the divine source known as the God, and we will look at how he is viewed in the Mystery Tradition of Witchcraft. The God figure is really a composite character comprised of various aspects. Each aspect or personification relates to how we interface with him, which is often associated with the seasons of the year. Just as we may look and act differently when we are at work, at home, or out for an evening of entertainment, so too does the God take on a persona appropriate to the setting in which we find him. It is through the integration of every aspect of the God that we can truly come to know him in a larger sense.

The oldest image of the God in Witchcraft is rooted in prehistoric concepts reflected in primitive art and iconography. Within the Mystery Tradition of Witchcraft, the rural concepts of pre-Christian European Paganism have been added and developed over the centuries. This development is something that is still ongoing in modern times as the Tradition continues to evolve. Because of this, we now possess a wonderful blend of things that are ever-ancient and ever-new.

The primary mythos of the God in Witchcraft depicts him as an infant born on the winter solstice, who grows to power, meets the nature

Goddess figure, impregnates her, then soon after, dies a sacrificial death and enters the Underworld. He is then reborn again at the winter solstice. Overall, the God is viewed as possessing several primary aspects, which are the Sun God of life, the Horned God of fertility, and the Harvest Lord of renewal. Within these aspects, others exist as well and will be explored throughout the book.

In 1948, poet and quasi-historian Robert Graves published his work titled *The White Goddess*. In Chapter One of his book, Graves writes of an essential "theme" that he believed was present in the popular celebration festivals we now call the seasonal rites or the Witches' sabbats. Graves also wrote that the theme *"...was also secretly preserved as religious doctrine in the covens of the anti-Christian witchcult."*

Graves describes his referenced theme as an ancient tale centered on the birth, life, death, and resurrection of the God of the Waxing Year. The author notes that an integral aspect of this theme concerns the God losing a battle with the God of the Waning Year. According to Graves, this battle is fought over the love of the "all-powerful Threefold Goddess," who he describes as the mother, bride, and "layerout" of the two brother Gods (*The White Goddess*, 1948).

In modern Witchcraft, the figures mentioned by Robert Graves relate to those referred to as the Oak King and Holly King. The Oak King symbolizes the waxing forces of nature, which begin at midwinter and end at midsummer. The Holly King symbolizes the waning forces of nature, which run from midsummer to midwinter. The brothers battle against one another at the beginning of each seasonal reign, and in the mythos, the loser withdraws into Caer Arianrhod (the Castle of Arianrhod) and awaits his time of power to return. According to authors Janet and Stewart Farrar (*The Witches' God*, 1989), the traditional mummer's play has preserved the ancient theme of the battling kings. Here, St. George is the Oak King, and the Turkish knight equates to the Holly King.

An interesting mythos exists in ancient Aegean/Mediterranean writings that present a similar theme as the one reflected in the Oak and Holly King myth. Roberto Calasso, in his book *The Marriage of Cadmus and Harmony* (1994), recounts Plutarch's references to the relationship between the Delphic Apollo and Dionysos. Plutarch wrote that in the freezing winter months, Dionysos is lord of Delphi, but when Apollo returns for the other months of the year, he reigns supreme. Calasso notes that no victory between the two is ever complete, nor does either last the whole year. He concludes that neither Apollo nor Dionysos can reign forever, nor can they do without the other or remain in one season all of the time.

An older mythos (one prior to personifying him in human form) exists among Tuscan Witches. In various traditions of Italian Witchcraft, the waxing and waning forces of the year differ from the Northern European mythos not only in personification but also in time of year. In the Old Religion of the region now called Italy, the wolf represented the waning year, and the stag symbolized the waxing year. The time of the wolf commenced on the fall equinox, and the time of the stag began on the spring equinox.

Some commentators have suggested that the symbolism of the God is related to the phallus and its characteristics. In the God of the Year analogy, we find the rise from a small child to an attainment of fullness in power (often associated with the spilling of life in sacrifice), and then a subsequent diminishment or disappearance. This parallelism to the mechanics of the male erection seems significant to themes related to a God of Fertility, which is the root symbolism of the Witches' God figure.

In Witchcraft, the symbolism of growth, fullness, and decline is connected to the God in all of his key aspects. As the Stag-Horned God, we note the seasonal growth of antlers, their use in adult mating battles, and then the following seasonal loss of the firm antlers. Examining the theme of the Sun God aspect, we find the three stages of dawn, noon, and sunset. As the Harvest Lord, we note the cycle of planting, growing, and harvesting. In the aspect of an Underworld God, we discover the repeating cycle of birth, life, and death (discussed further in the section of this chapter titled "The Underworld God").

Archaeologist Marija Gimbutas (*The Language of the Goddess*, 1991) views prehistoric images of the God figure as metaphorical depictions of "rising and dying vegetation." Gimbutas notes earlier images depicting a pre-agricultural era during which male figures in prehistoric art appear wearing masks designed as various animals and birds. The most famous image is that of the stag-horned man figure discovered at Les Trois Freres in what is now France. Archaeologists often refer to this figure as the "sorcerer."

The Horned God

The image of the God in Witchcraft is traditionally that of a stag-horned man. In various periods and regions of Europe, the God has also been depicted with goat horns or the horns of a bull. Historian Walter Otto (*Dionysus, Myth and Cult*) states it was an ancient belief that when river gods emerged from the water onto the land, they took on the form of a bull. This symbolized their fertile effect upon the land as a rushing and roaring body of water.

The early Christian Church tried to equate the Horned Pagan God with the biblical Devil or Satan figure. To this end, the Council of Toledo, circa 447, depicted Satan (who is never physically described in any biblical text) as a large, black, monstrous apparition with horns on his head, cloven hoofs, and an immense phallus. Such identification then conveniently paved the way for further connections between Paganism and Witchcraft and the Judeo-Christian Devil or Satan figure.

During the period of the Witchcraft trials throughout Europe, a horned figure is prominently featured. During the sixteenth and seventeenth centuries, those accused of Witchcraft in England and Scotland "confessed" to seeing the "Devil" in the form of a bull. During these same periods, in France, Italy, and the Basque region, the "Devil" is depicted with the horns of a goat. One of the earliest identifications with a goat-horned figure dates from Witchcraft trials in Toulouse and Carcassonne circa 1335.

In modern Witchcraft, the God is most commonly depicted with stag horns. He is known by many names including Cernunnos, Dianus, Herne, Pan, and Dionysos.

However, some modern traditions have replaced the Horned God with such figures as the Sun God Lugh. Yet many traditions still call upon the ancient Stag-Horned God depicted on the cave walls by our prehistoric ancestors.

The stag figure still calls to something primal within us. There is a seemingly magickal or mystical nature connected to deer antlers. This allure may have its roots deep in the human psyche, from a time when our ancestors hunted deer for survival. Our early ancestors used antlers for tools, weapons, and religious ceremonies. Perhaps the ancient memory of such an essential item is evoked within us when we see or touch a deer's antler, and we are now instinctively drawn to it. But perhaps there is something of actual magick here, as we shall see.

Mythologists and social anthropologists are well acquainted with what is called the "covenant of the hunter and the hunted." Joseph Campbell addresses this quite nicely in his book *The Masks of God: Primitive Mythology* (1991). A mythos arises from the covenant, which also appears in elements of the mythos within the Mystery Tradition of Witchcraft. The key points are the sacredness of the hunt, the sacrificial death of the hunted, and the renewal and resurrection of life for the one that is slain.

In our mythos, the sacredness of the hunt emerges as a metaphor that embraces the theme of the waxing and waning years overtaking one another in an endless cycle. The metaphor also extends to the God who faces a willing sacrificial death in the season of harvest. The sacrificial theme is extremely ancient and was practiced in many lands even outside of Europe.

The willing sacrifice manifests in the mythos of the God, surrendering his life for the well-being of his people. He was originally the Horned God of the woods, the stag whose body provided food, clothing, tools, and primitive weapons. In time, he evolved into the Harvest Lord, the spirit of the crops.

For our ancestors, as hunters, the renewal of life and the resurrection of the slain centered on the bone. The bone remained after the body decayed (in a sense, surviving death) and it was the bone that allowed the body to be animated. Therefore, the bone held significant meaning. From a magickal perspective, the bone could be used to restore life and return the slain to this world.

In hunter society, one of the primitive methods of returning the life of the slain stag was to place the antlers in a clearing just before sunrise. When the first ray of sunlight fell upon the antler, the hunter who killed the deer touched their arrow to the antler. Next, they drew their bow and released the arrow into the sky to fall back somewhere in the woods, thus returning the life of the stag into the woodlands. It is interesting to note a similar theme in the tale of *Robin Hood*. Here, the character fires an arrow into the air above the forest and asks to be buried wherever the arrow lands (*The Merry Adventures of Robin Hood*, Howard Pyle, 1883).

It was an ancient belief that some part of the life spirit of a slain stag remained in the hide and bone. To wear such an item allowed the merging of man and animal spirit. By wearing a hide cloak and donning the antlers, the power and secret knowledge of the beast could pass into the hunter (or priest). The primitive sorcerer or priest, wearing the ceremonial headdress of antlers, could reanimate the body and life of the stag. This fulfilled the covenant between the hunter and the hunted; for the covenant called for returning the life of the slain in exchange for the surrendering of the body.

The dependence upon deer and the resulting relationship with this creature formed several key elements of the mythos of the Mystery Tradition of Witchcraft. These elements relate to the characteristics of the Horned God as well as to the seasons of the year marked by the sabbats. In order to better understand this, we must become more acquainted with the deer itself. Here, once again, the antlers hold the key.

The growth and eventual shedding of their antlers mark the life cycle of deer. The further deer are from the equator, the more defined their antler cycle. For example, the deer in Northern Europe have a shorter window of when antler shedding can occur compared to deer in Southern Europe. In North America, the deer cycles are closer to those in Southern Europe than those in Northern Europe. In Alaska and Canada, the pattern blends well with the British Isles.

Deer shed their antlers annually as a prelude to the regeneration or regrowth of the new ones. In most species, regrowth generally takes place in the springtime, and the antlers begin to return almost immediately after being shed. While antlers are growing, a furry skin covering called *velvet* envelops them. The growth and hardening of the antlers is completed in late July or August.

In August, increased production of testosterone cuts off the blood supply to the antlers and velvet. The velvet dies away, dries up, and peels off. Further removal of velvet from antlers occurs during the mating rut. The increase of testosterone manifests in the stag thrashing his antlers against sapling trees and shrubs. This behavior scrapes off the velvet as well as polishes and stains the antlers.

The reduced daylight of winter diminishes testosterone production and causes the shedding of antlers. Mature males shed their antlers in February or March (younger males may retain their antlers until May). The entire shedding process takes about two to three weeks to complete. The phase of regrowth takes place over the summer. The speed at which antlers regenerate makes them the fastest-growing structures in the animal kingdom.

Bucks begin growing their antlers in late winter or early spring, within weeks of when the previous year's antlers are shed. At first, the antlers grow very slowly, but by late May, their growth increases rapidly and is usually complete by the end of August. The antlers are then ready to impress the female and to fight the competing males for the right to mate.

It is interesting to note that this cycle does not apply to the roebuck, one of the most ancient deer known to inhabit the British Isles. The roebuck is unusual even among the other deer that are native to the Isles. This particular deer is also an important symbol in the form of Witchcraft taught by Robert Cochrane. This tradition is detailed in the book *The Roebuck in the Thicket* (2001) by Evan John Jones.

The roebuck shed and regrow their antlers in the winter. As noted, other deer develop and grow antlers over spring and summer. The roe are born between late May and early June and are commonly twins (although triplets are not rare). The rut takes place between late July and early August. Bucks shed their antlers between October and December.

Various themes associated with personifications of the waxing and waning year present themselves in the observance of the deer cycle (those personifications being the Oak and Holly King in Northern European lore and the Stag and Wolf of Southern Europe). During the rut period of the roebuck, his seed is spilled, or "life essence" is surrendered during the time of harvest in the British Isles. In Southern Europe, the harvest period comes later, and so too does the rutting season of the deer. This likewise matches the harvest period.

The theme of the spilling of the seed or the "surrendering of the life essence" later appears in the Harvest Lord mythos (discussed later in this chapter). This was a direct evolutionary transfer of the hunter-gatherer perception to that of the following agrarian society. The ancient primitive hunter's view of the stag and wolf as nature symbols reflecting the seasonal shifts eventually gave way to the later "civilized" view of human imagery, which replaced the earlier form as humans developed farming communities.

Here, we find such images as the Oak King and Holly King, human personifications wearing leaf crowns that speak of their previous connection to the woodland deer.

In the book *The God Year* (1998) by Nigel Pennick, an illustration appears depicting the Oak King wearing a crown with acorns upon the spiked tips. The style of the crown resembles the horns of a stag. Here, the artist has captured a blended image of one extremely ancient and one very old concept of the waxing forces of the year.

In the Welsh tale of Culhwch and Olwen, the stag is one of the oldest animals in the world. The white stag, in particular, is associated with great antiquity and is also associated with the Otherworld or Underworld in Celtic lore symbol. This concept is related to the mythological view of the deer as a magickal creature able to move between the worlds. It is interesting to note that the Stag-Horned God of the Witches also possesses this ability as being both the Lord of the Woods and the Lord of the Underworld. Author Nigel Jackson (*Masks of Misrule*, 1996) notes that the white stag is a form taken by the Horned God in the Arthurian romances, where in various tales he lures the knights "deeper into the Otherworldly forests."

As Lord of the Woods, the Stag-Horned God is the Lord of the Beasts, ruler of the animal kingdom. All creatures that live within the woodlands are sacred to him. The symbolism of the Stag-Horned God and the Lord of the Woods come together in the tree itself. The antlers of the stag resemble tree branches, which shed their leaves like the stag antlers shed their velvet. Following this, both the antlers and the trees are left with a bare structure very similar in design.

In light of the ever-renewing antlers, the stag became associated with fertility and rebirth. The Celtic Horned God Cernunnos was depicted with the antlers of a stag and was associated with fertility and abundance. In Southern Europe, the Horned God of the woodlands was known as Dianus. Historian Julio Baroja (*The World of Witches,* 1961) notes that St. Martin of Braga wrote in the sixth century of his encounters with the Cult of Diana and of her male companion Dianum, which is the Latin form of Dianus.

Social anthropologist James Frazer (*The Golden Bough,* 1890) wrote of the god Dianus as a consort of the goddess Diana in ancient times at what is now Lake Nemi, Italy. Frazer associates Dianus with the sacred oak grove in the sanctuary of Diana. He also points to connections between Dianus and the Great God Jupiter/Zeus. Diana is also connected to a figure known as *Actaeon* who was transformed into a stag, and his death may be viewed as a type of sacrificial end (the price of the uninitiated seeing the Goddess unveiled).

When we consider the various elements and attributes that combined to form the Stag-Horned God image in Witchcraft, a very clear character emerges. From the hunted deer, we find his attribute of provider. In his fierce determination to mate during the rutting season, here is displayed the God of Fertility. As protector of the herd (or at least his female harem), we discover him as guardian. In the cycle of the stag's antlers, he is linked to the changing of the seasons. His swift disappearance into the woods and thickets speaks of Otherworld traversing. When we see his shed antlers upon the forest floor (as though this were all that remains of him), we encounter the sign of his Underworld nature.

For countless centuries, the stag and his antlers held much meaning to humankind. Not only was the stag a source of food, clothing, and needed tools, but he was also a spirit, and later, a god. However, even though the stag was a powerful being, his hide and antlers were to give way to a focus upon the green growth of the cultivated field. As the hunter spent more days behind the plow, the memory of the Lord of the Woods slowly began to ebb away. The image of another god was coming now to replace the old one of the forest.

The Green Man

The theme of the Green Man reflects the plant cycle of growth, harvest, and replanted seed. Here, the spirit of the Green Man grows in the grain and is bound up in the harvest. He is then returned to the earth through the planting of seeds taken from the ripe plants.

One of the earliest images of a Green Man appears carved on a temple wall in what is now Iraq (at Hatra) and dates from around 700 BCE. Green Man images also appear in Greek art of this same period. The earliest Celtic representation of the Green Man is arguably that of the stone carving known today as the St. Goar pillar. It was discovered in Germany and dates from the fifth century BCE. The style of the carving demonstrates a blend of Etruscan and Celtic art forms of the period.

It is revealing that blended images of humans and animals appear in art and iconography long before those of plants. This is not surprising when one considers that our ancestors depended upon animals for food and clothing for quite some time before humans developed agriculture. Therefore, the concept of the animal spirit preceded that of the plant spirit.

With the shift from hunter-gatherer to agrarian society, the religious and spiritual focus was likewise transformed. The old image of the horned Lord of the Woods became the leaf-faced Green Man. The connective imagery remained intact through the depiction of foliage in the mouth of the Green Man, for this was the remnant image of the stag eating the bounty of the forest while peering out through the thicket. With the passage of time, this imagery came to represent the bounty of nature issuing forth from the open mouth of the Green Man.

The popularity of the Green Man demonstrates a widespread acceptance of the spirit of the woodland animal kingdom now embraced as the spirit of the vegetable kingdom. His spirit could then be transported from the dark wooded places into the open cultivated fields. The Green Man then became the spirit of the land itself. This theme is essential to the transference of the Mystery Tradition from hunter-gatherer to agrarian society.

As humankind continued to become more "civilized" and develop communities with walls, gates, and structures, nature itself was pushed into an exterior concept. Nature became viewed as wilderness, and no longer as home. This severed (or, at the very least, obstructed) a deep inner personal connection to nature that was once equally shared by all living things of the Earth. Humankind had begun to establish itself as the "master of nature" rather than as a living part (and partner) of nature.

During the Middle Ages and well into the Renaissance periods, the Green Man image was placed in the architecture of many structures, including Christian places of worship. Many of the oldest cathedrals contain Green Man images on the pillars that support the ceilings. Oral tradition among Witches holds that the carvers were Pagan people wishing to view their own gods even though they were forced by social pressure to attend Christian worship. With the Green Man hidden high up on the pillars (often partially obscured by the foliage design), Pagans in attendance could look up and still pray to the Old Ones of field or forest. Historians state that such images were intentionally commissioned and not secretly added to the general foliage patterns common in the art style of the period. However, if these historians are correct, then they must answer why Christians would want the Pagan Green Man figures in their places of worship.

In some Celtic-based traditions of Witchcraft, there is a belief that the Green Man appears in the tales of King Arthur. Here he is seen as a figure such as the Green Knight, with whom both Gawain and Arthur have personal encounters. Some commentators view the conflicts that arise between the Green Knight and Gawain (or in some cases, Arthur) as representing the opposing forces of the waxing and waning seasons of the year.

Author John Matthews (*The Quest for the Green Man,* 2001) equates Arthur and Melwas as challenging seasonal symbols in the twelfth-century story *Life of Gildas.* Here, Matthews sees Arthur as the Winter King and Melwas as the Summer King. They confront one another over the maiden Guinevere, which Matthews views as the spring maiden of earlier Pagan myth or legend. In the *Story of Culhwch and Olwen,* Matthews equates Gwythyr with winter and Gwynn ap Nudd with summer. The two also have a confrontation over a maiden (Creiddylad) who Matthews equates with the spring maiden theme.

The theme to which Matthews refers is an old tale of the abduction of the spring maiden by the Winter and Summer Kings. The maiden bears many titles such as the May Queen, Spring Maiden, and the Flower Bride. Ritual combat to win her hand is fought on the first day of May.

Matthews mentions a Welsh folklorist named Marie Trevelyan who wrote of a May celebration in South Wales. The celebration contained various related elements to the theme Matthews describes.

In the folklorist's account, two captains each lead their own band of followers organized into winter and summer teams. The captain of the winter team carries a stick made of blackthorn, and the summer captain bears a willow wand. Ritual combat takes place with the winter team flinging straw and dried wood at the summer team, who defend themselves with birch branches, willow wands, and ferns. The winning captain (in this case, that of summer) then picks a May Queen for the continuing celebrations (Matthews, *The Quest for the Green Man*).

Festival activities were noted in 1610 at Chesterton in celebration of St. George's Day. The observer noted the appearance of *"...two disguised, called Greenemen, their habit Embroidered and Stitch'd on with Ivieleaves...z* An eighteenth century written description of Green Man figures states that *"They are called wouldmen, or wildmen, thou' at thes day we in ye signe (trade) call them Green Men, couered with grene boues...a fit emblem for those that use that intosticating licker which berefts them of their sennes"* (Simpson and Roud, *Oxford Dictionary of English Folklore*). In this description, we see a reflection of Dionysos, the God of Intoxication who wears a wreath of ivy on his head.

From the perspective of the Witches' Mystery Tradition, celebrations such as these helped preserve the pre-Christian Pagan themes among the populace, once Christianity had displaced the Old Religion. According to the oral tradition among Witches, there have been many periods in history during which members of the Old Religion directly or indirectly influenced (and in some cases, spearheaded) public celebrations and festivals. This included organizing street plays such as the mummers, symbolic dances like the Furry Dance, as well as introducing legendary characters such as John Barleycorn, Green Jack (or Jack-in-the-Green), Straw Bear, the Green Man, and others.

As we have seen in this section, the Green Man has been associated with the King of Winter and Summer and with the theme of growth and harvest. This association has led to identification with the willing sacrificial figure known as the Slain God (or Sacrificial King) in the Mystery Tradition of Witchcraft. Some of the deepest secrets of the Green Man lie within the teachings centered on the Slain God in aspect as Harvest Lord.

The Sacred King or Slain God

In the Mystery Tradition of Witchcraft, the Slain God or Sacrificial King represents the God as incarnate in the world of humankind. As a kingly figure, he rules over the land and its people. The well-being of the people and the fertility of the land are linked to the king's physical, ethical, and emotional state. The concept of the God in this aspect (and its connection to the Green Man) evolved from ancient tree worship. This is further explored throughout this section.

Our ancestors worshipped trees in ancient times, first viewing them as beings in and of themselves, then later as the dwelling place of spirits. Still later, the tree was considered to be the temporary abode of a god. This god could pass from tree to tree and thereby establish himself as the Lord of the Woods. It is here that the God takes on the form of a human personification.

In ancient art and iconography, sylvan deities are depicted in human form and bear a branch (or something related to the tree) in their hands. They traditionally possess the power to bring rain and have influence over the Sun. Mythological figures of a woodland nature are most often depicted carrying a club or staff, which is typically made of oak. Such images range from the Aegean/Mediterranean, where we find Sylvanus and Hercules, to the British Isles containing such figures as the Wild Man, Wild Herdsman, and the huge chalk figure in Dorset depicting a giant holding a club.

In Ovid's *Fasti*, there is an interesting legend connecting the horned woodland god Faunus and the hero Hercules. According to Ovid, one day, Faunus came across the beautiful Omphale (Queen of the Amazons), as she was arriving to attend the annual festival given in his honor. Hercules escorted Omphale, and they both went into a cave to pass the night. After drinking a large quantity of wine, at some point during the night, Omphale dressed Heracles in her own clothing and she put on his lion skin garment.

As Hercules and Omphale slept, Faunus crept into the cave intent on seducing Omphale. In the darkness, he felt the soft dress belonging to Omphale and slid his hand under it only to discover the hairy leg (and more) belonging to Hercules. His startled cry awoke both Hercules and Omphale, who then laughed at the embarrassed god. As a future preventive measure against a repeat of this event, Faunus then ordered from that day forth that all celebrants of his rituals must attend his rites fully naked. In modern Witchcraft, ritual nudity is referred to as being *skyclad*. Most of the older traditions still practice this, either year-round or during the summer months.

Robert Graves (*The White Goddess,* 1948) states that in the earliest legends, Hercules appears as a "pastoral sacred king." He is ritually married each year to what Graves calls "a queen of the woods." In this legend, Hercules can bring rain by rattling his oak club in the hollow of an oak tree and stirring a pool of water. As noted earlier, this is an attribute of woodland gods, which dates to great antiquity.

Graves describes the ritual death of Hercules drawn from a variety of sources. Here, Hercules is made drunk with mead on midsummer and is then led into a circle comprised of twelve stones encircling an oak tree in the center. The oak tree has been chopped to form a "T" shape, and before it is set an altar. Hercules is then bound to the oak in what Graves calls the "five-fold bond." This involves being suspended upside down with the wrists, ankles, and neck bound together with willow thongs.

Hercules is next beaten to unconsciousness, flayed, blinded, castrated, and then finally impaled with a mistletoe stake. His blood is then drained into a basin from which his tribe is later sprinkled in a type of sacred anointing. In his book, *Western Inner Workings* (1983), William Gray addresses many aspects of this type of Mystery theme.

In early tribal states, hunters and warriors held a significant and central place in tribal social structure. The bravest and most cunning tribe member was honored among the tribe and was generally regarded as a leader. As a key member of the tribe, the well-being of this individual affected that of the tribe. This is a theme openly found in the King Arthur mythos of Northern Europe. Merlin instructs Arthur that if he succeeds, the land will flourish, but if he fails, the land will perish. Arthur asks "Why?" and Merlin replies, "Because you are King. You are the Land, and the Land is you!" To understand this intimate relationship, we must look at the deepest connections hidden in the mythos.

Prior to the development of agriculture, our ancestors relied upon hunting to supplement the roots, berries, and nuts gathered in the woodlands. Hunting was essential to life because, without successful hunters, the tribe would face great hardships. Hunting was dangerous for many reasons, one of the primary being that primitive weapons required the hunters to be close to their prey. Personal injuries were common and many hunters lost their lives or were made lame as a result of the hunt. In time, the hunter became the warrior, further risking their life for the sake of their tribe. The needs of the tribe required sending out the best the tribe had to offer as hunters or warriors.

In time, this concept evolved into a connection within religion and its views regarding the relationship with deity. The concept of deity and its role in life and death took root within ritual and the system of beliefs in general. As an extension of the hunter-warrior theme of "sending out," the eventual idea arose of sending the best member the tribe could offer directly to the gods. Just as they secured food and needed supplies in the woods for the tribe, so too could they secure favors from the gods in the Otherworld. This was the birth of human sacrifice, and those who went willingly were believed to become powerful spirits or gods themselves.

In the Slain God mythos, the sending of the best is only part of the story, for the desire remains to retrieve the valued member and return them to the tribe. In the Mystery Texts of Witchcraft, we find a passage that reads: *"...and you must meet, know, remember, and love them again."* To accomplish this, rituals were designed to ensure the rebirth of the Slain God back into the bloodline to which he was formerly connected. Special maidens were prepared to bring about the birth. These were usually virgins who were artificially inseminated so that no human was known to be the father.

Over the passing centuries, rituals, practices, and beliefs matured and evolved. Human sacrifice shifted to animal sacrifice, which then gave way in time to plant sacrifice. Yet the same essence of the mythos was applied to plant sacrifice, and so we find the "consuming of deity" today in the ritual meal of cakes and wine (symbolic flesh and blood) within the Mystery Tradition of Witchcraft.

In the ancient tradition, it was through the connection of the body and blood of the Slain God, that the people were made one with deity. This is essentially the same essential concept of the Christian rite of Communion in which wine and bread symbolize the blood and body of Christ. At the Last Supper, Jesus tells his followers that the bread and wine on the table before them are his body and blood. He then declares that he will lay down his life for his believers and bids his disciples to consume his flesh and drink of his blood.

Blood was believed to contain the essence of the life force. The death of the Sacred King released the indwelling sacred spirit, which could then be distributed (through the flesh and blood) to the people and the land. Through such an act, heaven and earth were united, and the vital energy once contained within the Sacred King now renewed the entire realm.

The Sacred King/Slain God appears in various aspects throughout the ages. His image can be seen in the Jack-in-the-Green, the Hooded Man, the Green Man, and The Hanged Man of the tarot. He is the Lord of Vegetation, the Harvest Lord, and in his wild (or free) aspect, he is the Lord of the Forest. He does not take the place of the Earth Mother, nor does he usurp her power of generation. He is, instead, the compliment to her—her consort.

The Green Man is intimately connected to the mythos of the Sacred King/Slain God. He is the Spirit of the Land, manifesting in all plant forms, both cultivated and natural. He is the procreative power and the seed of life. The Green Man maintains the relationship of man to nature in his merged appearance as human and foliage. He is, in effect, our bridge between the worlds. He is One with Heaven and Earth, and to be One with him is to be One with the Source of All Things.

The goal of oneness is connected to the "taking in" of that which was "sent out." The mystical theme of consuming is at the core of the Mystery Teaching associated with the Sacred King or Slain God. The seed must go into the earth and the God must go into the soul. In essence, burial takes place in the soil and the stomach.

The "spilling of the seed" is a Mystery phrase associated with the mythos of the Sacred King or Slain God. It refers both to the ripe seed of the harvest, which must fall into the soil, and to the release of the life force in blood (or in semen). The harvest itself is the magickal act that begins the cycle of rebirth. The Harvest Lord is the spirit that assures the continuation of the cycle of birth, death, and rebirth.

The Harvest Lord

The Harvest Lord is essentially a title for the Sacred King or Slain God who is killed at his prime (the time of his ripened grain). Throughout Europe, he was called by many names such as John Barleycorn, Haxey Hood, or Jack-in-the-Green. By whatever name or image, he symbolizes the ever-repeating theme of renewal. This renewal is a "refilling" of divine energy back into the soil to replace what the crops have consumed, as well as back into the bodies of the people (wherein dwells the soul). By consuming the Sacred King or Slain God (before the passing of his prime), each individual was revitalized within the very center of their being.

In many cases, the sacrificial body is burned and its ashes scattered over the plowed fields to ensure (and restore) the fertility of the soil. This theme still survives in old European customs where effigies of mythical figures are burned at the closing of the year. This is performed to remove the negative influences of the past year and fertilize the potential properties of the next year. Even in popular public festivals, straw figures are lit on fire and are typically associated with the harvest (either past or future).

It is important to note the magickal associations related to the burning of an effigy connected to agriculture. Heat and light are essential to the growth of a plant and its production of fruit or grain. The fire represents the sunlight and moonlight which first gave birth to the agricultural deity. Just as the plant seeds and dies only to produce another plant, so too does the God die so that he may live again. Therefore, the Harvest Lord must return to his source in order to complete and initiate the cycle of life.

One of the oldest Scottish and English folk images is derived from the Corn or Barley God whose beginnings are rooted in the camps of primitive Neolithic farmers. An old Scottish folk song collected centuries ago tells of such a god. He is called John Barleycorn, a mythical figure cut down by three men seeking to prove their prowess. To many people, the image of John Barleycorn represents the Lord of the Woods, the Life Spirit, and the Spirit of Death and Resurrection.

The traditional ballad of John Barleycorn describes the planting of the seed or bulb in spring, the growth of the plant at the summer solstice, and the harvesting in the fall season. The ballad speaks of the tenacity of life and the ever-returning cycle within nature. It reveals that no matter how much humankind tries to master nature, nature will always prevail in the end. Here is the old traditional Ballad of John Barleycorn:

"There were three men come out of the west
Their victory to try
And those three men took a solemn vow
John Barleycorn must die.
They plowed, they sowed, they harrowed him in,
Throwed clods upon his head,
And those three men made a solemn vow
John Barleycorn was dead.
They let him lie for a very long time
'Til the rains from heaven did fall.
And little Sir John sprung up his head
And so amazed them all.
They let him stand til the midsummer's day
'Til he looked both pale and wan.
And Little Sir John's grown a long, long beard
And so became a man.
They hired men with the scythes so sharp to cut him
Off at the knee.

They rolled him and tied him around the waist
And served him barbarously.
They hired men with the hard pitchfork
To pierce him through the heart.
And the loader he has served him worse than that
For he bound him to a cart.
They wheeled him round and around the field
'Til they came unto a barn
And these three men made a solemn oath
On poor John Barleycorn.
They hired men with the holly club
To flay him skin from bone.
And the miller he served him worse than that
For he ground him between two stones.
Here's Little Sir John in a nut brown bowl
And brandy in the glass.
And Little Sir John in the nut brown bowl
Proved the stronger man at last.
For the huntsman he can't hunt the fox
Nor so loudly blow his horn
And the tinker he can't mend kettle nor pot
Without a little of the Barleycorn."

In this tale of John Barleycorn, we find that he is not only consumed but also provides raw materials. This is the same relationship humankind perceived in the hunted deer. So once again, we find the transplantation of woodland stag connections over to the Green Man spirit. In the development of the agricultural Mysteries, the mythos within the Mystery Tradition of Witchcraft was enriched and expanded.

With the advent of agriculture, our ancestors developed a stronger connection in magickal thought between an object, an act, and a result. Here, the seed is the object, planting is the act, and crops are the result. In addition to this theme, there arose another magickal concept, which is that of timing. There is a time to plow, plant, grow, and harvest. Although a similar cycle applied to hunting, in the agricultural society, the theme was more pronounced and readily observable to all.

In the early period before our ancestors fully understood planting, the seed itself was something of an object of power. Our ancestors believed that a spirit dwelled within the seed and that this spirit would produce the plant if treated appropriately; for not every seed sprouts, and not every sprout survives.

Ancient people viewed the plant itself as a manifestation of the spirit that once dwelled within the seed. When harvest time came, the plant spirit was believed to flee from bundle to bundle as the harvest was stacked in the fields. The farmers had to capture the spirit in the last bundle before it could escape the field totally, which would render the soil lifeless.

Once captured, the spirit of the land could be returned to the soil and thus ensure that the seeds planted in the spring would thrive. In the early farming communities, when a stranger appeared at the time of the harvest, they were regarded as the plant spirit trying to sneak off in the guise of a human. Therefore, the stranger was seized and sacrificed in the field next to the last sheaf. Their blood spilled back into the soil, returning the fertile spirit.

In modern times, such practices are now symbolic. There are still cases in which a visitor to a rural farm community at harvest time is captured and harassed by the locals. Often, this person is tied up and held for a time, all in good sport (or so say the locals). When no strangers appear at harvest time, the last reaper in the field becomes the personification of the Plant Spirit, and they are subject to the same treatment dished out to strangers. In this modified version of the old mythos, the plant spirit is driven out by the cutting of the last sheaf and must now take on another physical form. Therefore, they pass into the reaper who becomes the embodiment of the spirit.

What we see in harvest lore rites is the magickal art of imitation or mimicry. Such rituals are, in effect, an attempt to encourage nature through imitation to initiate the Wheel of the Year in a timely and fruitful fashion. This is basically what is referred to as *sympathetic magick*. Our Pagan ancestors believed that the forces of nature could be attracted and directed by personifying the principles of nature through ritual enactments.

In harvest symbols, characters, and rites, the participants evoke a mystical influence through sympathetic magick. This is performed to encourage the spirits to take up the drama in their own realm and thus produce the desired results on Earth. In other words, the hope is that what is done on the physical plane will be mirrored in the Otherworld, which will, in turn, empower the material form with the spiritual essence.

All things being equal, Witches never ignored the material world in favor of the spiritual realm. The elements of rain and Sun were understood as vital to plant growth. The life-preserving essence fell upon the fields from the heavens in the form of moisture, heat, and light. But from what source did this life itself come?

The Sun God

The Sun is one of the oldest symbols to appear in prehistoric art. Many sects were created in different parts of the world to venerate the Sun, and sacrificial offerings were an integral aspect of solar-oriented religions. Most, but not all, ancient European cultures viewed the Sun as masculine, and the associated deity was, therefore, a male figure. The ancient Celts attributed both gods and goddesses to the Sun, and some Germanic tribes viewed the Sun as feminine. For the purpose of this chapter, we will focus on the Sun as related to the God in the Mystery Tradition of Witchcraft.

The Sun God, in his mythos, is born on the winter solstice. He is the son of the Great Mother Goddess who gives him birth and receives him back into herself at death. This imagery is reflected in the rising and setting of the Sun. At sunrise, the Sun seemingly issues forth from the Earth like a child born from a womb. At sunset, the Sun sinks and declines as in death, until his light ebbs away and he enters into darkness.

Many attributes were given to the Sun as various associations came into place. The primary attributes were: Sky God, destroyer of darkness, protector/savior, restorer, life-giver, and all-knower/all-seer. The gods of all European sects fit into one or more of these categories. The process through which our ancestors associated the Sun God with various attributes is directly connected to our own biology.

Renowned mythologist Joseph Campbell (*The Masks of God: Primitive Mythology,* 1991) wrote that myths arise from the patterns of our own biological experience of the world in which we live and experience life. The imprints of our experiences are associated with the setting or situation in which the experience has a profound effect. This is what Campbell calls the "firm syndrome" of human experience.

In the case of the Sun, our primitive ancestors awoke from the night and the realm of dreams as the Sun rose and cast down its light. The night was a time of danger for early humans living in the forests or caves, and dreams often produced fearful situations. The rising Sun was a welcome release from this dark time. Therefore, the association of light with the dispelling of darkness itself and the dreamworld and night fears elevated the Sun to the status of rescuer and protector.

Here, we see an example of how human experience became patterned with biological responses to their environment (which then became the format and structure for the expression of our myths and the themes they contain). Campbell states that this reflects the unity of "the race of man" not only in its biology but also in its spiritual history which manifests as a "single symphony" expressed in the myths of all cultures (*The Masks of God: Primitive Mythology*, 1991).

In the old mythos, the Sun God was viewed as an invincible hero due to the fact that the Sun kept its shape in the sky (unlike the Moon, which faced away each month, a portion at a time). Throughout the year, the Sun descended into the Underworld each day only to reappear again unchanged in form. From this perspective, the roots of the resurrection mythos began to form around the Sun God of eternal life.

In the Mystery Tradition of Witchcraft, the "death" of the Sun God occurs in the harvest season, which reveals his identification with the Slain God or Harvest Lord figure. But his death is not a true death, as humans perceive it, because his form does not change. The only change in the physical form of the Sun was its absence from the sky. The ancients then surmised that there must be two Sun Gods, one visible and one invisible, one light and one dark. The latter is explored further in the section titled "The Underworld God."

At the close of each day, the Sun God descended into the Underworld. Here, he performed the "Night Sea Crossing" as he traversed the depths of the Underworld realm. This brought him into the land of the dead where the ancestral spirits dwelled. His light connected the dead and the living in the changelessness of his being. For his fire brought about transformation and his heat brought life-giving moisture and vitality. This teaching will become apparent as the Mysteries unfold in this chapter and throughout the book.

Fire was a very potent weapon and an associated attribute of the Sun God. The Sun God is frequently depicted with a sword representing the element of Fire and its ability to transform base minerals into fine tools. He is also often shown wearing spiked crowns, which are the rays of the Sun. Additionally, the spikes are stylized antlers of the ancient stag, revealing the identification of the Sun God with the Horned God of the woods (who we noted earlier was associated with rain and the Sun). Here, it is interesting to note that in ancient hunter society, the Sun was called the Great Hunter.

Like the stag, the Sun was viewed as a symbol of fertility. He was the Sun Groom and the Goddess was the Moon Bride. Together, they ensured the fertility of the three realms of Overworld, Middleworld, and Underworld. From their union, a host of beings come into existence in all worlds. Among their offspring are those humans who appear as royal incarnate gods, which brings us back full circle to the Sacred King.

A variety of myths (and, therefore, a variety of teachings) can be discovered in the legends associated with European Sun God figures. What becomes readily apparent is the differing view of the Sun God from an Aegean/Mediterranean perspective versus a Celtic one. This is because the Sun itself is experienced differently in these regions. The relatively severe coldness of winter in the north and the shorter agricultural cycle made the return of the Sun something of greater focus in Northern Europe as compared to the southern region.

One of the central Sun God figures in modern Witchcraft is the Celtic deity known as *Lugh,* whose name means "light" or "brightness." He was chief of the mystical group of beings known as the Tuatha de Danann. These figures are associated with an Elder race and with the Faery Faith of Old Ireland.

In the legends connected to Lugh, he appears as one skilled in all the arts. This "all-knowing" theme is classic in the depiction of a Sun God. Lugh later drowns in the sea and is buried in a castle on the shore. This is, among other things, symbolic of the Sun's disappearance beneath the waters of the western horizon. The festival of Lughnasadh (August 1) marks the beginning of the harvest season, which associates Lugh with the Slain God mythos.

Miranda Green, in her book *Dictionary of Celtic Myth and Legend* (1992), views the burial of solar amulets with the dead as symbolic of the connection between the Sun and death. The power to give life or renew life is attributed to solar gods in many cultures. Eternal life is also associated with the Sun God in various myths and legends. Larissa

Bonfante, in her book *Etruscan Life and Afterlife* (1986), describes an ancient mirror engraving that depicts the Sun God flanked on each side by the Goddess of Dawn and the God of the Ocean. Here, we see the ancient theme of the beginning (sunrise in the east) and the end (sunset in the west), with the Sun God set directly in the center of it all.

In Celtic legends, the figure called *Mabon* is believed by many to be identifiable with the Celtic god known as *Maponus*. Maponus was equated with the Roman god Apollo (a solar deity) and his name appears in various dedications such as those found at Corbridge. Like Apollo, Maponus is conflated with music and poetry. In modern Witchcraft, Mabon is associated with the autumn equinox, which marks the end of summer and the beginning of the decline into winter. This theme also resides in the mythos of the Slain God.

In Southern Europe, there were many gods associated with the Sun, such as Helios, Apollo, Jupiter, and Selvan. Selvan, an Etruscan god, presided over the light of dawn and was equated with the Roman god Silvanus. Silvanus was the God of the Woodlands, and here we see a reference to the power of woodland gods over the Sun again. In archaic Roman religion, much of which evolved from Etruscan religion, Silvanus was associated with the god Mars.

Mars was originally a guardian of fields and boundaries and was associated with agriculture. His rites were celebrated in the spring and fall and spread from Rome to the British Isles. An ancient inscription discovered at Uley, Gloucestershire, England, bears the epithet *"Mars Silvanus."* Uley was also the center of a cult devoted to Mercury, where he was identified with Mars and Silvanus. Another inscription discovered at Nettleham, Lincolnshire, England, reads *"Mars Rigonemetis,"* which means "Mars of the Sacred Grove." Silvanus was also known as Faunus, who was a tamer version of the two aspects

Faunus was essentially a pastoral god as well as a woodland deity. In his legends, he frequently appears as a hunter and a promoter of agriculture. Faunus was also an oracle god (in this aspect, he was known as *Fatuus* and *Fatuclus*) who revealed the future through sounds and voices in the grove. He also revealed the future in dreams for those who slept in the dark wooded places. Evidence for strongholds of his cult has been found in Latium, Italy, and Thetford, England.

Faunus was also known as Dianus who was the consort of the goddess Diana. As noted earlier, he is mentioned in the writings of St. Martin of Braga who kept a journal of his encounters with various Pagan sects during his sixth-century travels. James Frazer, in his book *The Golden Bough*, equates Dianus with Virbius who was the guardian of Diana's sacred grove at Nemi. Here, he bore the title *Rex Nemorensis*, which means the "King of the Woods."

The legendary figure of Rex Nemorensis protected not only Diana's grove but also stood guard beneath the sacred oak that was key to the worship at Nemi. Once a year, he could be challenged for his reign in ritual combat. Anyone who could break a branch from the oak tree with his bare hands earned the right to challenge in a battle to the death. As we shall see in other chapters, this theme of ritual combat and succession of reign is one of great antiquity. The theme of the Sacred King who becomes the Slain God is deeply woven into many facets of the Mystery Tradition mythos.

In Witchcraft, the Sun God is the fertilizing and life-giving power who traverses the world of the living and the dead. His essence is equally dispersed in both realms, and he renews all things in his presence. His myths depict the Sun God rising in the east from the Underworld where he collects the souls of those who died during the night. He then carries them into the Underworld, where the process of rebirth begins. While crossing the land of the living, he pours his vital essence down into the earth, which assures the fertility of crops and animals.

As an agricultural society, humans knew that fields could become depleted and no longer bear a fruitful harvest. All things, in fact, followed the theme of decline and death. Could it be that the Sun God himself would decline and pass away? If so, how then could he be restored?

The Child of Promise or the Divine Child

To ancient European cultures, the winter solstice marked the birth of the Sun God whose warmth had slowly waned from the time of the summer solstice. With daylight growing shorter, an association was made between the vitality of the Sun God and the plight of the world, which suffered the loss of light and heat. It is interesting to note that the earlier explanation of the seeming lifelessness of winter was attributed to a Mother Goddess figure and not to a Sun God. This is reflected in the ancient myth of Demeter and Persephone. This theme is covered in the next chapter.

The cycle of the year of the God begins with the Divine Child. In the Mystery tradition of Witchcraft, he is known primarily by the title of the Child Promise. He is born on the winter solstice as the new Sacred King. The Christian borrowing of the Pagan practice of offering frankincense and myrrh reflects this ancient theme. Frankincense denotes kingship and myrrh represents the sacrificial death.

The only direct references in Western literature to a Pagan Sun God actually being born on or near the winter solstice are Apollo and Dionysos. This does not mean that other European cultures did not have such a mythos; it only means we have no written records or references that serve as confirmation. However, the widespread celebration of Yule throughout most of Europe—which includes such Pagan symbols as the adorned evergreen tree along with mistletoe, holly, and ivy—indicates a commonality of ancient Pagan traditions associated with this season.

Yule, also known as Christmas, is now celebrated on December 25, which falls a few days after the winter solstice. In 274 CE, the Roman emperor Aurelian officially set the date of December 25 as the *Natalis Solis Invicti* (Birthday of the Inconquerable Sun) in honor of the Sun God. The festival took place just after the winter solstice when the days become longer.

The Roman Emperor Constantine (fourth century CE) was converted to Christianity. Alliances were formed between Constantine and the early Christian Church, and in 324, he made Christianity the official religion of Rome. In 349 CE, Pope Julius formally selected December 25 as the birthdate of Christ, and so began the celebration of Christmas in December and the arrogation of seasonal Pagan symbolism and religious theme.

The winter solstice, marking the shortest day of the year, denotes the "time of the greatest darkness." In Celtic legend, the figure known as Mabon is abducted from his mother when he is only "three nights old." Some commentators see a connection here between the infant Mabon and the infant Sun God born on the darkest day. Author John Matthews, in his book *The Winter Solstice* (1998) presents a thirteenth-century Welsh poem referring to the biblical Mary's baby as Mabon instead of Christ. This seems to lend support to those who view Mabon as associated with a December birth and, therefore, to an older solar connection.

In the Mystery Tradition of Witchcraft, the Yule log is associated with the rebirth of the Sun God. The underlying concept of this tradition is rooted in the Pagan beliefs regarding trees. In ancient times, there was a belief that fire dwelled within wood. Here, the spirit or deity dwelled inside this primal home. It could be coaxed out by focusing the Sun's light on the wood through a glass lens. Once the flame appeared, it was considered to be the living presence of the entity. Therefore, the burning Yule log represented the newborn Sun God's light and heat.

Just as life begins in the darkness of the womb, the flame resides within the dark depths of the wood. This theme of light dwelling within the darkness is central to the mythos of the God in the Mystery Tradition of Witchcraft. Here, we find his seed of light transmitted through the union of the Descended Goddess of the Overworld and the Dark Lord of the Underworld. This hidden scene of impregnation marks the ending and beginning of the continuous cycle of ascent and descent.

The secret mating of the God and Goddess is marked by the three-day absence of the Moon in the night sky. This particular mystical period of the New Moon falls prior to the festival at October's end, which is known by such names as *Samhain* and *Shadowfest*. Here, the light of the Sun and Moon are at home in the darkness to which they return each day and night. Here in the Dark Realm, the Child of Promise dwells in the womb of the Mother as the coming heir to the throne of the Sun God.

In the mythos, the Child of Promise must pass a test to prove his worthiness to be the new Sun God. In the Story of Taliesin, the Divine Child participates in a horse race with a total of twenty-four competitors. Some commentators view this number as representing the last twenty-four hours of the old fading year. The race itself takes place on the day of the winter solstice.

During the course of the race, the Divine Child defeats each horse by touching its haunch with a charred holly twig as he rides next to them. The holly is, of course, associated with the Holly King who reigns from summer solstice to winter solstice, where he is defeated by his brother, the Oak King. Here, the symbolism of the charred holly can be seen to represent the shift of seasonal reign. As we saw earlier, the connection between Sun God and Oak King is one of great antiquity.

In the Aegean/Mediterranean region, the Divine Child figure is best reflected in the god Dionysos. Dionysos was the only Olympian god born of a mortal woman. He is, therefore, fully divine and fully human as well. This theme is later reflected in the early Christian view of Jesus. Semele, the mother of Dionysos, was impregnated by Zeus. The Mystery theme here is an old one in which a maiden is impregnated by a divine figure. The Christian mythos surrounding the Virgin Mary is a newer form of this ancient Mystery tradition.

Semele dies during her pregnancy and Zeus removes the fetus, which appears as a bull-horned child crowned with serpents. In order to shield Dionysos from Hera (who wishes to destroy him), Zeus gives the infant to Hermes, who delivers him to Semele's sister, Ino. She disguises him in girl's clothing and begins to raise him as a girl. Dionysos is later taken by Hermes to be raised by the nymphs of Mount Nysa. He is transformed into a kid goat, and tutored by the satyr Silenus. Zeus provides Dionysos with twelve divine guardians, who are later transformed by Hera into centaurs as a reprisal for the thwarting of her plan to kill Dionysos.

Dionysos grows up to become a young, tender, beautiful god. He is most commonly depicted in ancient art and iconography as somewhat feminine in appearance. His dark hair is long and flowing in curls and his head is crowned with ivy and grape leaves. The effeminate nature of Dionysos is in sharp contrast to his half-brother Hercules. However, they both share a role in the understanding of the Mystery Tradition within Witchcraft.

Dionysos is frequently clad only in an animal pelt or a long robe. The animal skin speaks of his woodland nature and the linen robe reveals his agricultural roots (for linen is derived from plant fibers). Dionysos carries a wand known as a *thyrsus,* which is a fennel stalk topped with a pine cone. This symbol, in part, also unites his nature with the forest and the planted field.

Dionysos is frequently depicted wearing the pelt of a predator cat and sporting the horns of a goat or a bull. Here, we see the symbolism of the hunter and the hunted. As noted earlier, this is a theme of great antiquity associated with the mythical themes of Witchcraft as a Mystery religion.

The tales of Dionysos demonstrate a close affinity with the feminine, and in ancient times, his worshippers were mostly women. In the Mystery Tradition, the feminine plays an important role connected to the theme of birth, death, and rebirth. In this view, the Goddess brings life into the world through the womb gate and accepts it back again in death.

Between life and death is the liminal, the boundary of the Otherworld. In ancient tales, women are the key figures in tales of transitions related to the borders of life and death. Circe, in *The Odyssey*, helps Odysseus in his quest to contact the spirits of the dead. The Sibyl helps Aeneas enter the Underworld in a similar quest. In Celtic lore, mysterious female figures such as the Lady of the Lake and Queen of Elfland protect and guide various heroes seeking the Otherworld. The feminine and masculine sides of Dionysos join to reveal his role as a wild God of Nature and a liminal figure straddling the boundary between life and death.

The Child of Promise, in his role as the "Son of Light," serves as a mediator between the forces of life and death. He is the Sun God made flesh, incarnating as the heroes of various mythologies. In the world of humankind, he is a Divine King figure who must die a sacrificial death for the well-being of those who venerate him.

The Underworld God

Scholar Franz Cumont (*After Life in Roman Paganism*, 1922) notes that it was a common belief in ancient times that the dead accompanied the setting Sun to an underground world. In the Underworld, the Sun regained its vitality, as did the souls of the dead. Cumont goes on to discuss the importance of this union between the dead and the resurrected Sun. Here, it is through alignment with the Sun and identification with his birth and death that his followers die, only to be reborn.

In the Mysteries of Witchcraft, the Underworld God is seen as the renewer of all things. He is also depicted as the escort of the dead, the consoler and counselor of souls, and the Dark Lord of the Shadowed Places. This latter title connects him not only to the Underworld Realm but also to his aspect as the Lord of the Woods. Like the Underworld itself, in ancient lore, the dark wooded places concealed the entrances to the Faery Realm and other mystical worlds.

Entrances or thresholds have always been viewed as magickal or mystical. The threshold of a doorway is neither inside nor outside, but instead, is a place that exists in between. In the Mystery Tradition of Witchcraft, such a state of existence is often referred to as "the world between the worlds." In connection with the God, there are several such liminal points, including sunrise, sunset, and the threshold of the gates to the Underworld.

In various myths and legends, the entrances to the Underworld are guarded. Typically, the guardian is a dog, or one accompanies the guardian. In the mythos of Witchcraft, there appear seven gates of passage into the Underworld. These gates represent both various states of consciousness as well as mystical planes of magickal vibration. This is explored in Chapter Five.

The mystical Otherworld, like the Underworld, has its guardians as well. In most cases, the Otherworld is shielded or barred by either trees or natural phenomena such as mist or heavy fog. In Celtic lore, the trees known as oak, ash, and thorn stand together as guardians to form a mystical triad. Here, the thorn blocks access to the pillars of the portal, which are the oak and ash. Only the initiated or those called by the Fae may enter. See Chapter Five for further information.

Treasures or magickal objects are often hidden and protected in the Underworld or Otherworld. Sometimes the object is a cauldron or a sword, and in fairy tales, we find secret caches of coins or precious gems. What these items share in common is their ultimate origin, the very depths of the earth where minerals are found. Another thing they share in common is that they must be fashioned or transformed in some manner. This connection will eventually lead us to the Smith God, who appears in the last section of this chapter.

It is interesting to note that the name *Pluto* (the Aegean/Mediterranean Underworld God) is derived from the Latin *pluton* and Greek *ploutos*, which mean "wealth." Pluto was originally viewed as ruling over the wealth and abundance that issued forth from the Earth or could be drawn from its depths; for the Earth not only contained precious gems and metals, it also produced plant life. Here, it was associated with life and the cycle of seed, stem, bud, blossom, and fruit. In this, the earliest connotations of the Underworld, we find the Lord of the Dead also associated with the renewal of life.

In Welsh lore, the character known as *Gwyn ap Nudd* is often depicted as a Lord of the Dead figure. In the oldest literature to mention him, he is the ruler of Annwyn or the Otherworld and is accompanied by a pack of faery dogs. As noted earlier, he is identified with the summer solstice and the Holly King figure, symbolizing the forces of decline. In old Irish Lore, the character known as *Donn* is a dark, shadowy figure that summons the dead to his island abode. His name means "dark" or "brown." Some commentators identify him with Dis Pater, a Roman deity associated with the Underworld. The name *Dis Pater* means "father of riches" and in this regard, he shares a commonality with Pluto.

One of the earliest depictions of Dis Pater shows him wearing a wolf headdress. The wolf symbolizes the hunter. In Italian Witchcraft, the wolf symbolizes the waning year, just as the stag represents the waxing year. Here, we also see the interplay between the hunter and the hunted. This connection to the hunter is an interesting link to deities associated with the Underworld, Otherworld, and spirits of the dead in the mythos of Witchcraft.

The hunter figure takes us back once again into the forest. Here we find Cernunnos, a Stag-Horned God widely worshipped by the Celts. Cernunnos is related to both Donn and Dis Pater through myths and legends associated with Underworld powers, mastery over nature, and various tales regarding the souls of the dead. To this list, we may also add the figure known as Herne.

Author R.J. Stewart (*Celtic Gods and Celtic Goddesses,* 1990) points out that Cernunnos is a god of "hunting, culling, and taking" and that he maintains the natural order through selection or sacrifice. Sacrifice can be of what the God symbolizes or of the God himself. Here, the God is both the hunter and the hunted, beginning and completing an unending cycle. This cycle is often represented by the spiral design, which frequently appeared on prehistoric tombs and burial caves in both Northern and Southern Europe. This is further explored in the last section of this chapter titled the Hammer or Smith God and Lame God.

One of the classic representations of Cernunnos depicts him seated in a cross-legged position. In one hand, he holds a serpent, and in the other, a torc. Beside him is either a bag of coins or grain, the contents of which have partially spilled out.

The torc can be viewed in this context as a sign of his divine authority. The serpent is a very old symbol of the forces of the Underworld and of transformation itself. The coins are timeless offerings to the spirits of the dead, as is the grain. Coins and grain appear later as offerings to Faeries and ancestral spirits.

In the Mystery Tradition of Witchcraft, the Lord of the Dead is most frequently represented by the image of a human skull and crossbones. This image seems to be almost universal in the old Witchcraft traditions of Northern and Southern Europe. Nigel Jackson, in his book *Masks of Misrule* (1996), comments that the skull and crossbones represent the

Horned God as the Wild Hunter who guides the host of dead spirits across the sky at the time of Samhain and Yule.

The skull symbolizes many of the various Mysteries in Witchcraft and serves on occasion as a tool. In Italian Witchcraft, the skull symbolizes the preservation of ancestral knowledge and wisdom, the "body" of teachings that remain after each generation passes away. Here, it can be used as a vessel for bridging between the world of the living and the realm of the dead. One of the keys to activating the skull as a conduit for communication with spirits is to set a lighted candle on top of the skull image. This brings into play the property of fire and its powers of transformation. But what role does fire play in connection to the God of Witchcraft?

The Hammer or Smith God and the Lame God

The Hammer or Smith God is a mysterious figure, and he is even more so in his aspect of the Lame God. In most European cultures, the folklore surrounding the Smith God depicts him with an injured leg that causes him to limp when he walks. Many magickal powers are attributed to the Smith God, including the power to create ingenious tools and sacred objects. Smith gods are masters of elemental Fire and possess the ability to transform Underworld materials.

In various tales, the Smith God is in opposition to the Sun God, for he represents the fire that comes from beneath the earth (volcanic) rather than fire that falls from the sky (lightning) or can be drawn from the Sun (such as through a glass lens). He appears in Northern Europe in the guise of Goibhniu. In Western Europe, he is Sucellus, and in Southern Europe, the Smith God is called Hephaestos or Vulcan. Smith gods belong to a larger order known as Hammer gods.

In the book *Symbol and Image in Celtic Religious Art* by Miranda Green (1989), several ancient images appear depicting the Hammer God with a female consort. They sit side-by-side on separate thrones, with the female image holding a cornucopia and the male image holding a large hammer. When pictured alone, the Hammer God is often shown with a dog, and in addition to the hammer, he holds a pot. One image depicts the Hammer God wearing a leaf crown. The cornucopia is, of course, a symbol of abundance (particularly in connection with crops). The dog is a classic Underworld creature that often accompanies chthonic deities. The leaf crown can be viewed as a Lord of the Plant Kingdom symbol. The hammer is a symbol of the power to transform anything that comes from the earth.

Alexander Murray, in his book *Who's Who in Mythology* (1988), mentions that Hephaestos (Vulcan) was looked upon as one who aided the growth of vegetation. The suggestion is that this arose due to the association of volcanic soil with the fertility of plowed fields. The vine in particular thrives in soil enriched with volcanic material, and it is interesting to note that Hephaestos had a close friendship with Dionysos (who was, in part, a wine god). When we consider the images shown in Green's book, the connections between Hammer gods and agriculture are too close for sheer coincidence. The connective symbolism demonstrates that the Hammer God and the Harvest Lord share an association, as shall become even clearer. To that end, we must reintroduce another related character we encountered earlier.

In *Symbol and Image in Celtic Religious Art*, we read that stone and bronze images of the Hammer God depict him as a god of woodland, vegetation, and both the wild and domestic sides of nature (Green, 1989). His altars, even among the Gauls, bear dedications to the Roman forest god Silvanus. A statue appearing in the book *Dictionary of Roman Religion*, by Lesley and Roy Adkins (1996) portrays Silvanus holding a cornucopia and a sickle with a dog posed at his feet. The sickle, of course, is the tool of a harvester, and in the Mystery Tradition of Witchcraft, it is also the sign of the Harvest Lord or Slain God.

As noted earlier, Silvanus and Faunus are aspects of the same god. Faunus, a satyrlike figure, is frequently portrayed with goat horns and he carries a large club. The action of the Hammer God, in striking position, resembles a male goat in his classic standing and striking posture. The clang of the hammer and the crash of the goat's horns in a downward strike are similar and equally impressive. The goat, when standing upright on its two back legs (strike posture), walks in a hobble motion suggestive of the Smithy's limp. Here, we see a reflection of the cloven-hoofed satyr walking in the manner of the Lame God, or vice versa. Some commentators have suggested that the flickering flame (a symbol of the Hammer God's elemental Fire) is representative of his limping motion. The Horned beast/God takes us back once again (as all things do) to the Lord of the Woods.

Scholar Miranda Green points out that bronze images of the Hammer God depict him wearing a wolf pelt (*Dictionary of Celtic Myth and Legend*). As noted earlier, the Underworld God Dis Pater also donned the wolf. In the Mystery Tradition of Witchcraft, the Lame God figure leads a spiral dance into the Underworld and back out again. As also noted earlier, the spiral is an ancient symbol appearing on primitive tombs. The spiral dance draws its participants into the center from which the Lame God then leads them back to a wide circle dance (the dance of death and renewal). At the core of this mysterious dance is the lame figure leading the souls of the dead into the Underworld. To understand the connection between the dead, lameness, and the Lame Hammer God, we need only look to his veneration.

Altars dedicated to the Hammer God are commonly decorated with severed arms, legs, feet, and hands. Carvings of these items have also been uncovered in sites of Hammer God worship. The belief is that Hammer Gods could fashion new limbs for those who lost them so that in the afterlife, these individuals would be whole again. Here, we see the transforming and renewing powers of the Underworld God. For the Hammer God transforms the dead in the Underworld through the force of elemental Fire and the form of mineral, represented by his metal hammer.

The regenerative theme of the Hammer God and his Underworld associations appears in the magickal cauldrons that appear in many myths and legends. With the rise of Christianity, this older theme was commandeered from its Pagan roots, and during the medieval period, it was reshaped into the Grail mythos associated with King Arthur. Yet, even the chalice appears in the ancient myths of Hammer Gods. Goibhniu the divine smith and Hephaestos appear in ancient tales where they serve drinks from a cup to those gathered for feasting. In the case of Goibhniu, the guests are then transformed into immortals, while in the tale of Hephaestos, he serves drinks to those who are already the immortals of Olympus.

In the Mystery Tradition of Witchcraft, both the cauldron and the chalice are female symbols associated with the womb and with female body fluids. Here we find the sacred vessel of transformation, which is itself the gateway from the Underworld to the world of the living. Therefore, let us now turn our attention to the Goddess of the Witches, who awaits us in the next chapter.

CHAPTER FOUR

ᚷhe Uitches' Goddess

In Witchcraft, the Goddess is often primarily viewed from a lunar-oriented perspective. Here, we find the classic triformis nature divided into the aspects known as Maiden, Mother, and Crone. These, in turn, relate to the three stages of the Moon, which are waxing, full, and waning. Contained within this triple image are several key aspects of the nature of the Goddess that reveal some very important insights. Therefore, in the course of this chapter, we will examine the Goddess in all her rich diversity. Before we begin, it will be helpful to our larger understanding to first explore the triformis nature of the Goddess.

The earliest iconography (in what is now Europe) to depict a triformis nature clearly intended to represent a goddess (as opposed to, arguably, a simple female form) can be found in the Iunones imagery. The images discovered to date originate from the period of archaic Roman religion. They represent a female spirit flanked by an Iunones figure (a guardian spirit of fertility who served to ensure family lineage) and a nursing goddess. This same image later appears in Celtic regions as the Matres figure, depicting three mothers seated with an infant. Such figures were also called the *Deae Matres* or the *Matronae*. They are most frequently depicted with grain symbolism, infants, and children. It is noteworthy that the Iunones eventually evolve into a singular goddess image called

Iuno. She is more commonly known as *Juno,* the Great Goddess and consort of Jupiter. In Celtic religion, the Iunones concept appears in such singular forms as the goddess Matrona.

The ancient writer Catullus (first century BCE) equates Juno with the goddess Diana in his *Hymn to Diana.* Here, he writes, *"Diana whose name is Juno Lucina,"* and goes on to describe her as, *"filling the farmer's rough-walled barn with fruit and produce, vegetables and grain."* Aeschylus equates Diana with Hecate and depicts her as a guardian of the childbed. Varro refers to Diana as the "Trivian Titan" who is also called Trivia (of the three roads).

The ancient writer Lucan (first century CE) mentions a triformis goddess worshipped by Witches. In one of his classic works titled *Pharsalia,* a Witch refers to, *"Persephone, who is the third and lowest aspect of our goddess Hecate* (Riley, *The Pharsalia of Lucan)."* The third name (Diana) is easy to insert because Horace and other contemporary writers supply the three names of goddesses traditionally worshipped by Witches: Hecate, Diana, and Proserpina (the Roman name for Persephone). In Ovid's *Metamorphoses,* the Witch Medea says: *"I only pray that the threefold goddess will help me and come to give her blessing to our immense enterprise."* Despite such ancient references, historians such as Ronald Hutton maintain that the basic concept of a triformis goddess associated with Witchcraft is an entirely modern notion and invention.

The concept of a triformis nature associated with female entities also appears in the ancient concept of the Three Fates. In art forms (ancient and modern), they are depicted as a young girl, a mature woman, and an elderly woman. Such imagery makes sense, for it is meant to express the three stages of life: youth, maturity, and old age. Here, we see the classic Maiden, Mother, and Crone vision.

In the Mystery Tradition, the Maiden represents the freedom to explore and experience. The Maiden is self-focused, experiencing the world through a sense of being its center. Her energy is vital, initiating, compelling, and attracting. The Mother represents containment, the boundaries of family, hearth, and home. The Mother is protective, generative, directing, and controlling. Her energy is nurturing, life-sustaining, comforting, and sensual. The Crone represents wisdom, counseling, and preparation. Her energy is transformational, balancing, and predictive.

As should be clear at this point, the Triformis Goddess encompasses all aspects of goddesses that appear in the myths and legends of Europe. In the remainder of this chapter, we will explore the various goddess natures known to our ancestors. Here, we will uncover more of the wonders that reside in the Mystery Tradition of Witchcraft.

The Great Goddess

In prehistoric times, it appears that early humans had a vague sense that something controlled or influenced the world around, below, and above them. It seems likely that "divinity" was worshipped or venerated long before any firm or permanent image-form was created to represent the concept. It is probable that our very distant prehistoric ancestors perceived "divinity" as present in all things, seasons, and material forms. Therefore, no singular form, image, or expression was originally designed to contain the basic concept.

Eventually, humans began to create what we would today call statues or figurines. Among the earliest carvings, we find female figures, which are usually combined with bird imagery. In later periods, a variety of creatures appear in prehistoric iconography. Eventually, a theme emerges wherein three primary forms appear, which many commentators refer to as a Snake Goddess, a Bird Goddess, and a "Lady of the Beasts." There is some speculation that these forms represented the seasonal manifestations of a singular Great Goddess. It is interesting to note that these three forms fit nicely into the ancient concept of the Three Worlds: Bird Goddess (Overworld), Lady of the Beasts (Middleworld), and Snake Goddess (Underworld).

Sybille Haynes (a specialist in Etruscology) presents in her book, *Etruscan Civilization* (2000), archaeological evidence from the Bronze Age concerning a sacred spot in Tarquinia. Haynes examines the presence there of a great female divinity known as *Uni*, and associates her as a Nature Goddess and "Mistress of the Animals." The worship of Uni, in its primitive stages, appears to have focused on a natural cavity in a rock that sat in the center of the early human community. Haynes identifies Uni with Eileithyia the Goddess of Birth, and Juno the Great Goddess.

In the book, *Phases in the Religion of Ancient Rome* (1932), historian Cyril Bailey associates the Moon with Juno and notes that the day of the New Moon was sacred to her. Bailey states that Juno, through her association with the Moon, had certain functions as a sky Goddess. Juno was also known as *Juno Lucina*, the Goddess of Light and Childbirth. In this aspect, she was said to bring the newborn baby into the light, a type of escort of the soul. By the time Juno becomes fully established in the state religion of Rome, her ancient lunar connections had been altered and modified to fit the politics and agenda of the Empire.

The prehistoric Great Goddess was different in nature from the Goddess we find fully developed in the civilizations of Egypt, Greece, and Rome. In her primitive form, she was worshipped in part because early humans feared the Goddess. She dwelled in caves and took on the form of a bear, lion, or some other great and powerful predator. It was not until much later that the Great Goddess became the nurturing and protective deity we find in the historic periods.

Two examples of a Great Goddess image reflecting prehistoric concepts are found in the image of Diana of Ephesus and Minoan art. The statue of Diana at Ephesus depicts the Goddess with multiple exposed breasts. Upon her gown and headdress appear a variety of creatures: the hunters and the hunted. The arms of the Goddess are poised in a fashion that suggests an attitude of "behold all that I am."

The Great Goddess of Minoan culture appears with large, exposed breasts, and is accompanied by either trees and plants or a variety of animals. Frequently, two guardian lions, symbolic of a former fierce nature, flank her on both sides. The bull, stag, goat, snake, and dove are the most common animals associated with the Minoan Great Goddess. The primary symbols associated with her are the double-headed axe, bull horns, a crescent Moon, and a sacred pillar.

In Northern Europe, modified forms of the Great Goddess appear in such figures as Black Annis. In Leicestershire, England, she was sometimes called *Black Anna* or *Anny*. Here, she was associated with the "hare hunt" performed at the time of Easter and took on the form of a cat. In the local folklore, she was said to reside in a cave known as Black Annis Bower. Some commentators equate Black Anna with a Gaelic folklore figure called Yellow Muilearteach. She was a type of hag figure, often associated with the loss of domesticated animals in the woods.

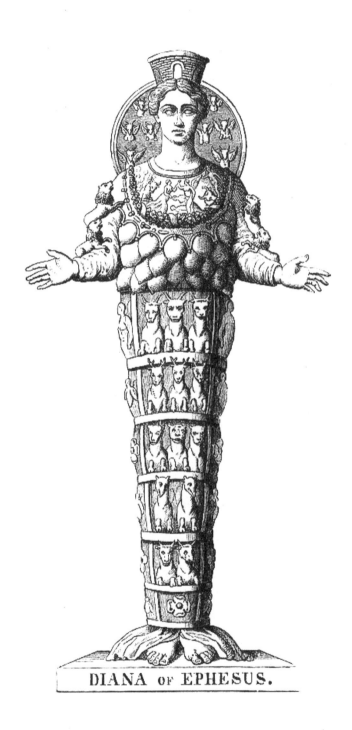

DIANA of EPHESUS.

In the period of her earliest formation, the Great Goddess appears to have been associated with the worship of stones, trees, wild animals, wells, rivers, mounds, and mountains. Her nature transformed and evolved along with that of humankind. In the period of human savagery, she was seen as savage. Here, she was the source of all that was creative and all that was destructive. As humans became more cultured and civilized, so too did the Great Mother image. In this latter period, the Great Goddess took on the attributes of a nurturing and protective Mother Goddess. Some commentators equate the Great Goddess with the Titan goddess known as Gaea, who gave birth to all things.

The Earth Mother

Robert Graves (*The White Goddess*) presents a twelfth-century prayer that originally appeared in an old herbal now residing in the British Museum. The original prayer reads, in part:

> *"Earth, divine goddess, Mother Nature, who dost generate all things and bringest forth ever anew the sun which thou hast given to the nations; Guardian of sky and sea and of all Gods and powers; through thy influence all nature is hushed and sinks to sleep...Again, when it pleases thee, thou sendest forth the glad daylight and nurturest life with thine eternal surety; and when the spirit of man passes, to thee it returns. Thou indeed art rightly named Great Mother of the Gods..."* (Harley Manuscripts, British Museum, 1585).

Here, we see not only the elements presented in this chapter but also several of the fundamental concepts also appearing much later in modern Witchcraft writings about the Goddess.

Many modern Pagans and Witches believe in the ancient origins of a Mother Goddess figure that dates to Neolithic if not Paleolithic times. Some scholars argue that even though these periods produced female images that appear pregnant with what can be viewed as fertility symbolism, such figures do not necessarily represent a Goddess image. Since we are dealing with prehistoric periods, neither side can wholly claim correctness on the issue, and we are left to a great deal of conjecture.

A reference in Hesiod's *Theogony*, written in the seventh or eighth century BCE, contains an interesting clue to prehistoric beliefs. Hesiod refers to a half-forgotten race of deities known as *the Titans* while writing about the deities of his own period (the gods of Olympus). This is interesting because he is writing in a period that today, we would call ancient, and he is referring to beliefs just as ancient to him.

For the purposes of this chapter, we are interested in the Titan named Gaia. She was the "Goddess of the Earth and reckoned as the Great Mother" in the tales we know concerning this goddess. According to the existing mythology, Gaia gave birth without impregnation by a male partner and brought forth the land, sea, and sky. Some commentators see a myth arising from the mindset of a matrifocal, if not matriarchal, society in the absence of a male figure.

Eventually, Gaia took Uranus as her mate (who was also her son) and their mating produced the Titan race of deities. The birthing of a son, who is also his own father, is not uncommon in myths related to Moon goddesses. However, in this case, the mythos relates to a Goddess of the Earth. This would suggest a possible lunar connection to Gaia, which we will explore further in this chapter.

In the birthing of the first deities, Gaia is the primordial element from which all the gods originated. Gaia is also said to have given birth to the first humans, and so she is called the Great Mother. The Mother image is indeed an ancient, powerful, and primal force. Whatever period in the past may have produced the original concept related to a Goddess image, the fact remains that the idea of a Great Mother Goddess was known in the earliest literary periods of Western culture. Here, they are then referred to as belonging to an even more distant past.

In the Mystery Tradition of Witchcraft, the Mother Goddess is viewed as the giver and receiver of life. Her symbols include caves, cauldrons, wells, mounds, hills, and mountains. Images that appear in the symbolic shape, which modern people would expect of a Mother image fashioned by ancient people, date to around 6000 BCE. Many people believe that the images appearing earlier in both Paleolithic and Neolithic art also express the concept of a more ancient Mother Goddess figure.

In the book *The Myth of the Goddess* (1991), by Anne Baring and Jules Cashford, the authors address figures from the Neolithic era, spanning from 10,000 to 3500 BCE. Reportedly, the sphere of influence related to the Mother Goddess "has clearly differentiated into three regions." These are mentioned as *"Sky, or the upper Waters, Earth, and the Lower Waters or the Waters Beneath the Earth."* The concept of three worlds is one we shall visit many times in the course of this book.

Some of the earliest art forms that many people associate with goddesses feature the bird figure. In prehistoric art, the bird appears to be connected to the theme of water, and the majority of images are waterfowl. Some examples are the swan, crane, duck, goose, and diver bird. Water fell from the sky and remained in lakes, ponds, and rivers upon the Earth. Birds seemed to be at home in the water and the air, linking the two realms together in connection to the bird image.

Prehistoric images, often labeled as bird goddesses, are frequently similar to those often referred to as Mother Goddess images. One of the similarities is the large buttocks. As Baring and Cashford point out, in prehistoric art, some female images have double eggs appearing inside the buttocks of the image. This has led some commentators to believe the symbolism represents the "egg sitter" nature of the bird, which is then extended to the Mother Goddess. Here, the large buttocks are seen as a symbolic requirement for "she who sits on the many eggs of all life."

Despite the fact that the Mother Goddess gave life, in prehistoric times, there appears to be no distinction between her as the Goddess of Life and the Goddess of Death. Neolithic art and iconography suggest that she was an image of life and death as a whole concept, undivided into polarities. Baring and Cashford suggest that life and death, and light and darkness were not antagonistic elements, but were instead the ebb and flow of the same thing. Here, we see a reflection of the bird image uniting earth and sky through its own nature. For just as the bird was at home in the sky and on the earth, so too was the Mother Goddess at home in life and death, light and darkness.

According to Baring and Cashford, it is not until the Bronze Age that clear divisions arise. These become apparent by the middle of this age, but earlier in the period, traces still appear of the Primordial Goddess. She is reportedly the origin of all the gods and goddesses who arise in the Bronze Age. She is also recognizable as the Great Mother Goddess of the Paleolithic and Neolithic eras. During the Megalithic culture, the Mother Goddess remained an essential spiritual focus just as she had in the Neolithic cultures of Old Europe. In Chapter Five, we will examine her connections to the great standing stones of Europe.

Another element associated with the Mother Goddess is the Moon. Ancient burial sites have revealed the dead in a fetal position, oriented to the east, and sprinkled with flowers and red ochre dye. Baring and Cashford report that lunar disks with a vulva symbol have been found in such graves. Is the red ochre symbolic of restoring life's blood, and is the dead person awaiting the rising of the Moon in the east in order to return to life as well?

Baring and Cashford suggest that the changing of the Moon in its monthly phases became the foundation for the primitive belief in rebirth. If the Moon could seemingly wither away and yet return to life anew, then perhaps joining with the Moon would bestow the same gift to the dead. This theme continues to appear in Moon lore in both Greek philosophy and European folk traditions through the centuries. Here, we find a belief that the souls of the dead dwell within the lunar sphere.

Is there a connection between life, death, and the sphere of the Moon? Is the Moon a realm to which the dead are guided? If so, then what powers or forces direct this process?

The Moon Goddess

The Goddess of the Moon is sometimes referred to as the *White Goddess.* In the book of the same name, author Robert Graves depicts her as the earliest European deity associated with birth, love, and death (*The White Goddess,* 1948). She appeared to the ancients as the New, Full, and Old Moon. To the ancient Etruscans, the Moon itself was a living goddess, and in their native tongue, there was no distinction between her and the Moon in the night sky. In Charles Leland's *Aradia: Gospel of the Witches,* we find a passage concerning Moon worship (versus Christian worship) that reads:

> *"I, like thee, was instructed when young by priests to worship an invisible god. But an old woman in whom I had great confidence once said to me: 'Why worship a deity whom you cannot see, when there is the Moon in all her splendour visible? Worship her. Invoke Diana, the goddess of the Moon, and she will grant your prayers.' This shalt thou do, obeying the Vangelo, the Gospel of (the Witches and of) Diana, who is Queen of the Fairies and of the Moon"* (Leland, *Aradia: Gospel of the Witches,* 1899).

The seemingly mysterious physical transformation of the Moon no doubt caused our ancestors to contemplate not only the seen but also the unseen forces at work. There was nothing obvious that seemed to be stripping the Moon of its light. Perhaps the answer lies in an invisible thing or an invisible realm. Whatever caused this phenomenon did not likewise affect the shape of the Sun. Was there indeed something invisible hiding in the darkness and unique to nighttime?

Our primitive ancestors knew that the Moon went unseen for three nights every cycle. This suggested a place in which the Moon resided, and from where it was reborn to begin its cycle anew. The realization that the Moon actually went through four stages of transformation (waxing, full, waning, and unseen) instead of just the three visible phases became one of the foundational hidden and symbolic elements of the Mystery Tradition within Witchcraft. This, of course, is the metaphorical meaning of a hidden principle.

Baring and Cashford suggest that the changing nature of the Moon may have been a catalyst for abstract thinking in humankind (*The Myth of the Goddess,* 1991). The reality of an unseen Moon that survived its disappearance perhaps led to the contemplation of an equivalent process for human beings. Here, the lives of humankind, which withered and disappeared much like the light of the Moon, were likened to the same process viewed in the cycle of the Moon itself. This may have led to the belief in an invisible realm where new life is regenerated. From here, both the dead and the Moon were reborn anew in some mystical cycle.

It is easy to see the cycle of birth, growth, decay, death, and regeneration as reflected in the phases of the Moon. Just as the Moon seemingly rises from beneath the Earth, so too does the new sprouting plant appear from beneath the Earth itself. The Moon grows in shape and fullness, just as the plant matures and swells with ripened pod or fruit. Then the Moon's light begins to wane, and something of the plant withers and dries up in its own cycle.

Eventually, the Moon falls into darkness, and so too does the seed slip into the dark earth, where it is likewise unseen while it awaits regeneration. Here, we find that we cannot truly separate the Mother Goddess and the Moon Goddess, nor is there any real reason to attempt such a division.

In the Mystery Tradition of Witchcraft, the phases of the Moon correspond to the seasons of the Earth. The traditional assignment is:

Spring:	Waxing Moon
Summer:	Full Moon
Autumn:	Waning Moon
Winter:	Dark Moon

The Moon plays a part in the mythos of the Mystery Tradition throughout the seasons, as we shall see in this section and throughout the book. Chapter Six in particular explores this mythos and the Moon in greater detail.

During the year, the Moon is called by many names in each month or season. The names vary according to the culture and region in which they reside. The following are common names found in some traditions of modern Wicca and Witchcraft. They are non-specific to any one tradition but seem to reflect a Northern European perspective:

January:	Storm Moon
February:	Chaste Moon
March:	Seed Moon
April:	Hare Moon
May:	Dyad Moon
June:	Mead Moon
July:	Wort Moon
August:	Barley Moon
September:	Blood Moon
October:	Snow Moon
November:	Oak Moon
December:	Wolf Moon

An older traditional list known to our ancestors in many regions was:

January:	Full Wolf Moon or Old Moon
February:	Full Snow Moon
March:	Full Worm Moon
April:	Full Sap Moon
May:	Full Pink Moon

June:	Full Flower Moon
July:	Full Stag Moon
August:	Full Fish Moon
September:	Full Harvest Moon
October:	Full Hunter's Moon
November:	Full Trapper's Moon
December:	Full Long Night Moon

Names associated with the Moon seem to underlie a connective tradition associated with hunting and farming. Both of these have an intimate association with the myths and legends found in the seasonal rites of the year. The mythos of the Slain God, Divine King, or Harvest Lord is featured in the seasonal rites.

As we continue, we will discover that the child of the Moon Goddess is the new Sun God who grows to hold the position of the Divine King. This figure in turn will become the Slain God or Harvest Lord of the year in which he reigned. The form in which we understand this masculine deity is rooted in the transformation that took place in the Bronze Age.

Beginning in the middle of the Bronze Age, we find significance placed on God images that does not appear to be indicated in the preceding eras. This is also the period of human history in which we find clear and distinct divisions of many kinds. During the Bronze Age, we find the emergence of caste systems wherein reside craftsmen, farmers, hunters, and so forth. Some commentators see in this era a rise of "Father God" images accompanied by a slowly receding focus on the Goddess as the God gradually moves to the center.

The myths of the Bronze Age appear to reflect a distinction between the whole and those aspects contained within the totality itself. Here, we see the Great Mother Goddess separated into various aspects and images of goddesses. We also find in this era the personification of a Son and Lover God intimately connected to the Mother image. In his earliest lunar connection, he is born with the New Moon, mates with the Goddess at Full Moon, perishes with the Waning Moon, and is reborn with the new crescent in the night sky. His true origins lie in previous ages, where he was the Divine Child, and the Sorrowful God (as well as the "Year God" of prehistoric periods).

Baring and Cashford note that the art and iconography of the Bronze Age connect the bull or bison to the son of the Mother Goddess (*The Myth of the Goddess*, 1991). This religious theme flows through Minoan culture and into ancient Greek culture. Scholar Donald Mackenzie, in his book *Crete and Pre-Hellenic Europe* (1917), notes that the Horned God of Crete was the son of the Great Mother. Mackenzie identifies her with Gaia.

During the Bronze Age, we also find the connection of the bull to themes of death and rebirth. However, earlier during the Paleolithic era, images of bulls with lunar-shaped horns appear on cave walls. This lunar-horn theme is also associated with stag antlers well into the Neolithic period. As we noted in Chapter Three (and will see in future chapters), the stag and the bull are key elements of the mythos in the Mystery Tradition of Witchcraft.

In the ancient mythology of some of the earliest cultures (such as the Sumerian and Babylonian), we find myths and legends associated with the theme of a Goddess and her consort. In these tales, the Goddess becomes separated from her consort by his death (either real or perceived). The God moves off into the Underworld where he is kept from the world of the living. In response, the Goddess descends into the hidden realm to retrieve him and return the God home. The mythos is always linked to the cycle of death and rebirth, descent and ascent. The Mystery teachings of this mythos are intimately connected to agricultural aspects, where the theme of planting, reaping, and replanting is essential. The mythos of descent and ascent also appears in ancient Greek and Roman Mystery traditions. The ancient Egyptian tale of Isis, and the death and resurrection of her consort Osiris, also belongs to the general mythos. The connective mythos of the God figure in Witchcraft and his Underworld association is further explored in Chapters Six and Seven.

Although the Moon Goddess is frequently associated with a masculine consort, she is best understood by examining her own specific mythology. As a unique deity, the Moon Goddess is best captured in her lunar forms and their inherent nature. At the beginning of this chapter, we noted the ancient references in Western literature to Witches and their triformis Goddess image. As we continue, our focus will now turn to the Maiden, Mother, Crone, and Enchantress, which represent the four phases of the Moon, respectively the Waxing, Full, Waning, and New or Dark Moon (as it is called). In this latter phase, the Moon is unseen in the night sky for three days.

The Maiden is the power of the Waxing Moon, the forces of vitality and growth. Everything awakens to her touch, and she "quickens" the life force of all she touches. Her light is the promise of coming fullness and maturity. As a Maiden, her form is lovely and her energy is delightful in its purity and innocence. Yet with her, there is a clear sense of the underlying power of potentiality within the Maiden.

The Mother is the power of the Full Moon, the forces of fertility and conception. Everything she touches is brought to fulfillment and completion. The light of the Mother is the promise of enlightenment in the places of darkness, the seed born to light from the darkness that once enveloped it. As a Mother, her form is full-figured and her energy is drawing and compelling.

The Crone is the power of the Waning Moon, the forces of preparation and introspection. Everything she touches is brought to examination and evaluation. The light of the Crone is the promise of renewal, the withdrawal of energy into a small, focused core from which regeneration occurs. As a Crone, her form is aged and her energy is contemplative and sage.

The Enchantress is the power of the New or Dark Moon, the forces of mystery and the obscure. Everything she touches becomes magickal and shrouded in mystery. The light of the Enchantress is the potential nature in all things, the source in which manifestation itself germinates. As an Enchantress, her form is sensual and alluring.

In Witchcraft, the Moon is often called "the symbol of the Mystery of the Mysteries." At the core of this lies the Moon Goddess herself. Penetrating her Mysteries and encountering her essence is the walk of the mystical labyrinth. She is everything around us, and the light of the Moon Goddess glows within the ancestral memory residing in our DNA. We still respond to her in the processes of our own biology, which, for example, is evident in the menstrual cycles of women.

The Moon Goddess awakens the primal nature and purifies the soul, which is essential for humankind because we have separated ourselves from the flow of nature. In our attempt to master nature and selfishly exploit her resources, we have broken faith in the soul of nature. We have, as a race, abused and forsaken our ancient Mother. Yet, the Mother still sends the magickal light of the Moon to fall upon her children of the Earth.

In ancient Greek and Roman Witchcraft, the light of the Moon was an important element of the Witches' Craft. Historian Richard Gordon (*Witchcraft and Magic in Europe: Ancient Greece and Rome*, 1999) notes an ancient belief in the magickal properties of moonlight. Gordon notes the ancient writings of Lucan that depict a magickal foam left upon the ground when the Moon is "lowered by incantation." Witches then collected this lunar substance left on the leaves of plants in a secret ceremony.

In the first century BCE, the ancient writer Horace (in his classic work titled *The Book of Epodes*) writes of the goddess Diana who commands "silence when secret Mysteries are performed." Horace writes of Witches who can chant the Moon and stars down from the sky. Here, he refers to a book of enchantments (*Libros Carminum*) used by Witches, who, in conjunction, call upon Diana and Proserpina. Horace attributes several abilities to the Witches of his era, such as the power to animate wax figures, evoke spirits of the dead, call down the Moon from the sky (*deripere lunam polo*) and brew magickal potions. The ancient writers Ovid and Lucan both refer to Witches using cauldrons that contain magickal liquids.

In Celtic myth and legend, we find a magickal cauldron rimmed with pearls. In the related literature, there seems to be no consistent account regarding the number of pearls. The two most common associations are either thirteen or nineteen pearls. The number thirteen suggests a lunar connection in general since there are either thirteen New Moons or thirteen Full Moons in any given year. For the number nineteen, we can use the Major Arcana symbolism and draw upon its antiquity as a numerical system in Western occultism. Here, we can turn to the cards one, nine, nineteen, and ten (the latter being the total of adding one and nine together). Number one is the Magician, nine is the Hermit, nineteen is the Sun, and ten is the Wheel of Fortune.

The symbolism of the Sun card (nineteen) addresses collaboration, partnership, and teamwork. This is the greater experience of community versus the individual. Therefore, the number nineteen reveals a macrocosmic connection to the cauldron. In the tarot, the Magician card bears the number one, and here we see the interfacing of the individual with the macrocosm. Number nine in the tarot is the Hermit card. This represents the principle of introspection, which the cauldron itself symbolizes in Celtic lore as wisdom/enlightenment. In the Major Arcana, number ten is the Wheel of Fortune. This symbolizes abundance, prosperity, and expansion. These are also themes associated with cauldrons in Celtic myth and legend. Here we see the cauldron as the vessel of regeneration.

The pearl imagery associated with the cauldron appears as both Cerridwen's cauldron and the cauldron of Annwn. The name *Cerridwen* links her to the color white, as *wen* means "white" (a form of the Welsh word *gwen*, expressing the same meaning). In Celtic lore, the color white denotes an Underworld or Otherworld association. Here, we see Cerridwen as a goddess of the Underworld or Otherworld. In support of this, we find her association with the sow. Pigs are traditional offerings to chthonic deities in many ancient European cultures. Ceres, the Roman Goddess of the Mysteries is also connected to the sow as an animal sacrificial offering. As we shall see in future chapters, Cerridwen and Ceres share many of the same attributes.

One of the attributes of Cerridwen's cauldron was the ability to restore life to the dead, which is a central theme of Underworld deities in the Mystery Tradition of Witchcraft. In classical literature, the Greek Witch named Medea also uses a cauldron to restore the dead to life. It's noteworthy that Cerridwen sometimes appears in Celtic tales as a Witch or a Faery woman. The other attribute associated with Cerridwen's cauldron is to bestow enlightenment. As noted before, in the Mystery Tradition, the Moon symbolizes "enlightenment in the places of darkness."

In the Mystery Tradition of Witchcraft, the cauldron is also attributed to the ability to give birth in a magickal and metaphorical sense. The cauldron is typically associated with the womb of the Goddess and is therefore also a Mother symbol. There is a connection between Gaia the Earth Mother and the Moon Goddess through the cauldron symbol. Gaia, as the Earth, gives birth to the Moon each month, symbolized by the Moon emerging from the body of the Earth (or so it seemed from a primitive understanding). Since the Goddess in Witchcraft is the Goddess of the Overworld, Middleworld, and Underworld, she is the "One Goddess" seen in three aspects. To our distant ancestors, the Goddess was both the giver of life and the receiver of life. Whatever the Goddess gave birth to, she reclaimed through its death.

As noted earlier in this chapter, the dead were believed to dwell in the Moon, and we have seen the ancient belief that Witches could draw upon the Moon as well as raise the spirits of the dead. We have noted that the Goddess of the Witches is also associated with the Moon and the Underworld. However, the Goddess in Witchcraft is not limited to the Earth and the Moon. In *The Charge of the Goddess,* we find the passage *"Hear ye the words of the Star Goddess."*

Star Goddess

Since ancient times, our ancestors have identified the stars with divine beings. An early indication of this is the ancient assignment of Aegean/ Mediterranean deities to various constellations. We find in Celtic mythology a goddess known as *Sirona,* whose name means "divine star." Her cult was once widespread from Hungary to Brittany. In iconography, she is depicted wearing a crown and with a dog at her feet. Sirona also bears three eggs and a snake coiled around her arm.

Author R.J. Stewart (*Celtic Gods, Celtic Goddesses,* 2005) notes that various Celtic deities were associated with constellations. Stewart also notes many gods and goddesses associated with nature in Celtic legend are "localized versions of stellar or cosmic figures." Stewart also mentions that the stars comprising the Pleiades were related to goddesses, but he does not name them. However, even earlier in history, we find the presence of a single Star Goddess: *she who wears the stars as a veil or gown.*

In archaic Roman religion, we find a myth associated with the goddess Vesta, which depicts her as a pure flame burning in the darkness of space. Here is the pure unformed presence of divinity, which is yet to be personified by humankind. This concept is unique to the star Goddess who is without definition and yet contains all that is definable.

In the Mystery Tradition of Witchcraft, there are several deity connections to the stars and various constellations. One example is the Celtic Goddess named *Arianrhod,* whose name means "silver wheel." While this indicates a connection to the Moon, the title *Caer Arianrhod* (Arianrhod's Castle) is a popular Welsh name for the constellation Corona Borealis. Here, we see an interesting stellar connection with the circumpolar stars that never set (from Welsh tradition). The star grouping we call the Milky Way today was known to the ancient Celts as *Arianrhod,* the Silver Road.

There is widespread disagreement from various sources as to how many stars comprise the constellation of Corona Borealis. The ancient commentator Eratosthenes referred to nine stars. Hyginus and Ptolemy spoke of seven stars, and Hipparcus addresses five stars. Some modern texts depict the constellation with seven stars and others with nine stars. The latter appears in the book *Star Myths of the Greeks and Romans: A Source Book,* by Theony Condos (1997). According to Condos, the constellation actually consists of nine stars lying in a circle. From the perspective of the Mystery Tradition of Witchcraft, one could view these glowing stars as nine pearls encircling the open mouth of a cauldron.

Mike Harris, in his book *Awen: the Quest of the Celtic Mysteries* (1999) refers to the *"...hitherto 'closed gates' where Ariadne, the Welsh Arianrhod, stands guard over what we now call 'the Celtic Mysteries' or more properly the Brythonic Mysteries."* In Aegean/Mediterranean mythology, Ariadne is intimately linked with the labyrinth, which is a more complex concept of the primitive spiral image. It is interesting to note that both Arianrhod and Ariadne are associated with horned gods, an important theme in the Mystery Tradition of Witchcraft. This is further explored in Chapters Six and Seven.

In Aegean/Mediterranean mythology, the Corona Borealis is the crown of Ariadne placed in the heavens by Dionysos. The crown itself was fashioned by the magickal Smith/Hammer God Hephaestus, who made it of gold, covered with sparkling gems. So bright was the crown that it cast its own light, which allowed individuals to find their passage through the dark labyrinth associated with Ariadne.

We get a glimpse of the Mysteries associated with Arianrhod and the Corona Borealis in one of the accounts of Taliesin, a sixth-century Celtic Bard of notoriety. In his poems on the "origins," he writes of being born three times, and of being held in Arianrhod's castle a total of three times. In the case of the latter, Taliesin is clearly indicating the stars in the night sky. Here, we see the basic principle of reincarnation still alive in Celtic culture during the early Christian era.

Caitlin Matthews, in her book *Mabon and the Guardians of Celtic Britain* (2002), depicts Taliesin as the consort of Arianrhod in her aspect as Queen of the Otherworld. Matthews also refers to the initiation of Taliesin into the Mysteries at the hands of Cerridwen. The latter theme appears in several tales, which depict Taliesin traveling to Cerridwen's secret island to be initiated. Some commentators believe this island later served as the prototype for the Isle of Avalon in Arthurian legend. The hidden realms of starlight and moonlight continue to be themes intimately associated with the Mystery Tradition of Witchcraft, as we shall see in future chapters.

One interesting element related to the Star Goddess (and Moon Goddess) can be found in what is termed the "star posture." This is a ritual stance used in Drawing Down the Moon which is a technique for interfacing with the Goddess and allowing the physical body to be used as an oracle. The classic image is a high priestess standing in the star posture while wearing a headband or circlet that features either a crescent Moon or a Full Moon flanked by a waning and waxing crescent.

The star posture represents the expansive and all-encompassing Star Goddess spread out upon the night sky. The Moon symbol headband or circlet represents the focus or delimited aspect of the Moon Goddess amidst the stars. The Moon symbol sits upon the forehead of the high priestess signifying her consciousness merging with the Goddess through the "third eye" or psychic center.

The posture of the Star Goddess also represents the Great Goddess who rules the three worlds or three realms. The arms extend into the Overworld, the trunk of her body is centered in the Middleworld, and her legs extend down into the Underworld. Therefore, the posture of the Star Goddess connects all three realms. The Moon then becomes the interface for the high priestess who channels the lunar consciousness through her body, mind, and spirit.

It is this oracular connection that requires a merging with the forces of the Moon, for Witches have always drawn their power and regeneration from the light of the Moon. In a magickal sense, the Full Moon attracts the energy of the planetary influences and focuses them like a lens. The Sun draws in the stellar influences, which are modified by the planets and then absorbed and emanated by the Moon. Since the Moon is the closest body in space to the Earth, it becomes the funnel within our solar system.

Oracle powers have been attributed to the Moon, the Moon Goddess, and Witches since ancient times. In fact, the Latin word *saga*, which means "fortune teller," was one of the earliest words used to denote a Witch. The Moon Goddess who ruled the Underworld, which has long been associated with an oracular nature, bestowed the power of divination upon the Witch. As noted earlier, the souls of the dead went to dwell in the Moon, and in ancient times, the dead were believed to possess knowledge of the future. Just as the Moon imparted light to the night, the Moon Goddess imparted mystic vision to those who gathered beneath the Full Moon to venerate her.

In the ancient writings of Homer and in the Celtic legends written at a later time, we find that the stars could be seen in the Underworld, as could the Moon. However, these were not the same stars and Moon of the Middleworld. They belonged to a mystical realm ruled by a mysterious Goddess. But who was this deity and what do we know about her?

The Underworld Goddess

In the last section, we encountered a constellation associated with Arianrhod/Ariadne, which connected it with an Otherworld theme and the mystical concept of reincarnation. In this chapter, we've also noted an intimate connection between the Moon Goddess and the spirits of the dead. Now we shall turn our attention to the relationship between the realm of the dead, the Moon, and the stars.

In the mythos of the Sun God (as noted in Chapter Three), he crosses the sky each day gathering the souls of those of those who died during the night. At sunset, he delivers them to the Underworld where the Goddess awaits. Here begins the process of rebirth. In some cases, individuals may achieve release from the cycle of rebirth.

In Aegean/Mediterranean myths, there are several goddesses associated with the Underworld, or connective themes related to it, as well as to the Otherworld. These include Manea, Proserpina/Persephone, Hecate, and Ariadne. In Celtic myth and legend, we find Morrigan, Sulis, Cerridwen, Rhiannon, and other goddesses associated with Underworld themes or symbolism.

One particularly interesting Celtic deity is the goddess Aeracura, also known as Aericura or Heracura. She bears many attributes that we also find in the goddess Hecate. Although Aeracura is associated with a male counterpart named Aericurus, she is often depicted with Dis Pater, the Underworld Lord. There is also a possible connection between Aeracura and the goddess Ailleann. The latter was a woman of the Otherworld who frequently took the form of a deer. In Arthurian legend, she led Arthur and his men off to marry various Otherworld wives, and she married Arthur herself.

The primary role of the Underworld Goddess is to restore the dead to new life. The idea that the dead remain "kept or locked" in the Underworld appears to have developed at a later stage than the original concept, which is closer to that of the Otherworld (particularly in Celtic lore). For the Celts, this mystical realm was a place void of sickness and decay. There in the Otherworld, food and drink were always in great abundance, and the soul refreshed itself in a realm where the season was always summer.

In the Mystery Tradition of Witchcraft, the Underworld Goddess receives the souls of the dead into herself, and then "births" them into the Moon as it rises from the Underworld back to the world of the living. The Moon, in its turn, births the souls into the world of the living. Those souls who have no need to return to the Material Realm are eventually birthed into the stars. It is from the star realm that avatars, the enlightened souls, sometimes return of their own accord to the physical realm in order to teach less-evolved souls.

In ancient times, there was a belief that, under certain circumstances, a soul could become lost or earthbound. This situation prevented the soul from being able to enter into the Underworld. Souls that were unable to leave the realm of the living were thought to inhabit the crossroads. But the Goddess would not abandon such souls, and in her aspect of Hecate, she took them into her company.

The ancient belief held that if the dead were buried without proper burial rites, the soul was denied entrance into the Underworld. The same belief applied to those who died "before their time" or those who died a violent death (other than in formal combat). These souls were forced to wander about without a home. In Chapter One, we encountered the College of the Crossroads where people either rejected by society or those who did not adhere to state-sanctioned religions and cults gathered to worship. Here, they venerated the old deities that were long ago displaced by the gods of Olympus.

The ancient Celtic people probably found themselves in a similar situation when the Romans conquered their lands. Many clung to their former beliefs and still gathered among the ancient standing stones and other sacred sites. Here, in secret, they venerated the Old Gods of their ancestors. Eventually, centuries of Roman occupation, followed by the spread of Christianity, displaced or modified many of their ancient beliefs with foreign and alien concepts.

The Underworld Goddess takes on many forms and images. To the ancient people who lived and worked closely with nature, these symbols were simply the basic signs of the natural cycles of life. But to modern people, many of these Underworld Goddess forms can be disturbing. By analogy, the average person today has not killed an animal, cleaned off its flesh, and then prepared it as food. More likely, they have simply gone to the grocery store and purchased it neatly wrapped in plastic. Our ancestors knew their food in its original form and participated in the process of transforming it into a meal. How many people today could kill, clean, and eat an animal without some degree of revulsion? Yet, every day, the lifeforms of nature consume one another in an endless cycle of life and death.

The classic forms taken by the Underworld Goddess include the vulture and the raven, which are carrion birds that feed on the dead. One of the few birds of prey that symbolize the Underworld Goddess is the owl. The color black is often associated with the Underworld Goddess, as black symbolizes the burial cave, the grave, and the night sky that receives the soul of the dead. But the Goddess is also associated with the color white, which denotes the sunbleached bone. She is often depicted wearing a white gown, riding a white horse, or in the company of a white deer.

The Underworld Goddess also assumes the form of a serpent, which is a creature that lives in tunnels, burrows, or rocky crevices. All of these were once considered to be entrances into the Underworld. Traditionally, the Goddess of the Underworld is the mistress of the Western Gate, which is the portal of death. In her form as the Mother Goddess, she is the mistress of the Eastern Gate, which is the portal of birth. The Sun and Moon pass through these gates each day, as metaphorically do the souls of the dead.

As human beings, we have a predisposition to personify, and this tendency causes us to isolate things. When we apply this to the Underworld Goddess, we fail to see her in the totality of her being. For *she who wears the black cloak of death* is also *she who wears the bright mantle of the Moon* and *she who wears the sparkling veil of the stars*. In ancient times, she could be encountered in her triformis nature wherever three roads came together, which, in ancient times, was a place known as the crossroads.

The Crossroads Goddess

It is a very old concept that the crossroads are a place of mystical and magickal encounters. In ancient occult belief, the crossroads were the best places at which to perform magick and the conjuration of spirits. In ancient Greece, rites of purification and banishment were assigned to the crossroads. In both Northern and Southern European traditions of Witchcraft, fateful events frequently occur at the crossroads. Here, too, is the place at which to make fateful decisions with the aid of the Goddess of the Crossroads.

In ancient Western writings, there are several goddesses associated with the crossroads, and the three most noted are Hecate, Diana, and Proserpina. In ancient Greece, women gave offerings at the crossroads to a deity named Kourotrophos. The pig was a sacred offering to Kourotrophos, which reveals an Underworld connection. Several ancient references appear to identify Kourotrophos as a "child-nurturing" aspect of Hecate. Some commentators equate Hecate with the Celtic goddess Aeracura or Aericura.

The image of Hecate at the crossroads is an interesting portrayal. Hecate belongs to the torch-bearing class of goddesses and is therefore lunar in nature. Her torches cast light upon the crossroads, and in this way, the three roads are revealed. The three roads symbolize the present, the future, and the alternative. The present road has been already walked to this point, and the person may remain in the present. The road to the future is the one that leads to that which the established patterns have set into motion. The alternative path is the way of personal will and vision. Sadly, this is often the road less traveled.

Hecate is a goddess who points out the path (the one we are on, the one that is probable, and the one that is possible). However, she does not guide one in the sense of suggesting or counseling. Instead, the choice always belongs to the individual who stands at the crossroads. Hecate is simply the light-bearer who, like the Full Moon at night, illuminates the path beneath our feet. But ultimately, the walk is our own.

In the mystical tradition, the crossroads is a place between the worlds. Where three roads meet, there is no coming or going; there is only the threefold center of choice. The center is neither in the road nor outside of the road but is instead a realm of its own. Here resides not only the portal to other realms but also the very essence of magick itself.

In ancient times, a pole known as a *hekataion* was placed at the fork of a crossroad. Upon the pole, three masks were hung, one facing each direction on the road. The ancient writer Ovid, in his classic work *Fasti*, refers to Hecate's face as *"...turned in three directions that she may guard the crossroads where they branch three separate ways"* (referenced in *The Rotting Goddess* by Jacob Rabinowitz, 1998). The designation of guardian implies an influence or power exerted over the crossroads and those who enter one.

The triformis nature of the Goddess at the Crossroads is an indication of the mystical process. The number three has long held significance throughout Pagan Europe. Many commentators believe that three represents an amplification of root power. Therefore, three would triple the power or significance of whatever was associated with or appeared with the number itself.

Pythagoras held the view that the number three represented the beginning, middle, and end. These junctures were often personified as three women known as the Fates. In both Northern and Southern

European lore, the three women are depicted as a young maiden, a mature woman, and an elderly woman. One pulls the thread of life, another spins it, and the last woman cuts it. This imagery represented the life of an individual being woven by external patterns. To some, these patterns were conscious aspects of a divinity that oversaw the lives of humankind.

The Fate Goddess

In ancient times, the power of the Great Goddess evolved into the concept of a Goddess of Fate. The earliest form of the Goddess as a deity associated with Fate depicts her as a bird or with the characteristics of a bird. The basic concept seems rooted in the Neolithic period where we find various bird deities accompanied by the imagery of triple lines above or below the bird goddess symbol.

The ancient deity forms of the Egyptians depict various gods and goddesses with bird heads. The vulture is a common bird Goddess associated with not only Egyptian deities but also with the Greek goddess Athena. In her myths, Athena could also transform into a dove, which we saw earlier as associated with the Great Goddess. The crow or raven is another bird linked to Fate. One of the common names for the Celtic Triple Goddess in Ireland is *Badh,* which means "crow."

In ancient mythology, various beings serve the Fates, as well as the decrees of the gods. Among them are the Sirens and Harpies of Greek mythology, which are birds of prey in the composite form of a woman. Their classic image features a human head, a winged body, and the feet of a vulture. Frequently, they appear in groups of three, which is the classic mythological theme. The mythological Siren possesses the power to lure a person through her song, which ultimately results in death.

Among the servants of Fate, we also find the Keres of Death. They appear to originate from the Old European Vulture Goddess or Bird of Prey Goddess. In the Mystery Tradition of Witchcraft, it is taught that the animals associated with a god or goddess are actually their earlier ancient totem forms. Here, we see a survival theme wherein the Goddess of Fate remains over the course of time.

In ancient Etruscan and archaic Roman religions, the Goddess of Fate held power over the "high gods" who ruled the heavens and the Earth. To the ancient Greeks, the Goddess of Fate was known as

Ananke. The Romans depicted her as the goddess Fatum. Over the passing centuries, the Goddess was divided into aspects personified as three sisters who were known as the Moerae or Parcae. Here, they represented the three stages of human life: birth, years spent, and death.

The Fates were believed to be the daughters of night. The night held the darkness, which symbolized the procreative forces that formed everything. It also represented the possibility that from darkness, anything could appear or issue forth. This is the essence of magick itself.

The three daughters of night were called Klotho, Lachesis, and Atropos. As goddesses of Fate, the sisters were weavers. The youngest was Klotho, and to her was given the task of putting the wool around the spindle. Lachesis then spun the wool into thread. To Atropos fell the task of cutting the thread, which brought an individual's life to an end.

Among the Germanic people, there were also three sisters associated with Fate. These sisters were known as the *Norns* or the *Wyrd Sisters.* The Germanics gave them the names Urd, Verdandi, and Skuld. They were also known as Wyrd, Werthende, and Skould.

In the Aegean/Mediterranean, the Moerae were associated with streams and fountains. The Norns originated from the fountain of Urd, the source of life from which the great ash tree Yggdrasil drew its strength. Like the three sisters of Aegean/Mediterranean myth, the Norns also spun the lives of humankind. In Germanic lore, Skuld (the youngest) cut the thread, while Urd (the eldest) wrapped the wool, and Verdandi (the middle sister) spun it.

In the Mystery Tradition of Witchcraft, the process of weaving, plaiting, and knotting comes under the auspices of the Fates. Here, the Moerae govern the Triple Mysteries: birth, life, and death; past, present, and future; beginning, middle, and end. The sisters are also aspects of the Lunar Mysteries and reflect the phase of the Moon: waxing, full, and waning.

Now we have come full circle back to the Moon, which is the symbol of the Mystery of the Mysteries. Therefore, it is time now to look deeper into the Mysteries themselves. Here, we shall discover the ancient wisdom and the hidden elements of Witchcraft. Let us turn to the next chapter where we shall encounter the Inner Mysteries of the Witches' Craft.

CHAPTER FIVE

Exploring the Inner Mysteries

The Inner Mysteries are comprised of two vital elements. One is the etheric or spiritual function, and the other is the material manifestation resulting from this "behind the scenes" process. The Inner Mysteries of Witchcraft meet and are understood in the way they interact within the physical realm. For the Witch, it then becomes a matter of knowing how to effectively interface with this mystical union, which is essentially something of the Otherworld.

It is the purpose and function of a Mystery Tradition to convey in myth and metaphor what cannot be understood by ordinary means and commonplace reasoning. Symbols that impact the psyche are also an important component. In the Mystery Tradition, they serve to invoke and evoke the response required to produce the needed alignments to what the symbol represents.

According to oral tradition, certain symbols were intentionally used to discourage certain types of people. The Mystery Tradition screened out any potential student to whom appearances alone were enough to discourage further involvement. Some examples are the Sabbatic goat figure and the gargoyle image. If such a disturbing sight alone could send a person running without first asking questions, then the potential student was thought to be untrainable in the occult Mysteries.

One of the most misunderstood objects appearing in Witchcraft is the skull. To many people, this is a disturbing presence and signifies death. However, in the Mystery Tradition, the skull signifies knowledge and wisdom. Essentially, the skull represents what remains of one's life experience. In this sense, it is symbolic of what our ancestors knew and passed on to future generations.

The crossbones represent guardianship. They form an "X" figure, which symbolizes power over the realm of death. In ancient art, the "X" appears on the thrones of deities associated with the Underworld, and among their general symbolism. In many ways, they symbolize the same meaning as crossed swords and denote a fellowship or secret order. In the context of the latter, the skull represents the preserved knowledge of the order.

Some commentators have suggested that among the Celts, the practice of headhunting was rooted in a spiritual tradition (as opposed to one of taking war trophies). If we hold to the view that the skull retains knowledge, then removing the head would keep such knowledge from leaving the body at death. There are many Celtic tales associated with the skull and with specific skulls, such as that of the hero Bran the Blessed.

In the tale of Bran, he instructs his men that, upon his death, they are to sever his head and bury it (at the site of what is now London). Bran states that this will protect Breton from being conquered by invaders. The implication here is that something of the power and spirit of Bran remains in the skull. The theme of retaining the ancestral spirit appears throughout continental Europe and the British Isles. In Northern Europe, it appears in what might be called the Cult of the Head.

In Southern Europe, the concept appears in the figure of the Lare, a spirit that personifies the ancestral connection. Here, the Lare serves as a link between the past and the current generations. It is interesting to note that the Lare spirits serve the so-called "head of the household."

Originally, the Lare were worshipped as spirits of the land. Offerings to them were made at the crossroads, which identifies them as spirits of the dead. Over the course of time, the veneration of the Lare was performed in the home. Here, Lare shrines were erected on or near the hearth.

In Chapter Two, we explored the connection between the hearth and the cave. Here, we found cave symbolism within the hearth and noted the connection of the cave as an entrance to the Underworld. We also discovered that through this connection, the hearth served as a living connection to those family members who dwelled in the Underworld.

As previously described, the classic hearth was made of piled and mortared stone, with a cave-like opening that housed the wood and fire. Across the top of the hearth was laid a mantle stone slab. In the Mystery Tradition, we see this slab as the remnant of the great standing stones that mark the ancient sites of sacred land. The fire of the hearth is the presence of divinity, and the wood is the ancient sacred tree of our ancestors. Here in the hearth, the standing stone (mantle), and the tree (log) meet in sacred flame.

In Hesiod's classic work, *Theogony*, he makes the statement that his teachings are not from oak and boulder. Instead, he claims that he speaks as directed by the divine Muses who were sent to him by the high gods. In his writings, Hesiod appears to have disdain for the beliefs of the rural peasants, and he places himself above them as being better educated. Hesiod tries to separate himself by claiming to be a philosopher rather than a rustic. However, his references to the oak and boulder are significant because they suggest older teachings preceding his own.

We know that our distant ancestors venerated trees (the oak in particular) and also erected great slabs of rock at their sacred sites. Therefore, the oak and the boulder (in a metaphorical sense) must have spoken quite loudly to our ancestors. Hesiod goes on to say that the Muses plucked a branch and gave it to him to use as a staff. In a curious turn, Hesiod then states, *"...but my theme is not of the oak and boulder"* but of the gods of Olympus.

Although Hesiod's *Theogony* is intended to record the lineage and nature of the Olympic deities, he also mentions half-forgotten things such as the Titans and the teachings of oak and boulder. The latter is of particular interest in our consideration of the Inner Mysteries of Witchcraft. What then can be said of trees and rock?

Standing Stones and Sacred Groves

One of the verses passed along in the oral tradition of Witchcraft refers to the tree and the standing stone. Author Doreen Valiente wrote a poem incorporating this theme in her book *Witchcraft for Tomorrow* (1978). A portion of the poem reads: *"Thee we invoke by the moonled sea, by the standing stone and the twisted tree..."*

It is an ancient belief that divinity dwelled within certain sacred trees. Within the Mystery Tradition of Witchcraft, there is also a belief that stone retains the memory of a place. Therefore, the great standing stones of prehistory are said to remember all that transpired around them. According to oral tradition, part of their use was to retain the essence of the rites and practices to which they stood witness. In effect, the ancient priests and priestesses intentionally passed all of this knowledge into the standing stones.

Initiations performed on the site of standing stones were designed to help the initiate interface with the memories contained within the material of the rock. This enabled the memory-chain associations, vital to any authentic initiation, to be passed to the initiate (this is explored further in the chapter). Any Witch or Pagan who ever visited one of these ancient sites will attest to the feel of the place, which suggests an emanation of some type coming from the setting itself.

Baring and Cashford (*Myth of the Goddess*, 1991) state that the raising of a stone is itself an act of remembrance. They also see a connective theme here with the erection of a headstone on a grave. Baring and Cashford mention a belief that the standing stones were thought to be the dwelling place or body of the dead. The souls of the dead could be summoned to the stone and reside there for an unstated period of time. This same essential principle applied to sacred groves in ancient times.

As noted in Chapter Two, the spirit of a god or goddess was believed to dwell within their sacred grove. From this ancient notion arose a teaching centered on the sacred branch. According to oral tradition, the staff of the priest or priestess represented their alignment to the deity with which the tree was identified. Through the spirit of the deity within the wood, the priestess or priest carried divine blessings to the villages, fields, crops, and herds.

To bear the branch as a staff identified the priest or priestess as an emissary of the associated deity. Traditionally, the staff was the full measure of the priest or priestess from head to toe. But to this length, another measure was added. This was the measure from the inside of the priest or priestess's left forearm, taken from the inside of the elbow to the tip of the middle finger. Because the arm can be extended or withdrawn by use of the elbow, this action represented the ability to extend their alignment with deity to another person, place, or thing. Therefore, the staff represented the personal connection to deity (one's measured height) and the ability to extend this connection to others (the reach of the arm when extended from the elbow).

In the Mystery Tradition of Witchcraft, it is not enough to simply cultivate one's own spirituality. The education and evolution of the self, if not shared with others, only serves the one. But spirituality is not about the self; it is about what the self brings to their community. In order to define anything, there must be something to compare it against. For example, *silence* can only be defined by knowing what *noisy* means, and *hot* can only be defined by knowing the experience of *cold*. Therefore, spirituality can only be discerned in the context of what one brings or fails to bring to others.

The classical image of the Hermit in the traditional tarot reflects this basic principle. Here, he is the "way shower," whose lantern sheds light for those who walk the path to which he guides. The traditional Hermit image of the tarot depicts an aged man in a hooded robe. He holds a lantern in his right hand and a staff in his left hand. The Hermit stands upon the summit of a mountain as he extends his lighted lantern out before him. Paul Foster Case (*The Tarot: A Key to the Wisdom of the Ages,* 1947), an acknowledged expert on the tarot, wrote:

"Although the Hermit seems to be alone, he is really the Wayshower, lighting the path for climbing multitudes below. He has no need to climb, hence his staff is held in his left hand."

The Hermit, like the priestess or priest, has trained and become enlightened. This enlightenment cannot be held within because it would deny the emanation of light. Therefore, self-enlightenment is only the beginning. It is an acquired state of "inner being" that is meant to be expressed in the outer world. By analogy, the divine spirit within the tree does not serve those who venerate it if it remains unexpressed within the wood. If it contributes nothing to the religion or spirituality of its worshippers, the divine spirit remains disconnected from meaningful purpose. It is only through bringing out the indwelling spirit that sacredness and holiness can be encountered and understood.

Ancient groves served as the spiritual center of the Mystery sect. Its priests and priestesses established an intimate relationship with the sacred tree that stood as the focal point or center of the grove. Offerings and adornments were placed on and before the tree. Chants drifted across the trunk and branches as members of the sect encircled the sacred tree. Within the tree, the indwelling spirit of the divine stirred in response. It was from this tree that the sacred branches were selected as staves. A modern version of this type of spiritual alignment appears in the custom of decorating the Yule tree, around which presents are placed and songs are sung.

Memory-Chain Associations

The beliefs, practices, and lore of our ancestors have been preserved in many ways. The earliest means were in the use of cave paintings and other prehistoric forms of art. Eventually, oral teachings arose, which gave birth to the bardic tradition. In time, humans created a written language, and this preserved a great deal regarding the beliefs and practices of our ancestors.

Over the course of many centuries, various concepts, beliefs, and practices were linked together and passed on to future generations. A tradition of training and aligning arose, and knowledge of these methods was retained by a handful of people within a tribal structure. In time, some elements of this eventually seeped into the general populace and became the root source for folktales, fairy tales, and folk magick. Those without training misunderstood it, and they lacked the knowledge of the alignments as well as the methods of interfacing. This is essentially the difference between esoteric and exoteric. It also reflects the difference between an initiate of a tradition rooted in what has been passed on, versus a person self-initiated into what they can piece together from whatever is available from various sources.

In the Mystery Tradition of Witchcraft, it is taught that ancestral knowledge lies deep within us all. In a mundane regard, our physical traits are passed to us by our parents. This passing on of genetic material constitutes an unbroken chain back to our earliest ancestors. We are, therefore, a living link to the past. But are we simply the product of inherited biological components, or is there more to our presence and existence?

From a metaphysical perspective, there is an etheric component attached to our material DNA, a continuation of the "life spark" passed from parent to child. It resides within the energy that renders the DNA into a cohesive pattern and keeps it intact. It is taught that many of our phobias, predispositions, and natural talents are imparted to us from the etheric component of our DNA. In effect, this non-physical element is ancestral memory. Therefore, we not only inherit our physical being—we also inherit our ancestral spirit.

Many modern Pagans and Witches are trying to reconstruct today what their ancestors knew ages ago. But the knowledge (and experience) of these ancestors already lies within us all. Therefore, there is no need to invent or reconstruct. In fact, all we may be doing is nothing more than remembering.

Skeptics often criticize writers of the Craft genre who deal with ancient beliefs, and state that such individuals are using modern minds to interpret and understand ancient ways. This view is void of the teaching and understanding of reincarnation. If we accept reincarnation as a fact, then we must accept that we are our own ancestors incarnate in the present. Through this view, we can come to an understanding that we can, in effect, remember what we knew when we lived in ancient times. The legendary, wise Solomon is credited with saying that there is nothing new under the Sun—what once was is now again.

It is no coincidence that within the Mystery Teachings, we find what is referred to as "the Cauldron in the Underworld." This is a metaphorical reference to retrieving ancestral knowledge from the soul memory. The process is involved and requires time, effort, and patience. Many myths and legends (particularly among the Celts) contain themes of entering the Underworld or a secret castle in a quest to retrieve a magickal cauldron. In such tales, the cauldron is most often associated with an Underworld deity or figure that rules over the dead. The fact that the cauldron (or its brew) must be "retrieved" from the land of the dead strongly suggests that it is linked to both the living and the dead. In a real sense, the same can be said of our DNA.

Many ancient myths and legends present themes of entering the Underworld on a quest. The common element in such tales centers on obtaining information or knowledge. This resides among those who have lived before, for to them is ascribed knowledge of the past, present, and future. Therefore, the hero of the quest must enter the dark realm in which the dead reside. In the tales of both Northern and Southern Europe, a sacred tree branch is required in order to safely enter the Underworld and then return from its kingdom.

The myths and legends within the Mystery Tradition contain hidden meanings that present themselves only when the reader is ready to understand what they convey. These tales are constructed in order to preserve and reveal the ancient memory-chain associations that link us directly to the knowledge and wisdom of our ancestors. The memory-chains are those things that link one concept to another so that in context and wholeness, the "master view" can be discerned. This can be likened to a jigsaw puzzle. As the connected pieces come together, so too does the appearance of a pattern. As the pattern expands through added connections, the original picture emerges.

In the Mystery Tradition, initiation is a process by which the memory-chain association alignments are passed. This makes it possible for the initiate to bring the ancestral pieces of the puzzle together. This begins to work automatically, much like tipping a domino that is lined up in a series with others. Once the first domino at the starting point is correctly set and properly aligned, then what follows is assured. In the Mystery Tradition, the symbol of the labyrinth is used to represent the inner process of retrieval and integration. At the center of the labyrinth lies the mystical cauldron of the ancestors, which sits nestled in the partially-exposed roots of an ancient tree. It is within the inner cauldron that the memory-chain associations reside. Here they await our arrival, at which point, the cauldron offers its brew of enlightenment.

How the memory-chain associations work is relatively simple. The core model works by linking whatever borders it to another related concept that incorporates both the core and the connecting concept together as one notion. This can be envisioned as a central octagon connected to other octagons. The center octagon represents the core concept of the Mysteries. Each directly bordering octagon represents an idea that helps define the core concept and makes it more understandable. In turn, other octagons that border those, that border the core, introduce ideas that connect previous ideas in relation to the core. Each octagon builds upon the other and connects its idea to the previous ideas, which all lead ultimately back to the core (from which they all derive their common origin).

It is through the study and contemplation of the ideas associated with the core concept that one can interface with the memory-chain associations. The first step is the alignment to the core concept, which is passed to the initiate through their initiation experience. During the ritual, subtle changes are made within the psyche. This is facilitated through the initiator who uses a combination of sound, fragrance, setting, and emotion. At the peak of the ritual process, the initiator raises and imparts a portion of the energy stream that they first received in their own initiation. This is directed into the center of the forehead of the initiate at a point just above the eyebrows.

Once the alignment has been made, a course of study begins. The new initiate must study not only the chain of ideas but also everything associated with each idea. For example, a study of a specific tree is not limited to its lore, magickal properties, and deity or spirit associations. One must also learn its physical properties and life cycle. When a deity or spirit is mentioned in connection with the tree, then this must be studied and searched for further links. Once these links are apparent, they must be examined for further links to the core concept and other ideas surrounding it.

The alignment that is established during initiation allows the memory-chain associations to fall into place during the course of study. From a metaphysical perspective, the associations are not being created but are instead a series of awakened memories leading back to the core concept. Through guided study, they properly connect to form the pattern from which the "master view" emerges.

The advantage of memory-chain associations is that they allow one to connect directly through time to the momentum of the past. This is a current of energy that flows from what has *been* to what is *now*. It can be thought of as a quantum thread connecting all time periods (very much like a thread in a spider's web is connected to the center and, therefore, to every other thread). When we connect to the memory-chain associations, we draw upon what is contained in the roots of this ancient tree of knowledge.

As we noted in Chapters One and Two, the sacred tree reaches into the Underworld with its roots and into the heavens with its branches. Between the worlds is the realm of the living where the trunk of the tree stands as a bridge. With the knowledge of ascent, symbolized by the branch, we can safely descend into the Underworld of our ancestors. The ancient tree is rooted in the Underworld. Rootedness is why we need to return, for therein is the tree nourished, and from its roots, we may draw what sustains us. But we cannot remain in the past if we are to serve as the bearers for a new generation that is to come. Therefore, we must carry the branch into and from the Underworld, for the branch declares that what we take is then extended to others. The cauldron will not offer its essence to those who serve only themselves.

The Inner Mechanism

In the Mystery Tradition, the view is held that every manifested object in the Material Realm originated from a non-physical energy imprint of that object. From a metaphysical perspective, there are other dimensions beyond the physical world in which "behind the scenes" forces are at work. These forces can and do have an effect on the material dimension. All occult and metaphysical principles are based upon our understanding of the inner mechanism of these other dimensions. Over the course of several thousand years, our ancestors have developed concepts, symbols, principles, and techniques for interfacing with the process of this inner mechanism. This knowledge and wisdom has been passed down to us through the traditional occult arts and occult correspondences.

The simplest way of understanding the inner mechanism is to imagine a series of interconnected and reliant planes of existence. Traditionally, there are seven planes, which span from the highest to the lowest.

7. Ultimate
6. Divine
5. Spiritual
4. Mental
3. Astral
2. Elemental
1. Physical

These realms are discussed in detail in my previous books, *The Wiccan Mysteries* and *Wiccan Magick*, therefore, I will only deal briefly with them here. Essentially, the order of planes begins with the "unknowable" realm. Here is the reality of how all things came to be, which is beyond our current level of human understanding. Therefore, we call this the Ultimate Plane or Dimension (ultimately to where everything can trace its origin).

The next plane, in descending order, is called the Divine Plane. This is the realm in which we envision divinity in ways that we can describe and relate to through our religious concepts. Following the Divine Realm is the Spiritual Plane. Here, we find the emanation of the Divine, which forms communication and expression from the Divine Plane. In a sense, this is the thought and the word coming from the Divine Source.

The Mental Plane is next in order, and here, the "thoughts and words" of the Divine become cohesive and discernable concepts to the human mind. In other words, what can only be sensed in the Spiritual Plane is then perceivable in the Mental Realm. In the Mental Plane, design appears and gives activity to the concepts flowing from the Spiritual Plane.

The Astral Plane is next in descending order. It is here where thoughts become forms as they flow into the astral substance. Unlike the etheric substance of the higher planes, the astral substance can be felt (much like a breeze or wind can be felt). From a metaphysical perspective, astral material forms around a thought or image and "coats" it with an enclosing shell. Here, it gives or brings out form. One way to imagine this is to picture dipping a small object into a bowl of melted wax and then quickly withdrawing it. The wax forms perfectly around it and the object now has a replica of wax surrounding it. If you could dip a thought into melted wax and then see it as a wax-coated image, this would better clarify the role of astral substance.

Another way of imagining the astral process is to imagine dipping a clear glass figurine of a horse into a bowl of melted colored wax. When the glass horse is withdrawn, all of the details of the figurine are now pronounced. The details are clearly visible because the color brings out the features that were previously unseen in the transparent glass.

Following the Astral Plane is the Elemental Plane. Here reside the building blocks of material creation, the elements of Earth, Air, Fire, and Water. Ancient philosophers, such as Pythagoras and Empedocles, spoke of creation being brought forth from chaos through the integration of the four elements. Each element represents a principle of creation. Earth represents cohesion, Air symbolizes expansion, Fire denotes energy, and Water signifies mutability. In occult philosophy, a fifth element exists, which is called Spirit. It is Spirit that draws, directs, and adheres the elements so that creation may take place.

The final plane in descending order is the Material Realm. It is here that the etheric substance of the universe vibrates at such a low frequency that concepts become tangible, solid objects. What appears to be a solid object in the Material Dimension is a tangible representation of the end result of a process taking place within all of the other planes of existence. For example, in the Material Realm, a tree is a plant. However, on the Elemental Plane, it is a process of cohesion into form. On the Astral Plane, it is an etheric replica. Within the Mental Plane, the tree is a perceivable or conceptual thought. On the Spiritual Plane, the tree is a formless expression or concept. Within the Divine Plane, the tree is a specific aspect of the divine nature. On the Ultimate Plane, the tree is the one thing (as all things are) that is the origin.

If we reverse this process and see it from the highest to the lowest, the entire concept becomes somewhat clearer. In order for anything to appear within the Material Realm, it must go through a metaphysical process. A tree was our earlier example, and we will now look at how the tree first came into existence and then manifested (from an occult perspective).

In the Ultimate Plane, we begin with the origin of all things. From this origin, a specific nature or characteristic then arises (Divine Plane). In our example, this "nature" will become a tree. On the next plane appears a formless expression of the isolated nature (Spiritual Plane). Following this arises a visual perception of the specific nature (Mental Plane). In turn, this gives way to an etheric replica form of this nature (Astral Plane). Next arises the "fixed cohesion" of this nature, which is a binding process (Elemental Plane). Finally, this nature, being bound, decelerates to a level at which it becomes tangible (Material Plane). What was once origin, nature, expression, visualization, replica, and cohesion becomes a tree as the process finalizes in "manifestation" within the lowest level (the Material Plane). In understanding this principle, we can say that the God and Goddess are in all things, for everything is a manifestation of an aspect of the divine nature.

In archaic Roman religion, we find a concept known as a *numen*. The numen is essentially a consciousness that exists within inanimate objects. It is the numen that gives an object a presence or character. Natural settings also possess a numen, which makes a place comforting, inviting, and pleasant. The presence of numen can also create the opposite reaction. It is primarily a matter of harmonious resonance between the numen and whatever comes into the presence of any specific numen.

In the Mystery Tradition, numen is viewed as an encapsulated spark of the divine nature dwelling with an inanimate object. It is more akin to radiation than to intelligence, although the numen does have a rudimentary awareness. It is not, however, a spirit or deity in the conventional sense or definition.

From an occult perspective, the animating forces within nature are spirit entities, which largely fall into the category of elementals or nature spirits. Within the Mysteries, such things as the appearance of a spout or the opening of a bud are viewed as the actions of nature spirits. In some rituals and spells, we find a verse referring to *"...by seed and sprout, and stem and leaf, and bud and flower_"* This addresses the mystical process behind the scenes, which manifests as the material results. The alignment of one's magick or ritual to "stem and leaf, and bud and flower" is to call upon the very forces that animate the process. An occult axiom states that "like attracts like" and in this principle, we find that mimicry draws the magickal to the physical and vice versa.

The divine role in this inner process symbolically appears in the myths and legends of Witchcraft. Here, we find a Goddess and a God within seasonal themes, as well as in the general themes of life and death. This speaks again of the Mystery tenet that views the divine within all things and the divine nature expressed in all things. Myths and legends are accounts of how it functions and what happens when we connect to the core of it all.

In the general mythos of the Witchcraft Mysteries, we find a God who is born and dies and a Goddess who loves him and follows him into the Underworld. Here, she hopes to return him to the world of the living. The mortal part of the God appears as subject to the cyclical process of birth, flowering, decay, death, and rebirth as are his worshippers. This is why one of his images is that of the Harvest Lord.

In the book *The Myth of the Goddess*, the authors Baring and Cashford present an insightful look into the Mysteries. Here, the Goddess is viewed as the totality of the lunar cycle. The God is seen reflected in the nature of the waxing and waning cycles of the Moon. In other words, the Goddess is the whole and the God is the part. This is not to suggest that he is lunar in nature, but simply to demonstrate that he is part of the Goddess as her consort, son, and lover. The Goddess and the God are, in effect, two dimensions of the one living principle.

In the ancient Greek Mystery cults, the words *zoe* and *bios* were used to indicate a connection between two dimensions of life. *Zoe* signified the eternal and infinite, while *bios* referred to the finite and individual life. The bios (as seen in the linear world) is simply a manifestation of zoe when some portion of it becomes isolated within the material world. The soul is the whole and the body is the part, and each is an expression of the life force. In the simplest of terms, the body is fixed and temporary but the animating soul is free and eternal.

The Goddess symbolizes the higher spiritual element as reflected metaphorically in the things of the heavens. The God symbolizes the incarnate nature of the spiritual element as reflected metaphorically in the things of the Earth (and specifically related to the agricultural year).

Together, they reveal the two facets of existence; eternal and transitory, unmanifest and manifest, invisible and visible. Baring and Cashford point out that the marriage of the Goddess and God symbolically reconnects the two worlds of zoe and bios. Through this sacred union, the Earth is then regenerated.

Birth, Life, and Death

To our ancestors, the cycles of life and death seemed to be mirrored in the phases of the Moon. It was also apparent in the seasons of nature. When we look at ancient rites and festivals, it seems clear that these intentionally marked the transitional points of the agricultural year. Rites of celebration were associated with the seasons of the waxing year, and rites of mourning were associated with the waning year.

Our ancestors, as an agrarian society, were not unaware of the analogy of the Moon with the life of plants and animals. They were also well aware of the Moon's influence on human biology. Likewise, in a metaphorical sense, our ancestors observed the symbolic connection between the cycles of the Moon, nature, and human existence.

Rituals associated with the Moon formed around primitive beliefs as well as religious and spiritual views. The Moon gave light to the darkness, demonstrating power over the night. It appeared to be born, grow to fullness, decline, and then disappear into darkness. Its ability to reappear again suggested that death was not the end. Here, darkness held no permanent power over light, and the Moon suggested that life always follows after death. Therefore, all light and all life held the promise of renewal and return.

Within the Mystery Tradition, the concept of reincarnation is rooted in the cycles of the Moon and the seasons. This essential theme was discussed in Chapters Three and Four, where we also noted various beliefs about the souls of the dead. Spirits of the dead and their association with the Moon appear among some of the oldest writings in Western literature.

An ancient view held that the souls of the dead dwelled in the ether surrounding the Moon. This was sometimes referred to as the sublunary world. This zone was imagined to border the atmosphere of the world of the living. The sublunary realm was said to exist "between the world of gods and men." Professor Franz Cumont explores these concepts in his book *After Life in Roman Paganism* (1922).

As we noted in Chapter Two, floating islands appear in the lore containing themes of death and the Otherworld. Both the Sun and the Moon are associated with conveying and containing the dead. Here, the theme of rising and setting associated both celestial bodies with the ocean and with the quarters of East and West. Among the earliest concepts, we find the Sun and Moon identified as the Islands of the Blessed, which was a Pythagorean concept as well.

In ancient lore, we later find the appearance of two mythical islands that float on the open sea called the *Islands of the Blessed*. This theme retains the earlier memory of the Sun and Moon (as well as the connection with water). The light of the setting Sun and the Moon creates what appears as a road or pathway on the surface of the ocean, which may have suggested to our ancestors a far-off realm at the end. Just before the Sun and Moon set, a "floating island" of light can be seen, which quickly disappears beneath the horizon.

In ancient times, the stars were also associated with the souls of the dead. This belief was rooted in the early concept that souls occupied a hidden realm in the air. Merging these ideas created a belief that the dead inhabited the sky in the form of stars. In a later philosophical era, this idea became more sophisticated. Here, the soul (about to be born in the material world) was seen to descend from the heights of the heavens and pass through the planetary spheres. As it descended through the spheres, the soul took with it a portion of each associated nature. The soul thereby acquired the dispositions and qualities of each planetary sphere. In this concept, we see the rooted principles of astrology.

After death, the departed soul was imagined to return through the spheres and divest itself of the impurities absorbed during its habitation within a material body. One interesting view held that the souls of the dead were drawn by affinity into the atmosphere of moonlight and came to dwell in the sublunary ether. Here, like the Moon itself, they took on a spherical globelike form of light:

"...souls, which are a burning breath, rose through the air towards the fires of the sky, in virtue of their lightness. When they reached the upper zone, they found in the ether about the moon surroundings like their own

essence and remained there in equilibrium. Conceived as material and as circular in form, they were, like the heavenly bodies, nourished by the exaltations which arose from the soil and waters. These innumerable globes of a fire endowed with intelligence formed an animated chorus about the divine luminary of night" (Franz Cumont, *After Life in Roman Paganism*, 1922).

When viewing various elements of ancient theory and philosophy, a composite view emerges regarding the soul. Here, we see the souls of the dead moving through different realms where they dwell for unspecified periods of time. These different realms are the Material, Lunar, Solar, and Stellar. In each realm, the soul takes on a "body" that is reflective of the particular realm in which the soul resides.

Within the Material Realm, the soul resides inside a body of flesh. In the Lunar Realm, it assumes an etheric body of lunar substance. It is from the sublunar atmosphere that the soul returns to the Material Realm during its binding to the process of reincarnation. Once the process of incarnation within the Material Realm is completed, the soul is then released into the Solar Realm. Here, it takes on a sun-like body. Once this cycle of existence is completed, the soul then takes on its final and true body among the stars.

In most modern Witchcraft traditions, the emphasis regarding the departed soul is focused on two primary tenets. These are the Summerland and reincarnation.

The Summerland

In the basic theology of Witchcraft, we find a teaching that involves the crossing over of a soul from the death of the body into a realm known as the *Summerland.* From a metaphysical perspective, the death of the material body initiates two significant events. First, without the functioning body, the life force cannot be sustained and energy is no longer available to nourish the indwelling soul. According to traditional occult teachings, the physical body absorbs etheric energy through the solar plexus. It is this energy that maintains the environment necessary for the soul to reside within a flesh vehicle.

The second event begins with the withdrawal of the elemental forces from the material body. Upon death, the soul leaves the material vessel, and this action removes the cohesive force that kept the four elements in harmony within the flesh body. Without the life force to keep the elements bound, they are released back into their natural realms. It is at this point that the material body begins to decay.

When the soul withdraws from the material vessel, consciousness is then transferred from the body to the soul. The lower consciousness of the personality is anesthetized and the higher consciousness of the soul awakens within the body of light. Between these two processes is a brief period in which a deep sleep takes place while the etheric cord is dissolved. This cord is sometimes called the *silver cord,* and its purpose is to tether the soul to the body during any given lifetime.

The silver cord is an important component related to astral projection. The nature of the cord is elastic, which allows the soul to journey in the astral body while the physical body lies unconscious. The cord ensures that the soul will be brought back to the body when the time comes to awaken. In an emergency, when the body is in danger, the cord is used to quickly retrieve the conscious soul in order for the body to be animated.

A very old teaching states that the soul remains in the vicinity of the body for three days. At this point, with the withdrawal of the elemental forces, the magnetic connection is abolished and the soul is free. The soul may then remain in the Material Realm for another three days, after which it is then drawn into the Otherworld. Therefore, the teaching states that the soul remains in the Material Realm after the death of the body for a total of seven days. The seventh day is the time of release from the Material into the Spiritual.

According to occult tradition, the soul is drawn into a non-physical realm that is harmonious in nature or vibration with that of the soul. Each lifetime and its experiences contribute to the energy and nature of the soul. Therefore, the soul is actually an accumulation of the experiences it has passed through, and its nature is a composite energy that resonates in accord with the resulting temperament of the soul. In other words, the nature of the soul reflects the integration of all the positive and negative experiences through which the soul has passed. The resonance of the soul reflects the resulting mentality, which is what constitutes the vibration of the soul.

In general, energies of love, compassion, forgiveness, and understanding tend to create high-frequency vibrations, which make the nature of the soul more etheric. This, in turn, draws the soul to the higher spiritual realms. Energies of hate, intolerance, resentment, and criticism tend to render the nature of the soul denser. This, in turn, draws the soul to the lower and more base of the spiritual realms. This follows the occult principle that "like attracts like" and ensures that the soul arrives where it needs to be in its present stage of evolution.

The Summerland is a term used in the Mystery Tradition of Witchcraft to refer to the realms in which a soul may find itself after the death of the body it previously inhabited. As we noted in previous chapters, the Otherworld has been perceived in many ways by many different cultures. These perceptions, although modified largely by cultural and religious elements, actually stem from a natural phenomenon. This is related to the experience of the Otherworld when we dream. The afterlife realm is partially known to us because we enter it through the dream gates each night. More often than not, the memory of the experience is not retained by the conscious mind but instead resides in the soul memory.

In the Summerland, the soul encounters a composite realm that is constructed of both what it expects or believes that it will find and what is most harmonious to its nature and soul vibration. Therefore, it is part of the Mystery Teachings to prepare the mind, spirit, and soul to encounter and experience the most beneficial realm. To this end, the Mystery Traditions have created specific images of the Otherworld. These include a description of the realm, its terrain, what it contains, and how one finds entrance. An interesting example from one specific tradition can be found in the book *The Roebuck in the Thicket* by Evan John Jones and Robert Cochrane.

Through meditation and guided imagery, it is possible to create an alignment that will draw the soul to a specific formed image within the Summerland. Wizards in the Middle Ages and Renaissance used paintings as a projection point through which the soul could enter the Otherworld. From this concept arose the idea of the astral temple, which is a constructed zone where the Witch can project for magickal purposes. I refer the interested reader to my previous book *The Witches' Craft* for further information.

According to oral tradition, the Summerland is a realm of rest, recuperation, and instruction for the soul. It is said that here the Witch encounters those who have come before, which addresses not only those souls still awaiting rebirth but also those who have ascended beyond the need for experiences within the Material Realm. In the Summerland, the soul first experiences the process of purification through which it is cleansed on all levels of its consciousness. This allows the soul to free itself of the contamination of physical life, which, in turn, resolves and then dissolves some of the karmic energy that has attached itself to the soul. This purification process places the soul in a situation where it will face its negative elements and discern its positive components.

Following the purification process, the soul is then revitalized. Once renewed, the soul then enters a period of reflection and instruction as it prepares for the next phase of its evolution. This can lead to either reincarnation within a material world, or to crossing over into a spiritual realm of existence beyond what the Material Realm can offer to an evolving soul.

Reincarnation

One of the oldest and most enduring of occult beliefs is the concept of reincarnation. This is a belief that the soul is essentially immortal and can live again in a succession of physical bodies over the course of time. The concept of reincarnation appears among the ancient Greeks and Celtic people as well as in India and other Eastern regions.

In the ancient Mystery temples, the art of astral projection and the teaching of reincarnation were taught in order to release initiates from the fear of death. The reality that the consciousness of the soul continued outside and away from the material body instilled confidence in survival after death.

Renowned occultist Dion Fortune once taught initiates to view life as a boat rising and falling amidst the waves of the ocean. Just as the boat descends from the crest of the wave, so too does the soul descend into physical matter through the gates of rebirth. At death, the soul then rises like a boat on the swell of a wave and ascends into the afterlife through the gates of death. Through this process, the soul moves through the rhythmical cycle of the tides of birth, death, and renewal.

The purpose of reincarnation is to teach and refine the soul in a process of evolution. This process hones the soul as it passes through a wide variety of experiences, which allows it to be rich and poor, healthy and ill, male and female, weak and strong, influential and menial, leader and follower, and so forth. Through the spiritual process of reincarnation, the soul is given the opportunity to nurture and develop love, compassion, integrity, and authenticity. It also provides an opportunity to shed negativity and karmic debt.

The time required for this process to conclude is ultimately up to the individual soul. According to occult tradition, between lifetimes, the soul enters into a "soul contract" which is an agreement of consciousness to achieve specific goals in any single life experience. The soul is also given knowledge of the key lessons the forthcoming life has to offer. This includes the type of parents, the general nature of the quality of life, and key events such as marriage, children, and so forth. Several possible deaths are also revealed. However, the concept of reincarnation in the Mystery Tradition of Witchcraft does not include the idea of a predetermined fate. The soul always has a choice, and may or may not succeed in fulfilling its contract. The willful actions of other souls can also alter the life experience and result in unexpected changes and modifications.

Dion Fortune taught that a soul could reincarnate in the past as well as in the future. This is because, from an occult perspective, time is not linear but is instead perceived as spherical. The core teaching holds that all time periods are functioning "in the present" as a simultaneous event. The time period in which a soul finds itself is a matter of what point within the sphere the consciousness of the soul is drawn to a physical form.

If we accept that all time periods run concurrent and that the soul dwelled within a material body in a different time period, then a question arises. How can the soul be in more than one body at a time? The most popular theory is that the soul is multi-dimensional, its consciousness simultaneously existing in different time periods in different bodies. On a mundane level, it's like a person steering a car, talking on the cell phone, working the gas and brake pedals, and looking for a road sign all at once. The "one consciousness" is divided into other areas of activity (i.e. other lives) all within the same moment.

For the soul, death becomes an ending of a specific connection within a specific point in time and space. In other words, a body dies and the consciousness of that soul is displaced. It will then seek a return to expression, and so begins the process of reincarnation.

According to the Mystery Teachings, when a couple is united in sexual union, an energy field arises, which is a harmonic blending of the couple's auras into a vortex of energy. Sexual energy stimulates the nervous system which engages the endocrine secretions of the body. This causes chemical changes to take place in the body. As the heart rate and breathing increase, a corresponding vortex of energy begins to swirl above the individuals, which is similar to the cone of power raised in a magickal ritual. The presence of the vortex creates an opening in the etheric matter that separates the physical world from the spirit realm.

Souls awaiting rebirth are drawn into the vortex if their vibratory rate is compatible with the energy present in the composite aura of the sexual participants. Different types of sexual unions draw upon different levels of the etheric realms.

In the Mystery Tradition of Witchcraft, sex magick is often used in order to draw upon the higher planes where souls dwell who have no need to return to the Physical Dimension. When trained and properly prepared participants engage in this type of sexual union, it is possible to draw prophets and avatars to the Material Realm. In the case of an avatar's birth, however, the spiritual entity can cross through the planes into any vortex of its choosing (regardless of the nature of the vortex). In such cases, the ritual serves primarily as a type of homing beacon for the advanced soul.

According to occult tradition, if conception takes place, then the womb energy binds the soul to the Physical Plane. As a result, the soul is then drawn into the physical substance of the egg and is eventually enveloped by the generated fetus. In the case of twins and other multiple births, there is usually a very strong karmic link between the souls, drawing them into the same space and time.

While in the womb, the soul is not fully integrated into the Physical Dimension but is suspended within the womb energy. Once the infant is born, a seven-day period begins during which the soul gradually merges deeper and integrates with the physical body it occupies. Day by day, the new body steadily connects the soul to its internal system, binding one physical function after another to the soul's consciousness.

An important Mystery Teaching holds that souls generally reincarnate in community groups that travel together through time. This offers the souls an opportunity to work out karmic ties between one another more quickly and efficiently than would random encounters throughout time. It also provides a continuation of the sharing of knowledge and wisdom between souls that have established an intimate relationship or association. In the Mystery Tradition of Witchcraft, this fellowship is an important aspect of the soul's experience.

The core of the teaching is reflected in a text known as the *Legend of the Descent of the Goddess*. Here, we find a passage that addresses the issue of rebirth:

> *"...you must return again at the same time and at the same place as the loved ones; and you must meet, and know, and remember, and love them again. But to be reborn, you must die, and be made ready for a new body. And to die, you must be born; and without love, you may not be born."*

These verses hint at why Hereditary Witches take their bloodlines very seriously. An old occult legend states that a Witch grows in power with each lifetime. This is amplified when the soul maintains the company of other Witches with whom it shared experiences in ritual and magick.

The Charge of the Goddess addresses the concept of rejoining with those who have passed from one existence into the next. Within *The Charge,* we find mention of the Cauldron of Cerridwen, which is the Holy Grail of Immortality:

> *"I am the Gracious Goddess who gives the gift of joy unto the heart of man. Upon earth, I give the knowledge of the spirit eternal; and beyond death I give peace, and freedom, and reunion with those who have gone before."*

The concept of rejoining those known in past lives is a common theme in the Mystery Tradition of Witchcraft. One of the teachings is concerned with what is called the *Star Gates,* or the *Four Gates of Atavaric Descent*. These gates are associated with the four cardinal signs of the Zodiac. Their symbolic images are Man (Aquarius), Bull (Taurus), Lion (Leo), and Eagle (Scorpio). Through these Star Gates pass great energies that can be used by spiritual forces and beings as pathways of descent into the Material Plane. The avatar descends through one of these gates at the time of conception and is born after the term of pregnancy.

Generally speaking, the gateway of Aquarius leads to a birth in November, Leo to April, Taurus to a birth in February, and Scorpio to August. There are many variables that alter these occult assignments, and certainly not everyone conceived at the time of a Star Gate is going to be an avatar or a highly-evolved spiritual being. Likewise, not every avatar is necessarily limited to a birth connected to a pathway of descent through a Star Gate.

One of the many important elements of rebirth lies in genetic memory, which is sometimes referred to as *ancestral memory*. Primarily, this is the belief that each of us carries the essential distillation of the memories of all of our ancestors within our DNA. In a physical sense, this provides us with the survival skills that ensured our lineage to us in the first place. In a metaphysical sense, this provides us with a living thread to the past through which we can awaken the memories of past Witchcraft practices.

In many ancient myths and legends, particularly among the Celts, we find a quest to retrieve a cauldron hidden in a secret castle or within the Underworld. This can be perceived as a metaphor related to connecting with and awakening the ancestral memory residing in one's inner self, the mystical cauldron within.

In Chapter Eight, we will further explore the principles and concepts that constitute the Mystery Tradition of Witchcraft. This chapter will help you to better understand the application of such things within your life, ritual, and magickal work. But for now, we must turn to explore the "hows and whys" of our ancestors as they understood the Inner Mysteries expressed within the world around them. Therefore, let us turn to the next chapter and enter into the ancient Wheel of the Year.

CHAPTER SIX

The Wheel of the
Year Mythos

In the Mystery Tradition of Witchcraft, the tides of power that flow across and through the earth are viewed as a wheel that turns with the seasons. This is not unlike a miller's water wheel that rotates as water flows, catching the wooden planks and turning the wheel as the water rushes beneath it. In a metaphorical sense, the seasonal energies are the water that turns the Wheel of the Year.

Our ancestors rightfully perceived an "otherworldliness" connected to events that occurred in the world around them. In the changing of the year from season to season, a mythos arose that personified and associated the events with divine beings. Here, we see an important component of the Inner Mysteries that reflects the belief in indwelling divine presence. In other words, within nature and natural events lies the presence and participation of the Divine Source of All Things. Therefore, various goddesses and gods take part in the process of nature. Another way of viewing this is that nature responds in correspondence to the actions of the divine.

Through a study, understanding, and experience of the Wheel of the Year, the Witch enters into an alignment with the divine process. Here, the soul begins to see itself and its journey as reflected in the unfolding pattern of the divine as viewed in the seasons of nature. In other words, such can also be seen as the seasons of the soul.

Throughout this chapter, we will examine the Wheel of the Year for connections to the Mystery Tradition. In doing so, we shall discover that various themes run parallel to one another and crisscross at intervals to form entwined and enchanted threads. Cycles and patterns are the keys to understanding the mythos underlying the Wheel of the Year.

It is also interesting to note that some of the earliest symbols used by our ancestors were spirals, net patterns, interlaced lines, and parallel patterns called *meanders*. All of these continued throughout the ages and appear within the ancient art of the Etruscans and Celts to name but a few. Such symbols give us a glimpse into the minds and spirits of our ancestors.

The Mystery Tradition within Witchcraft begins, as does life itself, with the Mother. Within the Mystery Tradition, she is viewed as rooted in Paleolithic times as the Great Goddess. In the Neolithic period, we see her nature as the Great Mother Goddess. By the time of the Bronze Age, she is the Mother Goddess who takes her son as a consort. In their mythos, the two become separated, for the son dies and falls into the darkness of the Underworld (just as the Sun wanes in its time and the world grows dark and cold).

The underlying myth of a mated Goddess and God of nature permeates the mythos of the Wheel of the Year. On one level, the Goddess and God represent the fertile cycles of nature (and vice versa) as they appear in waxing and waning periods of the seasons. The Goddess and God can also be divided into two separate and yet related Mysteries that each contain their own unique mythos. These are referred to as the Solar and Lunar mythos as they relate to the Wheel of the Year.

The Solar Mythos

In the myth of the Sun God, he is born on the winter solstice, which is the shortest day of the year. This symbolizes his infancy, the comparatively weak stage in the life of the Sun God. At this phase, he is the promise of light and power, the gift of hope in a time of decline. Here, he is known as the Child of Promise.

As the newborn Sun God grows in strength, he enters into a rite of purification in preparation for his forthcoming reign. This is marked by the season known most commonly as Imbolc or Candlemas. This period falls exactly midpoint in the year between the winter solstice and the spring equinox.

Following his purification, the Sun God grows into his fertile period of adolescence. The spring equinox marks this stage of the Sun God's cycle. Here, the Sun God is now the bearer of the sacred seed of light that ensures his own rebirth after his future death.

With the onset of young adulthood, the Sun God encounters the Goddess associated with spring and the renewal of life. The Sun God then courts the Maiden Goddess, and this rite of passage is marked by the season commonly known as Beltane, the first of May.

As the cycle of the Sun God continues, he is wed to the Goddess. This is marked by the summer solstice, which is the longest day of the year. Here, we find the Sun God at the peak of his power, where he then merges his life with that of the Goddess.

On the eve of August, commonly known as Lugnasadh or Lammas, the Sun God beholds himself as the father of the abundant harvest. This is symbolized by the pregnant Goddess and the ripened grain, which is the seed of the Sun God. The Goddess declares, *"I am the soul of nature who gives life to the universe."* The God declares, *"I am the seed of light that awakens the soul of nature."*

The Sun God meets his death amidst the fields of grain, symbolic of the sacrifice of the seed of light which he bears within himself. This event is marked by the autumn equinox, which sits opposite the spring equinox in the Wheel of the Year. The latter saw the Sun God come to the time of his fertile seed. In the former, the seeds are now supplied to renew life in their spilling forth, which is a metaphor for the ripe seed harvested in the cutting down of the stalk that bore them. Here, we see the Sun God become the Harvest Lord.

Following the sacrificial death of the Sun God or Harvest Lord, his spirit withdraws into the Underworld. This is marked by the season commonly known as Samhain, the time when the veil that separates the material world from the Otherworld grows so thin that beings may easily pass between both realms. The Goddess enters the Underworld seeking her lost consort. They meet again and join in sexual union, through which the Goddess becomes pregnant with the Child of Promise. He is born at the winter solstice and the cycle begins anew.

The Lunar Mythos

As both a Moon Goddess and Goddess of Nature (of the Year), her myth begins in the Underworld. She is the womb gate through which all life is born, even that of the divine essence. The dark Underworld, like the dark cauldron, is the state of procreation. Therefore, it is in the darkness that the Goddess is impregnated with the seed of light. This event is marked by the season of Samhain, which was an ancient fertility rite (as we shall see in Chapter Seven).

In the myth of the Moon Goddess, she gives birth to the Sun God on the winter solstice, and from her issues forth the Child of Promise. Here, the heavenly Moon Goddess who dwells amidst the stars is the Mother of God. This ancient Pagan theme appears in other religions, including Christianity.

Just as the Moon seemingly rises from beneath the Earth, the Goddess begins her journey to reach the Overworld of the living. Before her journey, she passes through a rite of purification, which is marked by the season of Imbolc or Candlemas. She is sometimes depicted wearing a crown of candles, symbolic of her divine light, which she bears even in darkness. This crown is also reflected in the symbolism of the circlet, which bears a crescent Moon as a sign of her divine light.

Following her purification, the Moon Goddess arises from the Underworld as a young maiden whose essence renews the Earth with her youthful vitality. The spring equinox marks this stage of the Moon Goddess's cycle. Here, the Goddess is now the herald that calls to the sacred seed of light, coaxing the young Sun God from the Underworld.

With the onset of young adulthood, the Moon Goddess encounters the God who is the bearer of the sacred seed. The Moon Goddess enters into courtship, a rite of passage marked by the season of Beltane where she appears as the Queen of May.

As the cycle of the Moon Goddess continues, she is wed to the Sun God on the summer solstice, which is the longest day of the year. Here, she draws from the Sun God a portion of his power, which is cloaked in the old axiom, "What men may never know and women must never tell."

On the eve of August (Lugnasadh or Lammas), the Moon Goddess is pregnant with the ripe harvest. In her declaration *"I am the soul of Nature who gives life to the Universe,"* we see her celestial nature merged with her earthen nature. For she gives birth to all things, even to that which impregnates her (the Sun God who is her lover, brother, and child).

Following the death of the Sun God or Harvest Lord, the Goddess begins her descent into the Underworld to follow after him. This event is marked by the autumn equinox. The Goddess seeks to gather the seed of light back into herself, the seed for which she yearned at the spring equinox. In the course of the year, the Goddess is impregnated twice, once to bear the fruits of the Earth and once to bear the fruit of the Sun. The first is material and the second is spiritual.

Following the sacrificial death of the Sun God or Harvest Lord, the Goddess arrives in the Underworld. This is marked by the season commonly known as Samhain and is, in part, reflected in the text known as the *Legend of the Descent of the Goddess.* In the Underworld, the Goddess meets the other light, her other half, which she desires to draw into herself. The essence of this mythos is captured in an old Witchcraft Mystery text that reads:

"And the Goddess saw that the light was so beautiful, the light which was her other half, and she yearned for it with exceeding great desire. Wishing to receive the light again into her darkness, to swallow it up in rapture, in delight, she trembled with desire. This desire was the Dawn" (Leland, *Aradia: Gospel of the Witches,* 1899).

The concept of dawn addresses both the idea of "becoming light" as well as that of beginning to be perceived or understood. In the latter regard, we find the Mystery of integration, the divine polarities of male and female form in oneness before dividing again into the forces of impregnation and fertile reception.

The Ancient Theme

Like the day, the year also begins with dawn in a metaphorical sense. In the Mystery Tradition of Witchcraft, the year begins in the darkness of procreation. Here, the light, which resides in deep, dark places, is drawn into the Moon Goddess. As we noted in Chapter Four, it is the role of the Moon Goddess to receive the souls of the dead into herself, so that through her, they may be reborn. This theme is deeply reflected in the legend of the Goddess who becomes impregnated with the seed of light and births it to the world.

Because of the extreme antiquity of the Witchcraft tradition, we find a blended mythos bringing elements of the hunter-gatherer together with aspects of an agrarian society. Here, we find composite images of the Horned God with the Sun God and the Harvest Lord. We also discover the Great Goddess with the Mother Goddess and the Goddess of the Moon. These are interesting traces of the "footprints through time" that confirm the survival of ancient themes within the Mystery Tradition of Witchcraft.

It is in the Bronze Age that we begin to see the composite images of what were once isolated elements to our ancestors. Here, we find the ancient Stag-Horned God, who became the Sun God, now appearing as a Bull-Horned God. Like his predecessors, the Bull-Horned God meets with a sacrificial death.

In the Mystery Tradition, the forehead of the sacrificial bull is adorned with a red rose, signifying his death and his passing into the arms of the Goddess.

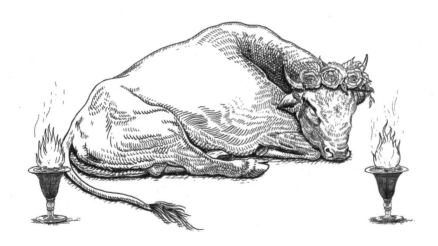

His life force is returned to the Goddess with the flow of blood into the soil. This is also the theme of the Goddess receiving the seed of light from the God into her womb. The forms within the mythos change over time, but the essence of the Mystery teachings remains in place.

The Horned God of Witchcraft, as a sacrificial figure, represents the generative principle of creation in a God figure. Here, he is not the Goddess but a part of the Goddess, her consort. The association of the God as the son of the Goddess retains the notion that he is born from her womb, and is therefore a part of what is the totality of the Goddess. His death returns that part to the whole, and then together, creation is again possible.

Within the Mystery Tradition of Witchcraft, we do not find any myths in which the Goddess dies. Even in the lunar myths that deal with the dissolving away of the Moon, there is no association with a dying deity. The essential theme is that the Goddess transforms into various natures (or goddesses) but does not perish. Here, the Goddess, as the source of manifestation, remains always a vessel of transformation and life. Her cycle is continuing and endless life, as opposed to the God who must rise, decline, and die.

The God is intimately connected to the seed. The ripeness of the seed in the plant kingdom begins the death process for the plant. The plant must fall and the seed must spill. This is the core theme within the God's Mysteries. The soil into which he falls is the body of the Goddess herself. Here, he resides in her womb until rebirth is gifted, and the God then breaks into daylight and recaptures his power, the light of the Sun.

By Seed and Sprout, and Stem and Leaf, and Bud and Flower

The tenacity of life is expressed within the visible signs of the power of nature. Despite the efforts of humankind to master and control nature, in the end, nature always rules the day. Walk down a typical sidewalk in any town and you will frequently see a crack in the cement. Appearing in that crack is most commonly a weed or clump of grass. Ultimately, nature will not be denied, and her tenacity is without match.

The power of nature, the very life spirit, is emphasized in an invocational or evocational verse that reads: *"Thee I (invoke/evoke) by seed and sprout, and stem and leaf, and bud and flower..."* These words of power refer to the process of manifestation itself as well as to the unconquerable power of nature. By calling upon such a force, the Witch aligns with the principle and becomes its channel.

The process by which a seed becomes a plant is a metaphor for the life-giving force of the Goddess. The seed itself contains the form that will become the plant, but without receiving the essence of the Earth Goddess, the seed will wither in lost vitality instead of becoming a plant. Therefore, from the Mystery perspective, the power lies in the earth and not in the seed.

In the Mystery Tradition, the God is the form, the detail, and the linear expression. The Goddess is the essence, the concept, and the cyclical expression. Each one united together makes manifestation possible. One without the other isolates the components, and therefore, manifestation or expression cannot take place. Here, all things remain within the Otherworld/Underworld and nothing may pass into the Middle World and be capable of taking root and sustainable form. Therefore, in the words of power, we find both the Goddess (process) and the God (material form) joining together to renew life in an endless cycle.

The journey of the seed through the year is a key element to the Mysteries that flow through the Wheel of the Year. These are highly marked by each solstice and equinox, which are solar-oriented periods. The seasonal rites that fall mid-point between them all occur on the eve before sunrise, which denotes them as under the providence of night and the Moon. Therefore, they reside in the realm of the Goddess. This is explored further in Chapter Seven.

The theme of the seed begins with life sleeping in death, the seed lying dormant beneath the snow or winter soil. The lifeless appearance of the land in winter symbolizes death. Here, we find that death is not the end, but simply a transitional period. For life awaits its re-emergence from the gate of death (winter) and through the gate of life (spring).

As the earth grows warmer, moisture begins to saturate the seed. The seed receives the moisture and begins to swell as the internal process of cell division and expansion begins. Here, we once again find the theme of water and the Underworld, which we explored in Chapter Two.

The first element to emerge from the seed is the root stem. Here, we find the bridge from the Underworld to the Middleworld. It is from here that the process of return begins. This is the preparation, all of which denotes that life exists in an unseen realm while the material world bears no witness.

Once the root stem emerges, then the shoot begins to form, and eventually, it breaks through the soil into daylight and the world of the living. The stem is the first sign of life, but beneath it lays the power of the process that is its foundation. Here, we find a testimony to the Goddess and the God; the process and the expressed form.

With the appearance of the sprout, there follows the stem and leaf (a sequence displayed differently by various plants). Here, we find the process of growth and maturity in progress. The vitality of the land, the Sun and Moon, and the air is joined with that of the indwelling spirit.

The maturity of the plant is reached with the development of bud and flower (from which the seed will eventually be produced). Here, we see the essence of male and female polarities joining forces to ensure the survival of the species. In primitive magick, it was held that the same entity returned, whether plant or animal, when death occurred. In other words, the seed or the blood returned to the soil the very same life from which it was shed. This formed the basis of the ancient covenant between the hunter and the hunted. I refer the interested reader to my previous book *The Wiccan Mysteries* for further information on this specific topic.

The relationship between the living and the Spirit of the Land was and is essential. Life itself seemingly came from the earth whether in the form of plants, trees, or animal life that emerged from burrows, caves, or crevices. This is one of the reasons why the grotto was one of the earliest places of worship, and with its connection to trickling water, the grotto was also associated with the Underworld.

The Underworld is a powerful theme that underlies the Wheel of the Year. For where is it that the Harvest Lord goes when he falls in sacrifice? He begins his journey on the river of descent, carried along in the Moon boat where he embraces the Golden or Silver Bough of the Goddess. Thus, he passes through the Horned Gate that allows passage into the Otherworld. There too, in her time, follows the Goddess on a quest. All of this is represented in the rising and setting of the Sun and Moon throughout the year and in relationship to the waxing and waning times of the seasons.

The sacred branch of the Goddess, whether called the Golden Bough or Silver Bough, is a powerful symbol in the Mystery Tradition of Witchcraft. The Silver Bough is of Celtic lore and is depicted as a branch from an apple tree adorned with nine apples. The Golden Bough is of Italic origin and is depicted as an oak branch bearing mistletoe and three apples. The former allows passage to and from the Faery Realm, while the latter provides the same safe passage associated with the Underworld.

In Celtic lore, the Silver Bough was also associated with the god Manannan, a powerful and magickal deity associated with the sea. In the book *The Magic Arts in Celtic Britain* (1970), author Lewis Spence describes the bough dangling with apples that gave forth enchanting magickal music, which none could resist. Spence recounts a tale in which anyone who hears the "sweet music-like bells" forgets all sorrow and care. He goes on to mention that the bough served as a link with the unseen world, and as a talisman that aided mortals to journey to the hidden entrance (Spence, 1970). According to Celtic lore, the entrance led to an overseas paradise.

The concept of the sacred bough transforms the plant kingdom into a mystical interface between the worlds. Here, divinity extends itself to humankind and draws mortals into the Spiritual realm. This links the Wheel of the Year to not only the cycle of plant life but also to the tree itself as a divine and sacred source.

In modern Witchcraft, we find a tree calendar marking the Wheel of the Year into lunar months associated with a sacred tree. The formula is based upon twenty-eight days of a lunar cycle divided into 365 days of a solar year, which renders thirteen months and one day. This is referred to as "a year and day." In modern Witchcraft terminology, this refers to a complete cycle of thirteen Moons, which is a metaphor for walking the Path of the Mysteries. This is why many Craft traditions require a year and day of study between each degree of initiation. The traditional calendar is given here with the Irish names for each tree:

1. **Birch:** December 24–January 20 (*beth*)
2. **Rowan:** January 21–February 17 (*luis*)
3. **Ash:** February 18–March 17 (*nuin*)
4. **Alder:** March 18–April 14 (*fearn*)
5. **Willow:** April 15–May 12 (*saille*)
6. **Hawthorn:** May 13–June 9 (*huath*)
7. **Oak:** June 10–July 7 (*duir*)
8. **Holly:** July 8–August 4 (*tinne*)
9. **Hazel:** August 5–September 1 (*coll*)
10. **Vine:** September 2–September 29 (*muin*)
11. **Ivy:** September 30–October 27 (*gort*)
12. **Reed:** October 28–November 24 (*ngetal*)
13. **Elder:** November 25–December 22 (*ruis*)

The Moon Tree

In the Mystery Tradition of Witchcraft, there is a symbol known as the *Moon Tree*. Depictions of this tree can be found in such ancient cultures as the Etruscans, Assyrians, Greeks, and Romans. Each ancient culture imagined the design of the tree in accord with their unique art style, and yet, the essential symbolism of the tree reflected a commonality of an essential concept.

As previously noted, trees have been viewed as symbolic Otherworld bridges for many centuries. In European folklore, doorways to the Faery Realm sometimes appear in the hollow of certain trees. In Northern European lore, the tree can grant enlightenment, as in the case of the god Woden who hung on a tree for several days. This theme is also reflected in the classic tarot image of the Hanged Man.

The theme of enlightenment regarding a tree is often symbolized by its fruit. The fruit itself bears the divine essence of the deity dwelling within the tree. This basic theme also appears in the cult of Dionysos where his spirit is passed in ritual wine, the fruit of the vine. The association of the Moon with a tree is quite ancient and links the Moon Goddess to the fruit of the tree.

One of the earliest representations of the Moon Goddess was a wooden pillar or tree stump, as in the case of Hecate. The archaic worship of Hecate included a wooden pillar (known as a *hekataion*) that was placed at the site of a crossroad. Here, we find the tree as a Goddess symbol in a place that represented the entrance to the Otherworld.

In ancient art, the Moon Tree is depicted as an actual tree as well as a truncated pole or a stylized pillar. In some ancient myths, the Moon Tree was cut down and carved into a boat for a Slain God or a coffin as in the myth of Osiris. Here, we see the roots of an ancient theme in which the sacrificed God journeys in a Moon boat following his death. This modified theme later appears in Arthurian legend where the body of King Arthur is taken to Avalon (the Isle of Apples) in a boat.

In ancient art, the Moon Tree is commonly depicted bearing thirteen blossoms or torches, symbolic of the fact that there are always thirteen Moons in a year (either Full Moons or New Moons). The typical Moon Tree is often decorated with ribbons similar to the European maypole. Sometimes, the Moon Tree appears enclosed in a shrine or trellis work. This recalls the fact that the Moon Goddess was first worshipped in a grotto or a grove of trees.

In the Mystery Tradition of Witchcraft, the inner teachings regarding the esoteric meaning of the Moon Tree are still retained. The Moon Tree symbolism is multi-layered and encloses the Mysteries themselves. A study and understanding of the Moon Tree symbolism brings one to the fruit of the divine tree. Here, one encounters a single white fruit, which is the sacred food of enlightenment.

In the mythos, the tree is located in the center of the sacred grove of the Goddess. It is guarded by the Hooded One, a powerful warrior who is not easily vanquished. The guardian of the grove represents our conscious mind which keeps us from embracing the mystical vision by always questioning and dismissing. It is only through allowing the experience of the mystical rather than the "rational" that one forms the mentality necessary to defeat the guardian. Once the guardian is bypassed, then the fruit of the Moon Tree is within reach.

As a Mystery symbol of the Goddess, the tree is also the receiver, the portal of death and rebirth. According to oral tradition, the Sacrificial God was bound to a tree and slain. The tree received his blood, and thus, the mother took back into herself the life essence of the God. This ancient Pagan theme is reflected in Christian mysticism where Jesus dies bound to a wooden cross.

In the context of a Wheel of the Year image, the Moon Tree symbolizes the periods of growth and decline as well as the portals of entrance and release. The tree stands at the center of the Wheel of the Year connecting the worlds together. Here, we see the agricultural year symbolized by the tree, as well as the Goddess and the Harvest Lord.

In the book *The White Goddess*, author Robert Graves mentions the ancient Cult of Artemis (Diana) and her consort the Oak King, who is sacrificed after a predetermined period of time. Most commentators view the Oak King as representative of the God dwelling in the tree, missing the point that his title reflects that he is consort to the Goddess who is the tree. Being the "king" of something does not equate to being that particular thing; it instead implies a relationship.

Graves equates the goddess Diana Nemorensis (Diana of the Woods) with the goddess Nemesis whose name is derived from the Greek *nemos,* which means "grove." Nemesis carries as her symbol a wheel, and in her hand is an apple branch. Here again, we see a strong connection between the sacred bough of the Goddess and the Wheel of the Year. Graves states that the goddess Diana was once worshipped in a celebration that included cider and a god roasted on a hazel branch. A bough of apples was suspended over the roast pit.

In one version of an ancient legend, Hercules (who we noted as a sacrificial figure in Chapter Three) is given the bough of golden apples by the Three Daughters of the West. Since ancient times, the direction west has been associated with the Underworld and the Otherworld. The Three Daughters in this tale can be viewed as the Three Fates or Faery women who await the Harvest Lord.

Apples have a long association with the theme of immortality, which is evidenced in the connection of the apple bough with the Faery Realm. In the cited myth of Hercules, we see the keys (apples) to the Otherworld passed to the future Slain God. The twelve labors of Hercules can be seen as a metaphor for the twelve months of the year, which connects him again to the Wheel of the Year. It is noteworthy that Graves also links Hercules to the ancient sacrificial rites of the Barley Mother, and depicts him in service to the Goddess of the Mill.

Graves, in his mythopoetic style, portrays the Great Goddess as the millstone of the Universe in her moods of creation and destruction. The theme of the millstone and of grinding the grain is connective to the mythos of the Harvest Lord in the Wheel of the Year. Graves states that another name for the Goddess of the Mill is Artemis or Diana Calliste, also known in ancient times as *Helice*. The latter means both "that which turns the wheel" and "willow branch." It is interesting to note that the willow tree is a powerful chthonic symbol. It is sacred to Hecate, who stands at the crossroads, which is the entrance to the Otherworld wherein resides the Moon Tree.

The Powers of Light and Darkness

As noted earlier in the book, our ancestors once viewed the seasons as divided into two halves, the waxing and waning year. These forces eventually became personified in such figures as the Holly King and Oak King, or the stag and the wolf. Over the passing centuries, there arose the concept of light and darkness associated with the two halves of the year.

In the Mystery Tradition, there is no concept of good and evil, and no attempt is made to depict the forces of nature in conflict with one another. Differences occur regarding the Northern and Southern European views related to the waxing and waning year. In Celtic lore, the shift takes place on the solstices, while in Aegean/Mediterranean lore, it occurs on the equinoxes. It is possible that these differences arise from the perspectives of a hunter-gatherer view as opposed to an agrarian standpoint. In either case, the essential concept is one of great antiquity.

The equinox periods mark the time when night and day are of equal length. Here, it is said that the forces of light and darkness are in balance. However, each equinox also marks the beginning of changes that dramatically affect the agricultural cycle. The spring equinox announces the return of life to the earth while the autumn equinox marks the coming season of decline. In this, we find a Mystery Teaching, for in the lifeless cold month of March begins the awakening of life. The autumn equinox, a time of ripe harvest and plenty marks the beginning of death.

The solstice periods mark the time when the light of day begins to either increase or decrease. Therefore, on the winter solstice, the power of darkness begins to wane and the power of light beings to grow. At the summer solstice, we find that the situation becomes reversed as the days begin to grow shorter. Here we find another Mystery Teaching, for within the beginning of bleak winter resides the key to regeneration. Within the summer solstice, with its ripening crops and abundance of living creatures, resides the key to degeneration.

At the core of the teachings related to the equinox and solstice periods, we find an even more important teaching. Neither season, event, nor resulting process is permanent, which indicates that life and death are part of something else that is far greater. Here, we find that existence itself is the macrocosm, with life and death as simple components. Existence is the process, and in nature, it never disappears. Instead, it bears with it the cycles of life and death.

In the Mystery Tradition of Witchcraft, nature is the blueprint, and within this, we discover the divine plan. Every single or specific thing bears within it the seeds of its own renewal and destruction. However, this applies only to its manifestation in form and not to its existence; therein is the essential Mystery Teaching. For while one specific thing in its form will eventually deteriorate and disappear, that which continues the process from which the form was generated (and animates the manifestation of that form) cannot vanish. If this were not so, then seeds would no longer produce plants and plants would no longer produce seeds. So too would the principle apply to all living beings.

This answers, in part, the age-old question: which came first, the chicken or the egg? From an occult perspective, the answer is that the process came first, and the first beings were essentially both the egg and the egg bearer. The process originated with the divine, but the answer as to the origin of the divine continues to elude human reasoning. In the Mystery Tradition, the trail to divinity suffices us while our souls reside in human form. In time, we will all become beings of "soul energy" without material form. Once void of the limitations of material brains, our minds will become more suited to understanding what the other realms of existence have to offer regarding the nature and origin of divinity itself. But for now, we must focus on the inner mechanism of the divine with nature.

Our ancestors understood the importance of the process or inner mechanism within nature. Because they also understood how energy affects material forms, our ancestors created rites of protection that centered on the seasonal cycles of nature. It was held in ancient times, that just prior to the emergence of an equinox or solstice, a period of three days arose that allowed influences to affect the coming season. Our ancestors called this period the *Ember Days*, a topic we encountered briefly in Chapter Two.

The English word "ember" (in the case of Ember Days) is derived from the Old English *ymbryne*, which means "recurrence" or "course of time." The English phrase is derived from the Latin word *ambi*, which means "to walk around." The modern word *ambulate* is derived from the Latin *ambulare*, a word also derived from *ambi*. The Greek word *amphi* shares the same root origin and means "to walk around" or "to walk about a specific area." All of these words originate with the Indo-European form *ambhi*, and one meaning is rendered to indicate "on all sides." The word *beleaguer* (as in "to surround with troops") is also derived from the word *ambhi*. In all of this, we see the idea of a cycle and an enclosing circle coming together.

Our ancestors believed that as the seasonal shift approached, the gateway between the worlds became accessible. This is not unlike the ancient reasoning that at Samhain, the veil between the worlds grew thin and penetrable. Access through the gateway of the year meant that the season could be modified through magickal intent. Here stood the forces of light and darkness.

As previously noted in Chapter Two, one of the most well-known examples of the Ember Day rites appears among a sect known as the *Benandanti*. Historian Carlo Ginzburg presents a wealth of information regarding the Benandanti in his book *The Night Battles* (1983). Here, Ginzburg describes ritual battles between the forces of "good and evil" over the outcome of crops and herds in the forthcoming season. These battles were fought during the Ember Days to protect village life.

While the literal notion of "good and evil" does not exist within the Mystery Teachings, the idea of participation and working with a common cause is an important component. It is the work of a Witch, as a practitioner of Earth Religion, to be a steward of nature. In the context of the Wheel of the Year and the forces of light and darkness, the Witch performs seasonal rituals in order to maintain a natural alignment. Here, the forces of light and darkness are balanced and remain true to their own nature and time of season without unnaturally influencing the other in its time of power.

To better understand this process of alignment, we must understand the esoteric nature and importance of the seasonal rites of Witchcraft. Once we examine the sabbats and their inner meaning, we can then embrace the internal alignment through external expression. Let us turn to the next chapter and explore the inner nature of the Witches' sabbats.

CHAPTER SEVEN
The Witches' Sabbats

In the Mystery Tradition of Witchcraft, the sabbats mark periods of energy shifts that occur on the Earth. These are related to Otherworld phenomena that manifest in the seasonal shifts. The myths and legends of various goddesses, gods, and spirits personify the forces at work during each sabbat. Through a study of the mythos that interweaves and permeates the sabbat, the Witch is aligned with the mystical forces that operate between the planes of existence.

The sabbats in Witchcraft are unique because they represent the patterns of both the Material and Otherworld Realms. Here, the Witch can experience the axiom "as above, so below" in the turning of the Wheel of the Year. It is in the understanding of patterns that the Witch begins to unravel the Mysteries and access the inner teachings.

Our ancient ancestors experienced nature more practically than most people do today. For them, there was no separation from nature to the degree that modern humans have reached. Because our ancestors worked the land, hunted, and lived in tune with the cycles of nature, the spirit of the land spoke to them freely, directly, and clearly.

Today, modern humans have collectively removed themselves from the intimate connection to nature that was once a part of everyday life. Few modern people grow crops, hunt their food, grind grain, or spin cloth. Most contemporary humans simply go to the grocery store, bakery, or department store for their needs. However, the ancient process continues, and it falls to a relative few to maintain the connection to nature so that her bounty can still be provided to humankind.

When we read about ancient times, we find references to waters teeming with fish. It is said that birds were so abundant that flocks cast a notable shadow when they flew across the sky. Thick forests covered many lands and greenery was everywhere in sight. Why then did the ancient rites call for fertility, abundance, and increase?

The answer can be found in the ancient view that nature required renewal. What was taken from the rivers, lakes, forests, and fields had to be returned in some manner. This was typically accomplished through rituals that raised the life essence of fertility. This essence was then bound to some object such as a bone, root, horn, or pelt, which was then buried in the soil or hung on a tree. Through such rites, the life force was returned to the process that generated the physical forms within the plant and animal kingdoms.

The sabbats that comprise the Wheel of the Year reflect the very essence of the process, which itself empowers the Mystery Tradition. Throughout this chapter, we will examine the myths and legends associated with each sabbat. For it is within symbolism, concept, analogy, and metaphor that the secrets of the Mysteries reside. The Mysteries cannot be understood by ordinary study or intellectual pursuit. Those who make such an attempt will discover little, and in the end, they will convince themselves that no such secrets exist. Thus, have the Mysteries been guarded since ancient times.

In order to penetrate the Mysteries, one must rely upon both the conscious and subconscious minds. The subconscious mind is the receiver and translator. The conscious mind is the retriever and integrator. Together they work in harmony, but if either one does not operate as an equal partner, then the path to the Mysteries is barred.

It is important to understand that the human mind is comprised of two halves, the conscious and the subconscious. In the Mystery Tradition, it is held that neither one separately constitutes the human mind. We are not the conscious waking mind, nor are we the dreaming subconscious mind. Instead, we are the merged consciousness of the two minds. However, the majority of non-initiates conduct their lives as though they are the waking mind and its personality. To such individuals, the subconscious mind is merely delegated to dreams, phobias, and psychological problems.

In reality, the subconscious mind allows us to understand what cannot be understood by human logic. This is because it comprehends meaning where none is apparent to the conscious mind. One example of this reality can be seen in the dream experience.

In a dream, a person can be riding in a car that suddenly becomes a bicycle. The dream mind allows the person to simply begin riding the bicycle with little if any recognition of how illogical the situation is. This is because the subconscious mind is concerned with the message and not with the messenger or the vehicle that conveys the message.

In the example presented, it is transportation, movement, or direction that is the message for the subconscious mind. The vehicle itself has little if any relevance, and it is simply a readily available and easily recognizable image through which to interface with the human mind. In other words, the process uses a familiar object in the dream to draw attention and transmit meaning.

The conscious mind, unable to grasp the illogicality of dream symbolism, applies the symbolism of the dream in a linear sense. It discards what cannot be understood and retains what can be deciphered through logic and rational reasoning. The discarded information falls back into the subconscious mind where it later reappears in another dream state. Here, it will either become the same image or something new until the conscious mind can find a way to discover its meaning and integrate it into the soul mind.

This essential theme is reflected in many myths and legends where it appears as a magickal cauldron hidden in a secret realm. Such tales are generally centered on a quest to discover and retrieve the hidden cauldron, which is most frequently located in the Underworld or Otherworld. It is not uncommon to find the cauldron hidden in the dungeon of a secret castle. Guardians are also commonly associated with magickal cauldrons. The cauldron itself contains a magickal brew or some mystical ability that is desired by the seeker who journeys on a quest into the dark Underworld.

As we noted earlier in the book, enlightenment resides within the darkness. The Sun and Moon themselves represent the principle that light is at home in the darkness. This is a metaphor for the subconscious and conscious minds and the interplay in their own rising and setting. In the case of the Wheel of the Year, it also begins in darkness and ends in enlightenment.

Samhain

In the Mystery Tradition of Witchcraft, the year begins in the place of deep shadow, when the stars of the Pleiades appear close to the horizon of the Earth. This season is marked by the eve of November with a rite commonly known as *Samhain* or *Hallowmas*. Another name for this sabbat is *Shadowfest,* the honoring of procreative darkness. Since most modern traditions use the name *Samhain,* we shall as well within this chapter.

Samhain is derived from the Old Irish *sam* (summer) and *fuin* (end) which renders the meaning of *Samhain* as the "end of summer." Among the ancient Gauls, this season began the new year, for it was an ancient belief that darkness precedes light. Therefore, the new year itself was born from darkness, as are all things that emerge from a womb.

Celtic scholar James MacKillop (*Dictionary of Celtic Mythology*) notes that Samhain commemorated (in part) Dagda's ritual intercourse with three divinities. These were Morrigan, Boand, and Indech's unnamed daughter. This strongly suggests that the ancient season of Samhain involved fertility rites. Supporting this notion is the fact that ancient belief held this time to be the most favorable for a woman to become pregnant.

Central to the season of Samhain is the theme of the Otherworld that lies beyond the realm of mortal humankind. An ancient European belief held that the borders between the natural and so-called supernatural worlds became passable. It was thought that the spirits and souls of the departed could come and go as they pleased during this time.

It was an ancient belief that the dead were attracted to blood and could be temporarily reanimated and given voice with an offering of this substance. In Celtic culture, Samhain was a time of slaughtering the animal herds in order to reduce the drain on feed in the coming season of decline. This is one of the reasons why the Full Moon near Samhain is sometimes called the Blood Moon. At the time of the slaughter, only the best breeding animals were spared. Here, we see a connection between death and blood in the season of Samhain. In modern Witchcraft, no such slaughter takes place as part of the Samhain celebration. The idea that blood carries the life force is found in the rite of spilling blood into the soil, which we find in the ancient slaughtering of the herds at this season. Here, the life force returns through the soil and into the

Underworld. The presence and flow of liquids in association with the Mysteries of the Underworld and Otherworld is an important theme, which we explored in Chapter Two.

The significance of Dagda's mating is found within the connection to water, a key theme in Underworld or Otherworld considerations. Here, we note Dagda's sexual union with Boann, a river goddess personifying the river Boyne. This act passes his seed into the waters that flow through the Underworld and rise in the sacred wells. Dagda also mates with Morrigan (a goddess of war and death) who he meets at Samhain. Thus, the womb of death receives the seed of Dagda, who is referred to in ancient lore as the "Father of All." MacKillop notes that some commentators identify Morrigan with Inanna, a goddess associated with a descent into the Underworld in order to retrieve her lost mate (*Dictionary of Celtic Mythology*, 1998). The classic *Legend of the Descent of the Goddess* in Witchcraft bears striking similarities to the tale of Inanna.

In Celtic lore, Dagda is a leader of the Tuatha De Danann, who later become the Faery race in ancient Celtic lore. He is associated with the Sun and with knowledge. Dagda is also a master of the arts of war, magick, and governing. He possesses a huge cauldron and a mighty club. In Chapter Three, we noted the carrying of clubs by forest deities such as Silvanus and Faunus, and we remarked on the club of Hercules. It is noteworthy that Dagda is also associated with trees in fruit and with swine. The latter is key to his Underworld connection, which we shall see as the chapter continues.

According to MacKillop, some commentators identify Dagda with the god Donn, the Irish ruler of the dead and the Underworld. Dagda is also thought to be a counterpart of Cronus, Hercules, and Dis Pater. These epithets all connect Dagda with various god themes in Witchcraft that we explored in Chapter Three.

Earlier, we noted that Dagda was associated with the cauldron and the sow, both Underworld symbols since ancient times. The goddess Cerridwen is also associated with the cauldron, and her sacred animal is the sow. Cerridwen can be identified with the Roman goddess Ceres, who is the goddess of the Mysteries and of the grain. Here, we see the symbolism of the seed, which is awakened to life by water and the warmth of the Sun. This is a metaphor for sexual union, a theme strongly connected to the Dagda during the season of Samhain.

The Agricultural Mysteries, governed by such goddesses as Ceres, appear in Otherworld themes related to Samhain. As previously noted, Dagda is associated with trees in fruit. The classic tree of the Otherworld is the apple tree. In Celtic culture, apples were first harvested at Samhain. Here, we see a connection between the apple, Samhain, and the realm that lies beyond the world of the living.

MacKillop notes that human sacrifices to the god Teutates were performed by the ancient Celts at Samhain. Teutates is connected to Dagda through the warrior aspect. The traditional method of sacrifice was by drowning the sacrificial victim. If we review the symbolism of Dagda, Samhain, and the Underworld, a Mystery theme readily surfaces. Here we find the cauldron, water, and apples. This comes together in the Samhain tradition of bobbing for apples, the food of the Otherworld that allows safe passage to and from the distant realm. This recalls the ancient sacrifice by drowning, and here, the person partakes of the sacred apple as they are plunged into the water. The apple ensures that the person shall return to life again.

In the Mystery Tradition of Witchcraft, the God is viewed as residing in the Underworld as the Dark Lord of the Shadows. This represents his procreative nature hidden in the shadowy process of the Mysteries. His followers who pass into his realm at death are given the apples of renewal. Through union with the God of the Underworld who rises again as the Sun, his followers also rise when united with his divine nature. This ancient Pagan theme also appears in the Mysteries of Christianity where the followers of Jesus consume his "flesh and blood" in order to unite with the sacrificed Christ figure.

The God in Witchcraft, in his aspect as Cernunnos or Dianus the Stag-Horned God, keeps his herd together through both the gates of descent and return. Here, the Witches are not among the "common dead" but are initiates who have tasted the faery apple from the sacred branch of the Goddess. Through this, they travel in a community of souls willingly bound in harmony to the Old Ways of their ancestors.

Ancestral veneration is an important element of the Samhain celebration. Tradition calls for the offering of food and drink to honor those who lived and walked the path before us. Time-offered meals included cakes, bean soup, bread, apples, cider, wine, nuts, and currants. One of the most ancient offerings is a blend of equal parts of milk, red wine, and honey. In popular tradition, a "dumb supper" is placed out in honor of the dead. This is most commonly a plate of food and a drink set at a separate table. Typically, a candle is set at the center of the table.

In connection with food and the dead, it is noteworthy that Dagda possessed a cauldron that magickally produced food so that no one ever went away from it with hunger. At Samhain, the spirits of the dead were believed to return and visit their former homes. The appearance of the Pleiades near the horizon (symbolizing the afterlife realm) was seen as a sign that the gateways were open. The spirits of the dead were then called back from the world of the living to a feast from Dagda's cauldron.

Charles Squire (*Celtic Myth and Legend,* 1919) mentions that Dagda possessed a "living harp" that caused the seasons of autumn, winter, spring, and summer to all proceed and keep in proper order. There is perhaps no better reason to place Dagda in the season of Samhain, which begins the new year in ancient Celtic culture.

Before ending our discussion on Samhain, we must also note the god Lugh. Author Lewis Spence (*The Magic Arts in Celtic Britain,* 1970) states that Samhain signified the decline of the Sun God Lugh. Spence goes on to note that hearth fires were quenched on Samhain to mark the "sleep of the Sun." Lugh appears later in the Wheel of the Year in the sabbat known as *Lughnasadh,* where he is the consort of the Goddess of Ripened Grain. Although not mentioned strongly enough in literary sources to solidly connect Lugh to Samhain as a primary deity, it is possible that he is a lost or forgotten aspect of Dagda.

Winter Solstice

Since ancient times, the winter solstice has been viewed as the rebirth of the Sun God. As noted in Chapter Three, he is also the Lord of the Woods, the Stag-Horned God of the forest. To honor him, the tradition arose of incorporating tree symbolism into his celebrations.

In ancient times, priests known as the *dendrophori* cut boughs from the sacred groves. These branches became offerings known as *strenae,* and were carried to the interior of the sacred temples. Here, they were placed before the appropriate gods and goddesses.

The Yule log featured prominently in the veneration of the Sun or Stag God. The log represented the Lord of the Woods, and fire symbolized the awakening of the divine forces of the Sun. Setting the log ablaze awoke the ancient spirit of the woodlands and united him as one with the bright Sun God. The hearth, a symbol of the gateway to and from the Underworld, contained the sacred log. This gateway served as a magickal doorway through which the Sun God could be evoked to return to the world of the living.

As part of the Yule celebration, a loaf was formed into the shape of a boar and then baked as an offering. Ancient belief held that the spirit of the Harvest Lord dwelled within the loaf. As a boar, he was the consort of the sow, which was identified with the Goddess of the Grain.

In the winter solstice celebrations, it is not difficult to see the continued appearance of the same symbolism also associated with Dagda. This is no surprise, for the newborn Sun God is Angus Og, the son of Dagda. He is also the Irish counterpart of Mabon/Maponus, who we shall encounter in the autumn equinox. MacKillop notes that some commentators equate Angus Og with Lugh. Another figure sometimes identified with Lugh is Llew Llaw Gyffes, whose legends share a common theme with those of Lugh (*Dictionary of Celtic Mythology,* 1998).

An important symbolism attached to the legend of Llew involves water. In one tale, Llew is cast adrift by his mother who places him in a coracle made of weed and sedge. This theme also appears in the myth of Dionysos (the Divine Child born on the winter solstice) who is set adrift in a harvest basket.

The water symbolizes the regenerative forces of the Underworld flowing back into the world of the living. The boat is both a sign of life and death. The boat is the harvest basket, which proclaims the new Harvest Lord placed there as an infant. As the container of seed, the basket symbolizes life renewed, and as the receiver of harvested grain, it symbolizes the death of the seed bearer (so that new life may emerge). Therefore, the basket/boat is both the womb and the tomb.

In the mythos of the Sun God, he is sacrificed, dies, and is taken by the Moon boat into the realm of the Underworld. This represents the force of the Goddess who generates all life and then draws it back again. The Western quarter has long been associated with the entrance to the Underworld, and it is where the Sun sets in Western culture. Here, we see the natural symbolism of the Sun God sailing across the sea and disappearing beneath the water, only to return in the east as a new light reborn.

In the Christian story of Jesus, he is placed in a crib within a manger, which connects him with the animal kingdom as a type of Lord of the Woods figure. Although Jesus is not set adrift on the water, he is instead set adrift from his homeland, for according to the tale, they must wander in exile. Like most divine sacrificial figures, his death is linked to the plant kingdom (death on a wooden cross). His spirit later reanimates the body, which is the symbol of the Yule log with its emerging flame.

In modern Witchcraft, we find another figure known as the Oak King who is also associated with the winter solstice. We encountered the Oak King earlier where he was noted as representing the waxing half of the year. Traditionally, the Yule log was of oak, which symbolized the Lord of the Woods. Mistletoe, commonly appearing on oak trees, became a Yule symbol. It was burned on top of the Yule log in a ritual of renewal, having been harvested on the previous summer solstice.

The harvest of the mistletoe on the summer solstice was performed to capture the full power of the Sun God on the longest day of the year. The mistletoe was kept safe until the winter solstice when it was burned on the Yule log, an act that passed the spirit of the Sun God back into the sacred fire (which symbolized the bright Sun God). In this ritual, ripe berries are harvested from fresh mistletoe and added to the old mistletoe spring cut at the summer solstice. This passes the fertile essence back into the Sun God amidst the Yule fire. It is noteworthy that mistletoe grows most readily on apple trees, which feature prominently in the Mystery Tradition of Witchcraft.

Another aspect of the Sun God in the Mystery Tradition of Witchcraft is the Child of Promise. We discussed him in detail within Chapter Three. His mythos begins the cycle of the divine Sun, and he is the old God of the previous year who is now renewed and born again into the world of the living. Just as Hercules was challenged to perform twelve tasks or feats, the new Sun God must now traverse the twelve months of the year that lay ahead.

The influence of the ancient Cult of Hercules is well-attested in Celtic lands. Its influence in the Aegean/Mediterranean is obvious and is therefore worthy of note in relation to its solar connections. In the tale of Hercules, Hera (the Great Goddess) suckles him as a baby. It is from this act that he receives his god-like strength, although he is also the son of Zeus, and, therefore, of divine nature himself.

The parallels between the legend of Hercules and the course and operations of the Sun are very similar, which suggests that the myth is a Solar Mystery Teaching. The first task performed by Hercules begins near his home, and each one thereafter takes him further West. His last task passes him into the Underworld but is preceded by the task of having to obtain the golden apples of Hesperides. Here again, we see the connection between apples and safe passage to and from the Underworld. The disappearance of Hercules into the Underworld through the far west evokes an image of the Sun setting in the west. Eventually, the twelve feats of Hercules were assigned to the Zodiac signs, which also suggests a strong solar connection.

In the early myths of Hercules, he becomes aware of his impending death delivered in secret through a potion. The potion was applied to a robe that Hercules always wore when he gave offerings. As the tale goes, Hercules climbed a high peak to make an offering, put on his robe, and absorbed the potion. Realizing his death was imminent, Hercules built a pyre of wood, climbed onto it, and was consumed in the flames. Here again, we see the symbolism of the Yule log ablaze with the divine spirit. However, the thirteenth-century Welsh tale of Hercules presents a classic Harvest Lord death, as we shall see later in this chapter.

Imbolc

The celebration of Imbolc falls mid-point between the winter solstice and the spring equinox. The ancient rite was traditionally held on the eve of February. The general theme is centered on purification and the element of Fire. As we noted in the winter solstice, fire signifies the presence of the divine. Fire draws out the divine within the wood, a process symbolized in the Yule log.

Since ancient times, fire has been a symbol of the divine, which originated as a feminine essence. We see this in the archaic myths of Hestia or Vesta, and the legends surrounding the Celtic goddess Brigit or Brigid. Brigit is a goddess of fire and smithing. She is also the daughter of Dagda and is strongly associated with Imbolc. Historian Peter Berresford Ellis (*A Dictionary of Irish Mythology*, 1991) states that Brigid appears to equate with Dana, the Mother of all the Gods.

In one tale of Brigit, she appears under the name *Bride*. She is held prisoner in a hidden castle by the Old Woman of Winter (Cailleach

Bheur). In a faraway land, Angus the Ever-Young (Angus Og) sees her in a vision in a well and becomes enchanted by her beauty. Angus leaves his home and goes to the land where Bride is being held. He searches for her for three days but cannot find her. At last, he encounters her in the forest gathering wood just outside her castle prison. The two fall in love at first sight, and their love is such that it breaks the spell of the Old Woman of Winter. This event brings the end of winter and is henceforth the celebration day of Bride/Brigit.

The symbolism within this tale is revealed in the Mystery Tradition. Bride is the Moon Goddess and Angus is the Sun God. The well of vision reflects the Moon on the water's surface. The journey of Angus is the course of the Sun as it follows after the Moon. The three days in which Angus cannot find Bride denotes the three days of the New Moon when it is hidden from view. In the mythos of the Sun God, Imbolc is the time of his developed adolescence. Brigit has long been associated with fertility, and at this season, she forges or quickens his sexual maturity with her divine fire. At Imbolc, the seeds of light (of which he is the bearer) begin to stir within the God. In ancient Rome, the rites of the Lupercalia marked this season.

Faunus, the Woodland and Agricultural God, we encountered in Chapter Three, was worshipped during the rites of the Lupercalia. Faunus was also known as *Lupercus,* and his priests were called the *Luperci.* On the festival day of the Lupercalia, the priests would run nude through the streets carrying straps made of goatskin, which were called *februa.* These straps were believed to possess the ability to bestow fertility. Therefore, the priests would strike people in the festival crowd and thereby pass the fertile essence to their bodies.

The theme of fertility, in context with the Sun God or Harvest Lord, connects once again to the harvest basket or Moon boat of the Goddess. The weed and sedge boat/basket of the Child of Promise we saw at the winter solstice now becomes the woven rushes figure known as Brigit's Cross. Rushes were traditionally laid down to form a mat in the birthing place. Here, the figure stands as a reminder of the life and death of the Sun God and a symbol of the fire within the wood that awaits rebirth.

In the Mystery Tradition of Witchcraft, we find the theme of mated pairs represented as either mother and son or sister and brother. The Moon Goddess of Witchcraft is mated with her brother who is her lover (a metaphor for the Moon and Sun). This is most notable in the mythos of Diana and her brother Dianus or Lucifero, a version of which appears in Charles Leland's *Aradia: Gospel of the Witches*. In Celtic lore, Brigit and Angus Og are brother and sister, their father being Dagda. The Mystery theme survived even in the popular folk customs surrounding Brigit at Imbolc.

The folk custom (although arrogated by the Cult of Saint Worship centered on St. Brigid or St. Bride) reflects the consort pair of Harvest Lord and Lady. Writings as late as the seventeenth century mention the custom of dressing up a sheaf of grain as a woman. It was also the custom to make a bed of grain and hay to which "Bridget" was called to come lay. The custom also included laying a wooden club nearby. The club, as we noted in Chapter Three, is carried by such figures as Dagda, Silvanus, Faunus, and other agricultural solar deities.

In the customs associated with St. Brigit/Bride, we see two themes. First (in the dressed sheaf) is the Grain Goddess, and the club represents the male consort. Second, in the bed of the grain and hay is the wedding bed of the Lord and Lady of the plant kingdom.

Historian Ronald Hutton presents an interesting custom in his book *The Stations of the Sun* (1996). Here, we find a tradition in which women make an "oblong basket in the shape of a cradle" that is called *leaba Bride* (the bed of Bride). They also make a woman figure from an oat sheaf, which is then decorated with ribbons, shells, bright stones, and flowers. The figure is called *dealbh Bride* (the image of Bride).

According to custom, the cradle and image of Bride are placed before the hearth (the goddess Brigit/Bride has long been associated with the hearth). The women then call for Bride to enter and lay upon the bed. Next, the image of Bride is placed in the cradle. Following this, a "peeled wand" is laid beside the Bride image. Ashes are leveled and smoothed in the hearth, and then the setting is left undisturbed. In the morning, the hearth is inspected for an impression in the ashes of the wand or of a footprint. Such a sign is considered a blessing.

The symbolism of this custom is readily apparent. The image of Bride is the Goddess, the cradle is the harvest bowl, the wand is the club or phallus of the God, and the ashes are a symbol of death and renewal. The ashes also signify the covenant between the Harvest Lord and Lady. To find marks in the ashes symbolizes the presence of the life force and the activity of the mystical process behind it all.

Despite the fertility symbolism and consort identifications, Imbolc is not actually about sexual union. It is instead a time of purification and preparation for the functional and active elements of sexuality in the spring season to follow.

At Imbolc, the seeds are still asleep beneath the soil. The Goddess wears a circlet on her head bearing nine candles, a symbol of the fertile dance of light between the Moon and Sun as they rise and set in an endless cycle. Her candles give light and warmth to quicken the seeds that await the coming season.

Spring Equinox

In the Mystery Tradition of Witchcraft, the spring equinox marks the return of the Goddess. This is seen in such myths as Persephone who returns from the realm of Dis, as well as in the legend of Bride who is rescued from the hidden castle of the Old Woman of Winter. Within the Mystery mythos, the Goddess emerges from a lake, which is a classic symbol of the passageway to and from the Otherworld.

In the season of spring, life returns most noticeably with the reappearance of life within the plant kingdom. It is here that the Goddess and God first return from their winter realms. The stirring of new life emerges in the woodlands, and here we find the Faery maiden and the Green Man. In the forest, the new antlers of the stag are covered with a velvet moss-like growth, linking the Green Man and the Stag-Horned God. Soon, he will emerge as the Sun God and take his throne in the sky.

In the Mystery Tradition of Witchcraft, the Moon Goddess bears the title Queen of the Faeries. Although the Sun God does not typically bear the title King of the Faeries, he is frequently associated with a Faery wife or lover. This is most likely a remnant in popular lore that recalls the old memory of the Goddess and God consort relationship.

In the tales of Angus Og and Llew Llaw Gyffess (Lugh), we find various versions of the Faery maiden. Angus beholds a vision of a beautiful woman in a dream and he finds himself pining away for her. This imagery reflects the Moon realm of dreams, a doorway to the Faery Realm. His infatuation with a woman he has never met is a classic theme of enchantment, and here, it can be no less than Faery magick. Once united, Angus and the Faery maiden are transformed into a pair of swans. Together, they fly off to an Otherworld realm known as Brug na Boinne.

In the tale of Llew, he marries a Faery woman named Blodeuwedd. She later falls in love with a hunter, and together, they plan to slay Llew. Blodeuwedd learns that Llew can only be slain under certain conditions. In order to die, Llew must be standing with one foot on a dead stag and the other in a cauldron. If he is speared in this posture, then Llew can perish. An expanded version of this tale can be found in *Myths and Legends of the Celtic Race* by T. W. Rolleston (1911).

In this tale, Blodeuwedd tricks him into assuming the vulnerable posture, and the lover who is hiding in secret then spears him. Llew turns into an eagle and flies off into an oak tree. The solar symbolism of the eagle and the oak is readily apparent in this tale. The key interest centers on the posture that Llew must take in order to die.

The Mystery Tradition symbolism of the stag and the cauldron are important elements in the legend of Llew. Here, Llew stands upon a dead stag, the symbol of the Slain God. Llew also stands with one foot in the cauldron, the symbol of the womb of the Goddess through which all life returns. Here, Llew stands between the worlds of life and death, decline and renewal. At the spring equinox, night and day are of equal length, and so the forces of light and darkness are held in balance.

In this legend, we can see a metaphor connected with the sunset. When the Sun is halfway beneath the horizon, one foot stands in the cauldron of the Goddess hidden in the Underworld. The other foot stands in this world as the power of the Sun begins to wane. Here, in a mystical sense, the Sun God stands with one foot on a dead stag (his symbol of earthly power in the world of the living). Here, between the worlds, he can be speared and perish because he has no power in either realm (being fully in neither) and is, therefore, vulnerable.

Although the theme of the death of the Sun God has no role in the spring season, its connection to his lover does hold meaning. Ultimately, it is his desire for her that leads to his death. Metaphorically, this can be seen as the absorption and return of the Sun God back into the Mother Goddess. His desire for her and her desire for his seed initiates the cycle of life and death. One might ask, does the seed freely fall to the ground or is it pulled to the soil?

In the Mystery Tradition of Witchcraft, the essence of the youthful Sun in spring is drawn into the new plant growth of the season. It is through this that the Woodland God (whether Horned or Hooded-in-Green) bears his solar nature. Here, such figures as Cernunnos, Herne, and the Green Man emerge.

In modern Witchcraft, the theme of spring centers on the youthful Goddess whose return from the Underworld signals the renewal of growth within nature. She is the young virgin maiden whose body also begins to bud and sprout in preparation for the coming season. The young God sports his antlers and tests his growing strength. Soon, the innocent playfulness of the young Goddess and God will turn into a mating of the two.

Beltane

The season of Beltane begins on May Eve as the stars of the Pleiades are distant from the horizon of the Earth. Here, the realm of death gives way to a season of birth, growth, and gain. In ancient times, Beltane was celebrated with fertility rites to honor and venerate these natural forces of the waxing year.

In the season of Beltane appear the May Queen and May King, personifications of the Goddess and God within the Mystery Tradition of Witchcraft. This is the period of courtship, and the old Rites of May allowed people to slip off into the woods and have intercourse with whomever they pleased.

The Horned God is not evident at this time and appears more commonly in his Green Man image. However, in keeping with the cycle of nature, he will soon begin to shed the velvet growth that covers his antlers. It is then that the Horned God can be clearly seen as he emerges from the foliage. In the meantime, at his side is the Green Woman who is the Queen of May.

Images of the Green Woman are rare, as are literary references. During the Middle Ages, legends of the "Wild Woman" depicted a female image dressed in leaves. Her hair was long, worn loose, and her face was one of wisdom. In some cases, the Wild Women were also known as the "Blessed Damsels."

The May Queen was also known as the "Flower Bride," which brings to mind the Goddess Brigit as well as the lore of the Faery maiden. In some of the customs associated with May Day, the Flower Bride is abducted. A struggle then takes place between the forces of winter and summer to win her hand. Here, we see the classic tale of the fight between Gwythyr and Gwynn ap Nudd who battled for the hand of Creiddylad (see Chapter Three).

In his earliest form, Gwynn ap Nudd is the Welsh ruler of Annwyn, the Otherworld realm. In his battle for Creiddylad, we see the last clinging attempts of winter personified as the longing for the Goddess who once dwelled in the Underworld. May Day games often reenact this mythos with mock battles fought by teams representing winter and summer. After much good fun and sport, the summer team always prevails. The prize, of course, is the favor of the Queen of May.

In the celebration of Beltane, we see the God and Goddess in their youthful courtship. The Goddess, as the Moon, appears as the Faery maiden and May Queen. The God, as the Sun, appears as the Green Man and May King. In essence, these are the youthful Angus and Brigit who have come through the seasons in many guises.

Summer Solstice

The summer solstice marks the longest day of the year. In the mythos of the Sun God, this is therefore the peak of his power. Several mystical themes appear and intersect at this season, which marks this as a particularly magickal time.

In the mythos of the sabbats, the Goddess and God wed on the summer solstice. It is this wedding that fully links the God with the Goddess. The Goddess draws in his life, only to give it back again in the coming season. The joining of the God to the Goddess begins the waning of his power as a separate light. As the days continue from the summer solstice, the light of day decreases.

In the Mystery Tradition of Witchcraft, mistletoe is cut on the morning of the summer solstice. This captures the peak life force of the Sun God before his decline. The mistletoe is then placed in a pouch and saved for use at the winter solstice. At midsummer, the berries are not ripe, but the flowers (produced between February and May) have declined and the buds have appeared. The familiar white berries will ripen between October and December. Instead of going dormant or dying during winter, mistletoe actually bears its fruit. This links it to the theme of the evergreen life cycle of the Sun God who dies but never perishes.

At the time of the summer solstice, the Holly King appears and challenges the Oak King for reign of the year. In some traditions, rooted perhaps in Druidic lore, the mistletoe is associated with the Oak King. One possible origin for the significance of mistletoe and oak is that mistletoe rarely grows on oak in comparison to other trees. This is because the hard bark of the oak makes it difficult for mistletoe to penetrate the tree where water and nutrients are available. Therefore, the mistletoe growing on an oak was considered especially sacred or magickal in some traditions. The fact that the holly begins to flower at the same time that mistletoe loses its own may underline the assignment of the Oak King and Holly King to seasonal shifts.

The summer solstice also introduces the revels of the Faery race in celebration of Midsummer's Eve. The Faery Folk belong to the realm of night, which is the doorway to the Otherworld. As the days grow shorter, the nighttime grows longer. Fireflies (once believed to be Faeries) mate on or near the summer solstice and are in great abundance. Their flight is dance-like and can be seen as a great Faery gathering. In the mythos, the Fae gather on the summer solstice to celebrate the marriage of their Queen, the Moon Goddess.

In the Mystery Tradition of Witchcraft, grain is associated with the Great Mysteries. At Midsummer, the fireflies swarm above the fields of wheat and barley. In the mythos, the fireflies (as Faery beings) impart their secrets to the grain upon which they land. The grain itself contains the secrets of the Underworld where it slept as a seed and where it sent its roots deep into the earth. Here, it drew the dark secrets to itself. As ripened grain, it then receives the second half of the Mysteries from the Fae, the teachings of light.

The symbolism of the grain, and the Mystery teachings associated with it, form the foundation of the ritual meal of cakes and wine in Witchcraft ceremonies. The sacred meal is also rooted in the Harvest Lord mythos. In its oldest form, the sacred meal represented the body of the Slain God/Harvest Lord, and the wine represented the blood or life-giving essence of the Goddess. To partake of this sacred meal was to awaken the Goddess and God consciousness within, which resides in the divine spark passed to our souls at our time of creation.

Over the course of time, the Mystery split into a second school of thought, which was due to the increase of importance regarding the masculine view of deity. As the survival of humankind came to depend more upon the hunter and warrior, the role of men took on more importance and increased in tribal life. This increased the religious and ritual focus regarding the God to which the men related.

In time, some Witchcraft Traditions absorbed the priestly view of the Mysteries. This resulted in perceiving the cakes and wine as the body and blood of the God. An ancient example of this can be found in the Cult of Dionysos where wine was considered to be his divine essence extracted from the vine. Once the role of men in impregnation was fully understood, the symbolism of the seed evolved and expanded.

In the Mystery Tradition of Witchcraft, the summer solstice marks two central themes. The first is the merging of the God into the Goddess, the beginning of the return of the isolated part to the whole. The second is the receiving of the sacred seed of light from the God, which has impregnated the Goddess and now brings forth the abundance of their union. Here, the symbolism merges with the ripe harvest grain that has emerged from the earth, the womb of the Goddess. In time, it will return to her in another season of the cycle of life.

Lughnasadh

This seasonal rite celebrates the ripe harvest and commemorates Lugh. In modern Witchcraft, he is identified with Lugos or Lugus, a Gaulish deity that the Romans equated with Mercury or Hermes. Since the Romans noted the similarities between Lugh and Hermes, it is worthwhile to examine Hermes in order to discover something of the nature of Lugh. The connections are significant as we shall see further in this section.

Hermes was originally a god of the proliferation and welfare of the animal kingdom (*Who's Who in Mythology* by Alexander S. Murray, 1988). In this regard, we can view him as the Lord of the Woods, and therefore, as a deity associated with the Sun as well (see Chapter Three). In early times, personal wealth was associated with herds, and herds were involved in trade. From this association, Hermes evolved into a deity of commerce and the communication needed for trade. It is interesting to note the tale of Angus Og, which credits him (and the sea god Manannan mac Lir) with the bringing of cattle to Ireland from India.

The association of commerce and communication led to the further evolution of Hermes as a divine messenger. In this role, he was granted access even to the Underworld, where he took on the name Psychopompos. In this role, he became the guide of departed souls. As noted in Chapter Three, this is also one of the roles of the Sun God, which strengthens the tie between the godforms associated with the Mystery Tradition of Witchcraft.

According to his myths, Hermes was born in the darkness of night, which denotes his connection as a Sun God in the Underworld who becomes the newborn Sun at the winter solstice. As the myth continues, we find Hermes born in a cave, a womb symbol associated with the Goddess. Hermes is the brother of the Sun God Apollo, which, in the Mystery Tradition, indicates another aspect of the concept.

As an infant, Hermes leaves his crib and steals the cattle of the Sun from Apollo (symbolizing the clouds in the sky). Hermes appeases the anger of Apollo by giving him a lyre or harp made from a tortoise shell. Then, Hermes invents the shepherd's pipe, which he keeps for himself. The association of the cattle and the shepherd's pipe (typically associated with the god Pan) appears as older memories of his Lord of The Woods nature.

In Celtic lore, the harp appears in the possession of both Dagda and Angus. Dagda's harp is made of oak, and the harp belonging to Angus is made of gold (the metal of the Sun). Here again, we see the connection between the Woodland God and the Sun God. According to legend, so sweet was the sound of the divine harp that no one could hear its music and not follow its sound. This reminds us of herding, and so we come full circle back to the animal connection.

In the myths of Hermes, he performs a variety of tasks that depict him as skilled and knowledgeable as Lugh in the arts. In the legends of Lugh, he is associated with the spear, and Lugh is known as the "long-armed" hero, which many commentators believe suggests his prowess in throwing a spear. The spear is Lugh's primary and favored weapon or tool and is symbolic of the rays of the Sun.

Hermes, in his myths, steals Poseidon's trident, the sword of Ares, the bow and arrows of Apollo, and the tongs of the Smith God Hephaestos. This suggests his power or influence over these arts. He is also a great inventor and creates a number of musical instruments. Hermes also instructs Palamedes in the art of expressing words in song, which is a bardic art as well as a poetic art. In the tarot, Hermes (Mercury) represents the Magician card, and Lugh appears in legend as a magician.

In the myth of Lugh, he approaches the citadel at Tara where he presents himself as the master of several arts. These include the warrior, smith, harper, poet, and physician. The latter is of particular interest when we compare Lugh and Hermes. This is because the primary symbol of Hermes is the caduceus, which has come to symbolize the medical profession.

As we noted earlier, Hermes was viewed as a guide, particularly of the dead. It became his office to assist mortal messengers and travelers as well. Evidence of this can be found in the object known as the *Hermae* or *Herms,* which was placed at the crossroads in ancient times. The Hermae consisted of a column or pillar that terminated in a bust or head figure. It served as an early signpost bearing directions to where each road led.

Travelers were obligated to place a stone beside the Hermae. Alexander Murray (*Who's Who in Mythology*) notes that this practice not only helped clear the planting fields of stones, but it also provided readily available material for building paved roads. This improved transportation and strengthened the connection between commerce and Hermes.

The idea of roads leads us to the notion of traveling to a destination. The sabbat known as Lughnasadh means to assemble or gather people together. This is derived from the Irish word *nasad*, meaning "to assemble," and the name *Lugh* (to assemble in the name of Lugh). The fact that Lughnasadh is celebrated on the eve instead of during the day places emphasis on the night. In the Mystery Tradition of Witchcraft, the night is associated with the Moon Goddess. This is reflected in the early Irish tradition that Lugh established this festival day to honor his foster mother Tailtiu.

The bulk of information regarding Tailtiu is found in the Celtic writings known as the *Lebor Gabala*, the *Book of Invasions*. MacKillop (*Dictionary of Celtic Mythology*) notes that Tailtiu is probably an older figure and possibly an earth goddess. In her tale, Tailtiu leads her followers to clear the forest at Caill Chua within one year and reclaim the meadowland. When the trees were all removed, roots and all, the area was named *Bregmag* and it became a plain blossoming with clover.

According to legend, the task took its toll on Tailtiu, and heartbroken, she fell into sorrow and weariness. This, in turn, brought about great illness, and so Tailtiu assembled the men of Ireland to receive her last behest. She then instructed them to hold funeral games to lament her deed. Out of this, the festival of Lughnasadh was established, joining together the theme of death and harvest.

This tale is of interest to us because it associates a feminine force harvesting a woodland domain. The metaphor for the Goddess drawing in the life of the Lord of the Woods is plainly evident. However, in the case of Tailtiu, she is not the mother of Lugh. Her consort relationship may be implied from a Mystery Tradition perspective, but its origins (if any) are lost in the maze of time.

In the legends of Lugh, it is Eithne who is his mother. Eithne is associated with a magickal impregnation, or at least with the attempted appearance of one. In one popular tale, Eithne is impregnated by a Faery who is sent by a Druid. Eithne eventually gives birth to Lugh. It is noteworthy that Lugh's mother in this tale is known as *Eithne* the Bride. Here, we see a reflection of Bride/Brigit who appeared in previous sabbat tales.

In the full tale, Eithne the Bride falls into a swoon one evening during a festival. When she awakens, Eithne tells of a beautiful country she visited and how she wishes to return. The next night, Eithne is taken by the Faeries and disappears from the mortal world.

Her husband leaves offerings at a faery mound in hopes of her return. Here, he learns that Finnbheara (King of the Faeries) has Eithne and is unwilling to return her. The husband learns further that the only way to retrieve Eithne is to dig a hole deep enough to allow the light of the Sun into the Faery Realm. However, all attempts to accomplish this task fail. At last, he learns that by sprinkling salt on the earth, Eithne will return. The husband uses the salt and his bride is thereby returned.

MacKillop notes in his *Dictionary of Celtic Mythology* that many commentators see a modified version here of the Greek myth of the rescue of Eurydice from Hades by Orpheus. He also mentions that Pluto, the Roman form of Hades, is known as the "King of the Faeries." The medieval tales of Sir Orfeo/King Orpheo appear in this classical tradition.

As we shall see in the next sabbat, the theme of the Underworld realm is one of the keys to understanding the Mysteries. In the mythos, both the Goddess and the God will descend into the hidden realm. Just as the Moon and Sun disappear beneath the horizon, only to reappear again, so too does the Mystery theme continue in the mythos of Witchcraft.

Autumn Equinox

The autumn equinox signals the official end of summer and the beginning of the fall season. In the mythos of Witchcraft, it is also the death of the Harvest Lord and the beginning of his journey to the Underworld. Within the Mystery Tradition of Witchcraft, the autumn equinox also marks the withdrawal of the Goddess from the realm of mortals as she goes in search of her lover and consort.

In the myth of Lugh, he is slain by three brothers. One is named Mac Cecht, whose name means "son of the plough." The second brother is named Mac Cuill, meaning "son of the hazel." The third brother is named Mac Greine, and his name means "son of the Sun." The three brothers encounter Lugh and kill him with a spear (in an act of vengeance for the death of their father at the hands of Lugh).

When we examine the myth, we find three things associated with the death of Lugh: a plough, hazel, and the Sun. The plough is a clear enough symbol linking the Harvest Lord with his life cycle. The "son of the Sun" is readily identifiable as the seed of the father, which, once spent, takes with it his life force. Therefore, he is his own death in the cycle of reproduction, for the plant dies when the seed is ripe. But what connection does the hazel have to the Harvest Lord/Slain Sun God? In order to penetrate this Mystery, we must look to the lore of the hazel.

In modern Celtic Witchcraft, the hazel marks the ninth month of the Celtic Tree Calendar. The number nine is the magickal numeric of the Moon, and it is said to take nine years for a hazel to produce a full crop of nuts. In Celtic tree lore, the hazel is believed to bestow wisdom and inspiration. We see the numeric of nine reflected in the nine maidens who tend the Cauldron of Inspiration (and the nine Muses who keep company with Apollo).

In Celtic lore, the hazel appears as a type of Tree of Knowledge icon. Bards favored the hazel and believed that it aided the poet. In Irish and Welsh lore, the hazel was considered to be a faery tree and there was a strict taboo against burning it in any hearth fire. So sacred was the hazel that at one time, the felling of a hazel tree brought the death penalty (as did the felling of an apple tree).

Hazel is associated with Hermes, whose caduceus is made from its branch into the form of a wand. In Celtic lore, Angus Og is also associated with the hazel and is said to have carried a hazel staff. The hazel tree appears in the lore connected to Boand, the mother of Angus. In her tale, Boand is transformed into the Boyne River. At the source of the river, there is a sacred well known as the Well of Segais. Nine hazel trees surround it, and nuts from the hazel drop into the water and are consumed by salmon.

Ancient lore ascribed the properties of wisdom, knowledge, and inspiration to the hazelnut. Therefore, the salmon that ate the nuts were blessed with its nature. One particular salmon is featured in connection with the mythos associated with the autumn equinox. This salmon appears in a tale featuring Mabon, a legendary figure in Celtic lore.

It is generally agreed that Mabon is a form of Maponos, a god of music and poetry (the bardic arts). MacKillop points out that Maponos is identified with the Gaulish Apollo, and also equates with the Irish Angus Og. This brings Mabon into the seasonal mythos as viewed in Witchcraft. In some traditions of modern Witchcraft, the autumn equinox sabbat is known as Mabon.

Mabon appears in a tale called "Culhwch and Olwen," yet plays a relatively minor role. Mabon is needed by several characters that are on a quest. The quest is to retrieve a razor and comb from between the ears of a magickal boar named Twrch Trwyth. In order to overtake the boar, the seekers need a magickal dog named Drudwyn. They are then told that only Mabon can hunt with Drudwyn. However, no one knows his whereabouts or whether is he alive or dead.

As the story unfolds, we are told that Mabon was taken from his mother (Madron) when he was only three nights old. From the perspective of the Mystery Teachings, this is a reference to the three days of the New Moon when it is absent from view. This is reflected in the story of Mabon being taken away, the implication being that his mother (the Moon Goddess) was not present when he was kidnapped. It is widely accepted that Madron is identifiable with Matrona, a Divine Mother figure in Gaulish lore. Here, we find, once again, the mother and son pair that is key to the Mystery Tradition in Witchcraft.

On the quest, Gwrhyr Gwastas Ieithoedd, who knows the language of birds and beasts, accompanies the seekers. This indicates that the journey involves the Otherworld. During the quest, a series of animals are encountered. Each one is asked if they know anything of Mabon, son of Madron. The birds and animals each indicate the great periods of time in which they have lived but still know nothing of Mabon. Some commentators view these creatures as totems belonging to Mabon: the blackbird of Cilgwri, the stag of Rhedynfr, the owl of Cawlwyd, the eagle of Gwernabwy, and the salmon of Llyn Llyw.

In the tale, it is the salmon that takes the seekers to Mabon. He is found imprisoned in a castle, where Mabon is then rescued by Cai and Gwrhyr. Mabon joins the seekers on their quest, and with the aid of the magickal hunting dog, the boar is tracked down and the razor and comb are retrieved.

The hound or hunting dog is a classic companion of the Moon Goddess. From the view of the Witchcraft Mysteries, the reason only Mabon can control the dog is because he is the son of the Moon Goddess. The salmon, who ultimately reveals the location of Mabon, has eaten the hazelnuts and, therefore, possesses knowledge, wisdom, and intuition. Knowledge is information, and wisdom is applied experience (from the integration of knowledge). Both of these are worldly accomplishments, but intuition is something of the Otherworld and is separate from knowledge and wisdom.

In Mabon's tale, the salmon is found in a lake, which is a classic entrance to the Underworld. When questioned whether the salmon knows of Mabon, it answers that while swimming about, it has heard lamentations coming from a castle. The salmon has no direct knowledge of Mabon, nor has it seen Mabon. Instead, it is the salmon's intuition that leads it to conclude that this is the person of the seeker's quest. It is this Otherworld sense that leads the salmon to Mabon.

The lake passage to the Underworld/Otherworld takes the salmon (carrying Mabon's rescuers) to the hidden castle, which itself represents containment within this mystical realm. Mabon cries out that his captivity is "grievous" and he longs to be released. Here, the symbolism can be applied to the agricultural Mysteries.

In some traditions of Witchcraft, Mabon is viewed as the seed buried in the earth. This is represented by Mabon's imprisonment in the castle. Water is the element that leads to Mabon's rescue, and it is water that initiates the sprouting of the seed. The sprout is the release from the Underworld, the longing of the Sun God or Harvest Lord to return to the world of the living.

It is of interest that the boar plays an important part in the story. Pigs have been associated with chthonic deities since ancient times. They appear in both Northern and Southern Europe as animals linked to Underworld deities, deities associated with grain, and goddesses of the Moon. The hound's ability to overtake the boar suggests a lunar relationship.

Mabon's name means "youth," and many commentators believe this points to his infancy and his seed connection. In his tale, Mabon is unknown to the oldest living creatures because he predates them. Therefore, some commentators see him as the youngest and the oldest of beings on the Earth. This has led some traditions to view him as the Year God, the traveling Sun God who becomes the Harvest Lord. The Harvest Lord falls into the harvest and is buried so that he may rise again. This essential theme is reflected in an Etruscan mirror etching that depicts the Sun God (Uslan) flanked by Nethuns (Neptune) on one side and Thesan (Eos, the dawn) on the other. Here, the Sun God stands between the east and the west, the beginning and end of his journey.

The Celtic figures of Mabon, Angus Og, and Lugh form an interesting triad within the mythos of Witchcraft. From the perspective of the Mystery Tradition, it is possible to view Mabon as the seed, Angus Og as the sprout, and Lugh as the fruit. All three are contained within Dagda, the father from which they ultimately issue forth.

In the Mystery Tradition of Italian Witchcraft, we find some interesting parallels to the Northern European depictions. Due to the antiquity of the Italian system, instead of encountering human personifications of the seasons (such as the Oak and Holly Kings), we find animal forms. Here, Lupus is the Wolf God, representative of the waning forces of nature. Cern is the Stag God, symbolizing the waxing forces of nature. These gods are also referred to as the powers of light and darkness.

The mythos of Cern and Lupus centers on the equinox periods, unlike the Celtic mythos that embraces the solstice periods. As the story goes, Lupus sets out on the day of the spring equinox to hunt a deer. During the hunt, Lupus is struck by a bolt of lightning shaped like an arrow and seemingly perishes. However, the next morning, he rises from the Underworld as the Sun.

The only physical remains of Lupus are his wolf skin, which is found by a hunter in the forest. The pelt is magickal and has the power to transform men into wolves. The hunter discovers the powers of the wolf pelt and becomes a priest of Lupus. Gathering others to himself, the hunter forms a secret society that he names the *Luperci* (the wolves).

Cern learns of his brother's demise and assumes reign over the world of mortals. Here, he attains Sun rulership over the mortal world. This presents us with the notion of two Sun Gods, one light and one dark (the waxing and waning rulership of the year). From the Mystery Tradition perspective, we find the "as above, so below" principle reflected in the Overworld and Underworld Sun Gods. The setting Sun of light displaces the dark Sun that is already within the Underworld. Therefore, the dark Sun must rise in the night, unseen against the black sky of darkness. For is not the night a shadowed Sun?

In this mythos, we find the rivalry of opposing seasons, "brothers" that are necessary balances in the scheme of nature. Lupus is slain during the hunt, in which Cern is the hunted. He is slain by a Centaur who is given a bolt of lightning for his bow by Dianus (having been persuaded by his sister Diana). Cern is later slain on the autumn equinox by Mars during a hunting incident.

It is interesting to note that the centaur in the constellation Centaurus is aiming a bow at the constellation Lupus, the wolf. In mythology, the centaur was beloved by Apollo and Diana who instructed him in many of the ancient arts. Diana and the stag are strongly associated with the Witch Cult, and in her classic Roman statue, she is portrayed standing with a stag. It is also noteworthy that the wolf was sacred to Mars. Here, we see a possible vengeance slaying within the myth of Cern and Lupus.

In the legend of Lugh, we noted that he was slain with a spear by three brothers, one of whom is the "son of the plough." In archaic Roman religion, Mars was originally an agricultural deity associated with the plough. When fertile lands became targets for raiding parties, Mars evolved into a god of war.

The Cult of Mars was carried into Celtic lands by the Roman legions, where it took root in local culture. At Uley, Gloucester, England, Mars Silvanus was worshipped. Here, he was equated with Hermes or Mercury. An inscription at Nettleham in Lincolnshire indicates that Mars Rigonemetis (Mars of the Sacred Grove) was worshipped in this region. Discoveries at Thetford, England, point to the worship of Faunus, the Pastoral and Woodland God. Here, he also appears as Fatuus or Fatuclus, an oracle deity who revealed the future in dreams and through voices in the grove.

In the Mystery Tradition of Witchcraft, we find the essential commonality of mystical themes that dovetail into one another, despite regional and cultural differences. This can be viewed as the "one truth" spoken in many different ways. The places at which we enter the Mystery path may differ, but the journey is the same walk upon the ancient trail.

Let us now continue our walk and turn to the next chapter. Here, we will encounter the Mystery Teachings that have been preserved by our ancestors. The Wheel of the Year has turned, and a year and day have ended. Before us now is the ancient tome of the Mysteries themselves.

CHAPTER EIGHT

Occult Principles in Modern Witchcraft

It has been a longstanding tradition within any Mystery Society to preserve its foundational beliefs and concepts. These beliefs and concepts serve as the keys to unlocking the inner meaning and symbolism associated with the ritual and myths of the society. It is generally the custom to refer to such material as the Mystery Teachings. These teachings record the knowledge, wisdom, and intuition of the ancient masters.

The masters who developed the method of recording the Mystery Teachings constructed rituals of initiation that were designed to prepare neophytes for a period of formal study and training. These rituals were called the *rites of initiation*. During the ritual, a mental alignment was established through which the memory-chain associations were passed to the initiate. Each phase of the Mystery experience was marked by a degree or level of initiation, which further prepared the initiate for the understanding necessary to penetrate and comprehend the Mystery Teachings.

An important component of each degree of initiation required the taking of an oath of initiation. Typically, these oaths bound the initiate to secrecy and required that they abide by the ways of the inner society. This called upon the personal code of honor for each initiate.

In the book *Crete and Pre-Hellenic Myths and Legends* (1917) by Donald MacKenzie, the author provides some interesting information regarding oaths. According to MacKenzie, it was the ancient custom to gather at a certain oak in Charnwood Forest. Beneath the oak, a type of rustic court was held, which was called a *mote*. The mote frequently heard claims pertaining to forest rights. The convening of a mote put a person's word on the line. In this light, the Witchcraft axiom "so mote it be" refers to one's word among their peers (literally, "what I say before the mote is so"). MacKenzie states that in Scotland, the custom of the mote was also practiced.

According to MacKenzie, it became the custom to plant a pole of oak in the center of a field. Here, it was called the "Column of May" and the area was called the "Fields of May." Here, a peasant court passed judgment on governors and royalty for various wrongs. MacKenzie concludes that the motes and maypoles are relics of tree worship. He envisions a past when the representative of the Goddess sat beneath her sacred tree and dispensed justice.

In ancient Aegean/Mediterranean culture, it was the practice to swear a public oath to Ge or Gaia in order to cement an alliance. A Gaelic custom involved lifting a piece of earth in one's hand and shouting out an oath (typically one of vengeance). Here, we see swearing an oath in the name of the Great Mother.

Hesiod and other ancient writers state that before sacrifices or offerings are made to any deity, a person must first go before Hecate. This is because Hecate is the keeper of the gateway and the mediator between mortals and divine beings. She is involved with all beginnings and all endings.

One of the earliest focuses of her worship involved the erection of a wooden pillar at the crossroads. This pillar is the material counterpart of the Moon Tree that resides in the Otherworld. In the Mystery Tradition of Witchcraft, oaths of initiation are performed by placing one hand upon the earth and the other upon the pillar of Hecate. Here, the initiate kneels before the gates of the Otherworld in the presence of the Goddess of the Crossroads.

In the Homeric *Hymn of Demeter,* Hecate appears in connection with the abduction of Persephone. In this ancient tale, Hecate hears the cry of Persephone as Hades, Lord of the Underworld, kidnaps her. Hecate goes to Demeter, the mother of Persephone, and announces something to her (but the myth does not reveal what was spoken). Once Persephone is returned to the mortal world, Hecate appears again to welcome her. Homer then informs us that from that day forward, Hecate attends Persephone.

Professor Sarah Iles Johnston (*Hekate Soteira,* 1990) points out that Hecate *"was involved more intimately in the descent and return than the Hymn tells us."* Johnson bases this upon certain wordings in the Greek text that indicate Hecate accompanied Persephone to and from the Underworld. Here, she served as both a guide and a protector. Homer states that Hecate continued to accompany Persephone after her return from the Underworld, which means that she journeys with Persephone each year when she must go back to the Underworld.

The Legend of the Descent of the Goddess (into the Underworld) is a classic element of the Mystery Tradition of Witchcraft. The primary importance of the story is that the Goddess never dies; she simply descends into the realm of death in order to renew the life of the God. He can die, as does the body, but she cannot die, for she is the soul.

The return of the Goddess and the God from the Underworld symbolizes the ever-repeating cycle of life. This basic theme is an essential part of the Mystery Teachings and is foundational to many tenets of belief in the religion of Witchcraft. Witchcraft, as a nature religion, looks to the microcosm in order to gain an understanding of the macrocosm. Here, we can find our place in the greater order of things.

Over the course of many centuries, ancient Witches formulated various occult principles, and others were adopted from outside sources. Since recorded times, the Witch was rarely the ignorant country bumpkin. The earliest writings in Western literature depict Witches involved in some fairly complex ritual and magickal performances. Witch trials from the Renaissance show evidence of Ceremonial Magick incorporated into Witchcraft from medieval grimoires. One example is that of Laura Malipero (1654) in whose home a copy of the *Key of Solomon* was found, from which she had been copying various sections into her spellbook.

At some point in history, the inclusion of the four tools of Western occultism came to Witchcraft. These are the pentacle, wand, blade, and chalice. Tarot cards also became a part of the Witches' sect as the centuries passed. Here, we see that an occult tradition within Witchcraft was evolving over the course of time.

The remainder of this chapter is devoted to discussing the occult principles that now reside within modern Witchcraft. Each tenet requires its own focus of study as each concept has a large body of material devoted to it in various books. In the course of this chapter, the essential core teachings are provided, and I encourage the reader to investigate these tenets in more depth. They have been touched upon in previous chapters, but appear here as an expanded teaching.

The Source of All Things

Our current state of human consciousness does not allow us to comprehend what ultimately created the universe or what initiated the process. We cannot comprehend what divinity truly is and how it originated (if indeed it had an origin). Therefore, we draw a line between our ability to conceive and that which is inconceivable. The line is our ability to grasp an understanding. Above that line, we place the Source of All Things. In occultism, this is often called "The Great Unmanifest."

The next step is to look at what we perceive regarding the Source, and what the experience of it has been regarding our ancestors. For thousands of years, humans have practiced religions and spiritualities that evolved from what was perceived, experienced, imagined, and intuited. The process itself, as well as the reason for seeking an understanding, all contributed to what humans came to believe regarding divinity.

From a metaphysical perspective, any generated energy or action must cause a reaction. Attempting to communicate with the Source of All Things is no exception. Shamans, mystics, Witches, occultists, and others have meditated, channeled, and explored non-material realms for centuries. What was encountered, received, and interpreted now comprises the traditional material upon which we draw.

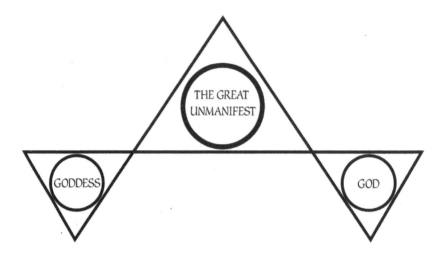

An important element for Witches is the concept that the Source is comprised of what we call *feminine* and *masculine* polarities of consciousness. To simplify this notion, we use the terms *Goddess* and *God*. It is our human nature to personify, which helps us relate. By trying to relate, we can interface with a different consciousness and reach an "agreement of consciousness." This agreement becomes a compromise between reality and our perception of it. Let's look at an example that can help clarify this concept.

If you were to travel back in time and try to explain the mechanics of a flashlight to primitive humans, you would find it quite difficult to be fully understood. Instead, you would need to use their ideas and communication abilities to convey what a flashlight is and how it operates. Here, you would only be partially successful, but the primitive humans would come away with their own understanding. This understanding would be partially what you communicated and partially what they can comprehend. The meeting point between reality and perception becomes an agreement of consciousness as to what a flashlight is all about. This same scenario can be applied to the human understanding of the divine.

In Witchcraft, the interfacing of our ancestors with the Source has led us to conclude that the divine manifests and operates as goddesses and gods. These deities possess specific natures, personalities, and characteristics. They also have likes and dislikes, just as humans do. This is our agreement of consciousness.

As Above, So Below

In the Mystery Tradition, there is an axiom: "That which is below, is as that which is above. And that which is above is as that which is below." Essentially, this means that whatever is found in cosmic principles also applies equally to the human condition (and that of the soul). Therefore, what we know regarding the universe can be applied to understanding ourselves. Likewise, what we know about ourselves can be applied to understanding the universe.

Occult teachings hold that the universe is made in the image (representation) of the divine. Humankind is made in the image of the universe. This means that the pattern is the same principle. Therefore, one is a reflection of the other. This concept is conveyed in the words inscribed above the entrance to the ancient Greek Mystery temple at Delphi: "Know Thyself."

It is said that each soul is a divine spark generated from the Source of All Things. It is here that the microcosmic pattern resides and is connected to the macrocosm. This is why mystical traditions incorporate meditation, a going inward to enlightenment. This is the "stillness" point where we can interface with our divine origin. In the Mystery Tradition of Witchcraft, we discover a verse that reads:

"But to all who seek her, know that your seeking and desire will reward you not unless you realize the secret. Because if that which you seek is not found within your inner self, you will never find it from without. For she has been with you since you entered into the ways, and she is that which awaits at your journey's end."

In the classic tarot image of the Magician, he is depicted holding a wand upward with his right hand while pointing toward an altar with his left hand. Mercury is assigned as the ruler of this card because the cosmic association here is communication. The Magician communicates with the mystical forces of the cosmos and then directs manifestation within the material dimension.

Nature as the Great Teacher

From the perspective of the Mystery Teachings, nature contains the divine blueprints of the process and inner mechanism of the divine workings. This is because the nature of the artist goes into the artwork. Therefore, studying and understanding the artwork provides clues to the nature of that which created it. In a sense, as a Mystery Tradition, we examine the material for clues as to the spirit that animates it.

According to the teachings, we enter the material dimension as souls and become housed in physical bodies. These bodies allow us to explore and experience material existence. In this view, life on Earth is a learning experience with nature as the active teacher.

In Witchcraft as a nature religion, we look at the ways of nature to see what teachings they hold. In the rising and setting of the Sun and Moon, we see our own physical existence. Just as the Sun and Moon rise, reach their peak, and descend beneath the horizon, so too is the cycle of our lives.

The changing of the seasons points to transition and transformation. The only constants in nature are transition and change. In this concept, we are taught that it is the process that remains, and everything is drawn into the process. Each state of being is temporary and yet cyclical at the same time. Picture a boiling pot of water with beans in it. The bubbles lift the beans to the surface where they appear for a moment and then descend again to the bottom of the pot. The metaphor here is that each appearance is a life experience for an individual consciousness. Each descent is a transition back through the process, which ultimately transforms the individual involved in the process.

The animals of nature teach us ways of living, enduring, and surviving. They are closer to nature than most humans are, for we have removed ourselves from the natural order. Therefore, we turn to the creatures of nature so that through a connection with them, we can draw closer to their alignment with nature. This is the root of the relationship with a Witch's animal familiar.

One of the most important teachings in nature is to participate and live in common cause with nature. Trees are a good teacher in this regard. A tree remains present and in constant accord with what is happening in nature around it. The tree does not love one season and hate another; it is simply a tree in its season.

Teachings of the Tree

In the Old Ways of Witchcraft, the tree is a sacred symbol that represents many things. It is also a great teacher through the metaphors we see within the tree. In this lesson, we will look at what the tree has to reveal. Here, we will discover some of the reasons why our ancestors worshipped or venerated the tree.

As a symbol, the tree speaks of the three ancient realms that our ancestors called the Overworld, the Middleworld, and the Underworld. The Overworld is the mythological realm of the heaven worlds where the gods and goddesses dwell. As previously noted in the book, in prehistoric times, birds featured prominently in divine symbolism and representation. Therefore, the nesting of birds in trees, and the abundance of myths in which birds are messengers of the gods, strongly connect the branches of the tree with the divine realm.

The roots of a tree are hidden beneath the earth. To our ancestors, the earth seemed to generate life from below the surface. For not only did plants spring forth, but snakes, insects, and various animals also emerged from the earth. This naturally led to the idea of a realm that existed beneath the earth. In time, this place came to be called the *Underworld*. Over the centuries, this realm was believed to receive the departed souls of the living, just as it received the setting Sun and Moon. The mystery that surrounded such a realm led to many tales and legends. One such legend spoke of the tree, with its deep roots, penetrating the Mysteries of the Underworld. Here, the tree became a "knower" of that which lies hidden deep in the earth. Thus, it knew the secrets of birth, life, death, and renewal.

The trunk of the tree stood in the Middleworld where mortal beings dwelled. It was perceived as a bridge to the Overworld and a doorway to the Underworld. In fact, in many legends throughout Europe, the trunk of a tree contains a secret hidden doorway into the Otherworld. Rituals and ecstatic dances were often held around large trees in order to venerate the place where the three worlds came together. Two of the great legendary trees were the oak and the walnut, both of which have a long history of association with Witchcraft and magick. Other sacred trees include the ash and the hawthorn, which, along with the oak, appear in legend as a triple image. The oak and ash form the two pillars of the gateway and the hawthorn blocks the uninitiated from entering.

In ancient times, our ancestors believed that a god or goddess dwelled within one of the sacred trees. From this belief arose the practice of carrying a branch from the sacred tree as a staff. The staff signified a priest or priestess of the sacred grove, one who served as a messenger and emissary of the divine presence. By carrying the tree branch (and therefore, the spirit within it), the priests and priestesses brought the divine presence into the boroughs and villages to which they ventured. Through the priests and priestesses of the Old Ways, the blessings of the God and Goddess were carried to the people, crops, and herds.

Trees teach us many things. They speak of rootedness, position, and strength. The roots of a tree remind us that a great deal is unseen by our eyes. Here, we come to understand that we must look beneath the surface to understand what seems apparent on the surface. The tree also tells us that it is the roots that provide nourishment and that sustain life. In addition, they provide foundation and strength, keeping the tree sound against adverse conditions. While branches may break away and the trunk become damaged, if the roots survive, then so too shall the tree. In this, we understand that the roots must be fed if the tree is to produce fruit.

The branches teach us about age and youth and the importance of both. Fruit grows only on the old wood of the branch. Here, there is nourishment and seed for future generations. The new branches of a tree quickly produce flowers and attract the process of fertilization and renewal. Together, the old and new branches contribute equally to the future of the tree and the future of the grove.

The spirit of the tree speaks to us, serving others as we serve ourselves. While the tree stands and proclaims its place in the world, it also provides shade, shelter, home, and food for other beings. From its center, it teaches us the lessons of its spirit:

• Have a position with deep roots in your understanding of it and stand firm in your place within the world.

• Reach upward to touch lofty things and outward to extend yourself to the world.

• Provide shade for those who need rest and shelter for those who come to you.

• Bear fruit and be abundant.

• In the winters of your life, conserve your resources. In your springs, take advantage of the opportunities for new growth. In your summers, expand, thrive, and reach new heights. In your falls, release what no longer serves, make preparations, and await renewal.

• When all is said and done, leave behind some seeds.

Momentum of the Past

It is an ancient teaching that when something is repeatedly performed consistently over the course of centuries, it builds up a momentum of energy. This energy is a living current that flows from the past into the present. All that is required is to trigger the inner mechanism through a specific ritual, symbol, or gesture. Once the release is accomplished, then the flow of energy rushes like a wave into the present.

Effective techniques that have been preserved respond and operate in accord with the original intention and design. They are actually independent of the user's knowledge of them (although such knowledge is preferred when working with potent energies). This is why secrets do exist within Witchcraft, which minimizes the misuse of powerful forces by individuals who are unprepared to use them in an appropriate manner.

In the Mystery Tradition of Witchcraft, symbols connect to concepts, much like a light switch connects to a circuitry. Concepts connect to energy in the way that circuitry connects to electricity. The symbol must be activated in order for the current to flow and manifest the desired results. By analogy, it is ineffective to simply have a light switch if one does not know how to operate it. Possessing a symbol and not activating it ensures the same lack of results.

The pentagram, or pentacle, is a popular symbol in Witchcraft. It reflects an ancient Greek philosophy rooted in the teachings of Pythagoras and expanded upon by the philosopher Empedocles. The concept depicts the four elements of creation held in equilibrium by the activity of Spirit. This is the quintessence of magick. In ancient philosophy, the quintessence was the fifth and highest essence above the four elements of Earth, Air, Fire, and Water. The quintessence was believed to be the substance of the cosmos and was latent in all things.

The pentagram symbolism connects to the concept of creative energy that is stabilized and available for use. To activate the pentagram, it is necessary to establish the proper alignments. These alignments link the consciousness of the Witch to the inner mechanism behind the form. To accomplish this alignment requires a conscious acknowledgment of each component of the symbolism within the pentagram. This must be done within a formal setting.

To begin creating the alignments to the pentagram, the Witch sets it on their personal altar. Each of the points of a five-pointed star are identified and named out loud. Next, the star is traced from the top point (Spirit) with the index finger downward and then following the line in a clockwise manner (returning to the top point). As the pentagram is being traced, the Witch recites:

"With the ancient star, I trace this day
The elements bound as is the way.
Water, Earth, Air, and Fire
From Spirit birthed at mind's desire."

Next, repeat the above and add a visualization of color for each element. The occult assignments are:

Spirit: Purple
Earth: Yellow
Air: Blue
Fire: Red
Water: Green

The last step is to repeat the technique a third time in which the pentagram is anointed with a special oil. The oil serves to associate the concept with a scent (the scent should not be one you use in everyday life). This brings the sense of smell into play, which is a powerful tool of recollection. Everyone has the experience of a fragrance that reminds them of something or someone from the past each time the scent is noticed. This is a testimony to the power of scent in the occult context of evocation or invocation. When using an oil for the pentagram alignment, the choice of Master Oil is best. Most metaphysical shops carry this blend.

The advantage of creating an alignment with the pentagram is that the concepts become established in the psyche and are always operating in the mind. This allows the energy to readily flow through the wearer or possessor of the pentagram wherever and whenever magickal creativity is required or desired.

The concept of the "momentum of the past" can be activated to evoke or invoke many other connections. This is particularly powerful regarding ritual work. By bringing time-honored and time-proven correspondences into a ritual, the levels of power (and therefore, efficiency) increase substantially. This requires a careful study of traditional correspondences and associations.

The Triangle of Manifestation

In order for manifestation to take place, there are three things that must be simultaneously present. These are time, space, and energy. The time is the moment in which you perform a ritual or spell. The space is the place in which you perform, and the energy is what you bring to bear on your desire. If any one of these things is absent, then nothing will manifest.

In order to understand how manifestation occurs, we must first look at the occult formula. From a metaphysical perspective, every material object is the manifestation of a formed thought. The book you are now reading is one example. Before it became a physical book, it was an idea, something I first conceived of in my mind. If you are sitting in a chair as you read, the chair too was first visualized and imagined before it ever became a material object. In effect, you are holding and sitting upon the very fabric of magick.

When viewed as the core mechanism, there are three realms that form a magickal triangle of manifestation. These are the Astral, Elemental, and Physical Realms. Each of these plays an important role in the manifestation of desires. In the context of magick, these three realms are interdependent.

The Astral Dimension is a realm where thoughts become things (the process is discussed in Chapter Five). It is here that concepts blend with visual images. These visual images originate in the Physical Dimension whenever we visualize or imagine. The images we raise are drawn into the Elemental Dimension because they are creative energies. Therefore, a magnetic attraction exists between the nature of the image and the nature of the element (or elements) to which it is suited as an energy form.

This magnetic attraction occurs due to an occult principle known as "like attracts like." Essentially, this means that things of a like nature are drawn to one another. On a mundane level, this principle is why groups, clubs, gangs, and social cliques form. It is the magnetism of the concept or image that creates an attraction and holds a group together.

In Chapter Five, we envisioned the elemental forces as a river back and forth between the Material and Astral Dimensions. This is because the elemental substances share a likeness to both astral and physical substances. Therefore, an attraction to both planes exists, which keeps the elemental forces in a revolving movement. The elemental nature of binding or adhering shares an affinity with matter. The elemental nature of creativity and etheric substance shares an affinity with the astral.

Manifestation occurs when thought-forms generated from the Material Realm are of sufficient energy to cause an attraction to an elemental nature. This draws the thought-form into the Elemental Realm. Here, the thought-form is applied by the merging of elemental energy, which causes an attraction from the Astral Realm. This arises from the creative energy of the elemental influence upon the thought-form, which stimulates the astral substance to envelop and replicate the thought-form.

Once enveloped, the astral substance increases the density of the thought-form, which causes the Elemental Dimension to react to the change in creative form. The elements then draw the astral form back into the Elemental Dimension. This is followed by an attraction from the Physical Realm arising from the density of energy, which causes the elementally charged astral form to be drawn into materialization.

Deity Forms

Earlier in this chapter, it was noted that the Source of All Things became personified into a Goddess and a God. These first two manifestations that were generated from The Great Unmanifest are what we call *archetypes*. In this case, we call them the Great Mother and Great Father. From the archetypes themselves are generated various goddesses and gods that have specific and more finite functions such as the Moon Goddess and Sun God. Here, we see the "as above, so below" principle at work in the Divine realms.

The formula of the Triangle of Manifestation and the Physical, Elemental, and Astral Dimensions apply to the creation of divine images. Through this process, the images given to goddesses and gods by humankind are empowered by elemental force and given form within the Astral Dimension. However, something happens in this case that does not happen in the standard process.

The divine images appearing in the astral substance contain a higher vibration than simple thought-forms. This is because the elemental forces have amplified the energy of worship or veneration attached to the thought-forms. These emotionally charged thought-forms carry not only a different vibration but also the energy of a different intent. They are not the thought-forms of personal desire but of the awareness of something greater than the self.

The higher nature of the energy causes an attraction from the higher planes beyond the Elemental and Physical. The Mental Plane is attracted to the expansive concept not rooted in self. This draws the astral form of a Goddess or god into the Mental Realm where sentience awakens. The Spiritual Plane is attracted by the stirrings of pure sentient energy and draws it upward. Here, the deity form becomes charged with spiritual essence.

The Divine Plane is attracted to the spiritual energy blended with consciousness. Within this, there is also the recognition of the intent of the vessel as well as the core energy charge of worship and veneration. Here, the Archetypes imbue the entity with divine consciousness, passing into it something of their own essence. At this point, a specific goddess or god emerges. It is a blend of human design with divine consciousness and power. In occult terminology, these are called *egregores*.

An egregore is greater than the sum of its parts and should not be mistaken as anything other than a divine being. They are as real and individual as you are, even though you are comprised of materials supplied by your genetic parents. Your blending of genetic material from your parents did not create your soul; it only contributed to your form. But your nature and your soul are different from those who served in the process from which you were created. In this same way, the nature and divine essence of the egregore are different from the source of its origin.

In the book *Inner Traditions of Magic* (1970), renowned occultist William Gray refers to egregores as "telesmics." Gray explains that the ancient Greeks used the term *telos* to indicate fulfillment or the end product of something. Another form of this word is *teleo*, which refers to initiation into the Mysteries. By joining the meanings, it becomes clear that telesmic images are associated with the result of a process for the initiates of a Mystery Tradition.

The key to understanding this can be discovered in the fact that a relationship exists between the soul and its creators. Creating something establishes a relationship with what is created. Therefore, a relationship exists between our divine origin and ourselves. The same is true between an egregore, the humans that generated the image, and the divine source that made it a goddess or god. For, as we noted in the principle of "as above, so below," the divine, the universe, and humankind are images of the pattern containing the same principle. One thing is a reflection of the other.

The Source of All Things communicates with us and we try and communicate with it. The tools that we use are images, concepts, and religious beliefs. One tool it uses is the process or inner mechanism within nature. The other tool is the "agreement of consciousness" through which interfacing is possible. The egregore is a key agreement of consciousness within the Mystery Tradition of Witchcraft.

It is important to understand that the egregore form is created in accord with our own creation since we possess the pattern and principle of the divine within us. Therefore, the ancient Mystery Traditions provided myths for goddesses and gods. In these, they have parents, are born, receive a name, grow, and have adventures. They also come to be proficient in a task or purpose, which becomes their specialty. Some examples are a god of war, a goddess of love, and so forth. Through their forms, we connect with the concept, and through the concept, we connect with the energy. The energy differs in its polarity field, which we call either *feminine* or *masculine*.

Feminine and Masculine Energy

The occult concept of feminine and masculine energy is not gender specific, nor is it meant to indicate the nature of a man or woman. The teaching is concerned with the nature of these energies and how they work. Both are necessary and functional principles that help us better understand our deities and ourselves.

Essentially, feminine energy is expansive and conceptual. It embraces concepts and holistic views, which emphasize the importance of the whole instead of the parts that comprise it. Masculine energy is focal and analytical, emphasizing the importance of the parts that comprise the whole. Men and women possess both types of energy, but in most cases, one polarity is more pronounced than the other.

If we look at this in terms of the divine mind, then we can begin to better understand the applications of polarity. Let's look at a goddess of love as an example of our concepts. The pure feminine expression of this would be the totality of love, being there for everyone but not directed toward anything specific. This makes it difficult, if not impossible, to be received or tapped.

The pure masculine expression would be directed towards individuals, being a readily available stream of energy but not one that carries the conceptual energy of love. This makes it difficult to manifest what the whole contains. However, when the masculine and feminine polarities work together, concepts arise in the feminine and are delivered by the masculine. This is why mated pairs of deities appear in the Mystery Tradition of Witchcraft.

From an occult perspective, feminine energy is receptive, receiving concepts and retaining them. Masculine energy is active, channeling and directing specific elements pertaining to the concepts of which they are a part. As with electricity, feminine and masculine energies have a polarity charge. Feminine energy is a negative charge and masculine energy is a positive charge. Together, they allow energy to flow and manifest a desired result.

As an energy, the feminine polarity is magnetic and the masculine polarity is electric. The former draws and the latter transmits. We have within us a flowing current of feminine and masculine energies. In Eastern mysticism, they are frequently called the *Ida* and *Pingala* currents. In Witchcraft, they are known as the *Goddess* and *God* currents.

In a magickal and spiritual sense, the Goddess and God currents create receiving and transmitting terminals. These are the hands, and the right is transmitting, while the left is receptive. In spiritual practice, the left polarity receives what is extended to the person. Therefore, when an object is handed to an initiate, it is received with the left hand.

The right polarity transmits outward, and therefore, an initiate uses the right hand to give to another person. When both hands of an individual join together (to receive or give), this is a sign of equilibrium. In a spiritual sense, it makes the statement, "I share the blessings with you." In this sense, the energy is not divided into separate polarities but blends as one. Here, both people give and receive in harmony.

In magickal practice, you will find that by passing the palm over an object, you can feel its energy. The passing of the right hand sends energy into an object. Placing both hands over an object stabilizes energy. This use of hands is beneficial in healing work as well.

In the art of scrying, the left hand draws images into clarity and the right hand focuses the imagery. This is performed with circular passes of the hand in a clockwise manner over the bowl or crystal sphere. Holding both palms steady over the bowl and crystal stabilizes the image, which helps to lengthen the time the image remains visible.

Widdershins and Deosil

The nature, flow, and behavior of energy is an important part of magick and ritual within Witchcraft. Energy is typically divided into waxing and waning patterns or influences. Our ancestors knew this as *deosil* or *widdershins*. Deosil means to move with the direction of the Sun and widdershins is to move against it. Naturally, this is a metaphor that speaks to the nature of energy patterns.

Deosil energy is used to establish ritual and magick circles in which to perform various rites. This type of force raises, draws, and focuses energy. Its waxing nature creates an atmosphere that is conducive to manifestation. Deosil energy also keeps a current established and flowing.

Widdershins energy is a waning force. It disperses, releases, and dissolves. Its waning properties create an atmosphere that releases bound energy, allowing the ritual setting to return to its natural equilibrium. This is important because, without this equilibrium, the waxing energy remains active in the setting and is therefore out of balance with nature. The natural order within nature is the back-and-forth exchange of waxing and waning energies.

The waxing and waning exchange within nature cleans and purifies the earth. Decay becomes absorbed and transformed, and the life essence of the soil is renewed. If this does not take place, then contamination will occur and disease will prevail. However, the waning forces remove the buildup of contamination, whether magickal or material. The waxing forces raise new and pure substances (again, magickal or physical).

In regards to casting a circle, deosil energy raises new, untainted magickal properties. As a ritual proceeds, the circle absorbs both positive and negative energy. This comes from the auras of the ritual participants which contain the energy pattern of their psyche. Dissolving the ritual circle widdershins then removes and cleans the astral debris and any lingering etheric contamination.

The exchange of deosil and widdershins forces ensures that magickal and etheric residue does not remain to contaminate future rites and the casting of new circles. It also severs the ritual participants from the mixed residual energy that exists following any rite. This is important because if residual energy remains, the participants will carry it with them.

Once residual energy is absorbed into the aura, it will create etheric pressure in the psyche, which frequently exacerbates psychological and emotional problems. The participants will then bring that to the next ritual, where their auras will introduce this energy to the circle (and so the pattern continues and builds momentum).

The Nature of Magickal Links

Previously, we encountered the concept of the divine spark that was passed from the creators to each thing that was created. In this concept, we find that everything is connected to everything else through the divine essence shared by all things. We can liken this to the strands of a spider web, which all connect to the center where the spider rests. Here, the spider is aware of any disturbance of any strand.

From an occult perspective, everything has a connective thread of energy that ultimately connects it to the Source of All Things. When we consider the axiom of "as above, so below," we discover that the cells of our bodies share the same relationship that we do with the fabric of the cosmos, and therefore, with the Source. Each cell is separate and yet intimately joined and interdependent upon the wholeness of the body. The state of the body affects its cells and the state of the cells affects the body.

Each cell is linked to the whole because it shares the same energy pattern. Through this connection, there is awareness and communication. How does our brain make our hands move? What mobilizes white blood cells to attack invading viruses or bacteria? Where and how is the imprint of the "remembered enemy" retained so that the body can later reproduce the specific antibodies needed to combat the return of the same invading organisms?

From a metaphysical perspective, communication continues to exist between the body and its parts, even when the direct physical connection is severed. The occult connection remains and functions on an astral level until that connection is destroyed in some fashion. This concept is the root of the belief that such things as a lock of hair or fingernail clippings can be used to magickally influence the person from which they came.

In a more expansive view, things of a similar nature have a more immediate or closer tie than connections that are further removed. This is why something like a green candle is believed to be able to aid the attraction of money (the color of our paper money being green). This conforms to the principle of "like attracts like." Here, the mind establishes the connection and completes the circuit between symbol and concept, concept and energy. This draws the energy to the source of the desire (the spellcaster) and carries with it the concept. The concept, in turn, attracts the symbol, which then attracts that which it represents.

The principle of the relationship between symbol, concept, and energy provides a vast supply of occult correspondences. These correspondences include color, scent, sound, shape, image, and affinity (among many other things). All of the occult correspondences are designed as catalysts to draw whatever is desired or required.

Once a symbol becomes an "agreement of consciousness" between the concept and the thing it represents, then the memory of it is stored in the so-called Akashic Records. This is an occult zone corresponding to the magnetic field surrounding the Earth.

If a memory is awakened, then the momentum of its connection arises. This flow of energy carries with it the connection to the concept. In the Mystery Tradition of Witchcraft, it is believed that such memories can be stored within the soul and carried from lifetime to lifetime. Here resides everything we knew and experienced when we were our own ancestors.

The Genetic Memory Factor

From an occult perspective, our ancestors passed on to us more than just our physical traits. We also inherit the essence of their experience, which helps to explain any natural talents we appear to be born with or predisposed toward. This is not to discount the soul's memory of the lives it has lived. The genetic factor is simply part of the retaining and transmitting process.

Reincarnation is a blending of the memories the soul has retained from previous experiences, with the imprints of experience carried in our DNA. The soul chooses the next physical body by accepting birth through a specific set of parents. This may or may not be an ancestral lineage (nationality) that the soul has already experienced. Therefore, it has access to genetic or ancestral memory with which it may never have had a previous association. This is the equivalent of a person reading another person's biography and obtaining information that can then be applied to the course of one's own life.

Some people wonder why we don't readily remember our past life experiences. The reason is that we are fully focused on our current life, and in effect, have surrendered to the stimulation of the present incarnation. Therefore, it's not that we don't remember past lives; it's that we're too busy to take the time to search for the memory. On a mundane level, the longer we live, the harder it is to readily recall memories from events that occurred decades ago. But with time, patience, focus, and a few linking reminders, we can draw back the recollection. So too is it with past life memories. Do you remember being one year old? The fact that you don't remember doesn't mean you never had the experience.

In the discussion of the nature of magickal links, we noted that a connection exists between the part and the whole. This connection continues even when the two are no longer directly linked together. Here, we may also apply the occult principle to the ancestor and the descendant.

The living genetic material that is passed by parents into the creation of a fetus contains energy. This energy is the same fabric of the cosmos from which all things are formed. In other words, it is the microcosmic pattern of the source of life itself. Through the binding of this energy to a fertilized egg, life and soul are joined to a material substance. This substance is the developing fetus that forms into a new being.

The energy that binds things together is the same energy that is represented by the upper point of the pentagram. It is the fifth element of Spirit, the divine activity. Just as this binds the four elements in order to establish equilibrium, it also keeps order down to the very level of subatomic particles and beyond. But what is of value to ancestral memory is that it binds our DNA and maintains its integrity and equilibrium. The essential memories, or the imprints of experience, are contained within the microcosmic fifth element of our DNA structure.

In the occult order of the Planes of Existence, the Mental Plane borders the Astral Plane. The Astral Plane is an etheric substance, while the Mental Plane is etheric energy. The substance contains thought (as in thought-forms) but is not thought itself. In other words, the body contains the mind but is not the mind itself. Therefore, it is the mentality that accesses and interprets what is recorded within energy patterns.

It is a longstanding tradition in Witchcraft to achieve altered states of consciousness for ritual and magickal purposes. This can be used for a variety of purposes, including the perception of other realms of existence. It is for this reason that rituals in the Mystery Tradition are designed to induce an altered state of consciousness within its practitioners.

Interfacing Through Ritual

Within the Material Realm, communication occurs largely through sound. Birds, mammals, insects, humans, and a host of other creatures all use sound to communicate in some manner. Sound causes vibration, and vibration stimulates the physical receptors of living beings which allows them to hear.

In the Elemental, Astral, and higher realms of existence, communication occurs through imagery. Images, and the thoughts and concepts connected to them by energy, serve the same purpose as sound in the Material Realm. This allows a representation of communication through symbols.

Rituals are constructed around symbols, gestures, and interpretive dance. These serve to convey the intent or purpose of the ritual to non-physical beings in non-material realms. In the Material Realm, the evocations, chants, ritual scripts, and dialogue all contribute to creating states of altered consciousness. This is also true of the sights, scents, and emotional stirrings.

Once an altered state of consciousness is established, then the sounds, sights, scents, and emotional energies overwhelm the conscious mind. Once the conscious mind is in a trance, then the subconscious mind assumes dominance. The subconscious, or dream mind, communicates well through imagery and symbolism. This altered state of consciousness then aligns with the Otherworld vibration in which imagery is communication. Here, we see the occult axiom of "like attracts like."

In the Mystery Tradition of Witchcraft, it is said that the ritual circle is the "World between the Worlds." This means that it exists in a space that is neither fully in the Physical Realm nor a non-physical realm. It is, in effect, within a corridor between two planes of existence. Here, the nature of both realms exists, which creates an environment that both physical and non-physical beings can occupy for moderate periods of time.

In the World between the Worlds, vibration becomes image and image becomes vibration. This exchange allows both physical and non-physical beings to communicate an inner level of understanding. Spirits interpret the images, signs, and gestures much like deaf people use sign language. The ritual participants interpret the responding vibrations through intuitive and psychic senses. The latter form of communication is sometimes called "hearing the voice of the wind."

It was an ancient belief that spirits wrapped themselves in the air, which made them invisible. Ancient philosophy also held that spirits resided in the sublunar atmosphere, a realm associated with Air in occultism. Therefore, hearing the voice of the wind is a reference to communicating with spirits.

As a relationship develops over time, a mutual understanding occurs, and in a sense, beings of the non-physical and Physical Realms learn each other's language. At this stage, beings of the other worlds will often use images through which to communicate with physical beings. This frequently begins in dreams but can extend to waking visions as well. Here, the Witch receives and interprets astral images they are shown.

Beings of the other worlds will often use images in order to interface with material beings. To achieve this, the entity merges consciousness with the Witch. Through this, the entity accesses mental images stored in the psyche that are attached to the emotions. Once it finds an image known to the Witch, the entity will focus on manifesting the apparition. The emotional reaction of the Witch to the apparition is an important component of manifestation. This is because the resulting energy is needed in order to maintain appearance within the Material Realm once the Witch perceives the manifestation.

The more an image evokes an emotional response, the greater the intensity and longevity of the manifested vision. This is the source of such apparitions that appear even in other religions, a common example being the appearance of the Virgin Mary figure associated with Christianity. Non-physical entities will often use familiar and comforting images through which to communicate. It is not uncommon at death for spirits to assume the appearance of departed loved ones in order to make the crossing from life less stressful.

Rituals that involve guided imagery meditations are powerful opportunities for interfacing with entities in other realms. Among the most effective structures is one that includes a quest to retrieve something or to encounter a being. This immerses the Witch in imagery and intent, allowing beings of the other realm to use the receptive state of consciousness for direct interfacing in the Astral Realm (or whichever realm has been reached).

Effective guided meditation journeys include a series of stages that are effective to incorporate. The exercise should begin with a change within the Witch's perception of being in the Material Realm. Typically, the meditation supplies the notion that the body feels light and begins to rise up and away from the setting.

The next stage is to introduce movement and direction, and here, the Witch imagines that they are sailing through the sky. Incorporating the image of a broom is effective because it contains a "momentum of the past" of its own. In occult correspondences, the four directions each have a mythological association. North is the realm of the Overworld deities. East is the realm of beings of light. In the South reside the astral beings of legend. Through the West are the ancestral beings and the Faery Realm.

Once the journey begins, there are three things to include that will assist the Witch in accessing the Otherworld. One is the inclusion of a tree or forest, as this links the Witch to the three realms of Hecate: Overworld, Middleworld, and Underworld. The second feature is a pond or a lake, which represents the water that flows to and from the Otherworld or Underworld. The last inclusion is an access point, such as a cave, portal, tunnel, or doorway.

The guided meditation then guides the Witch downward from the sky, introducing the idea of feeling heavier. Next, the Witch is guided through the forest or past the tree, taking note of its appearance. This helps establish an alignment. The Witch is then directed through the entry point or passage.

What exists on the other side of the doorway can be designed according to the cultural tradition of the Witch. It can be a mystical realm or a simple grotto. Somewhere in this setting, the Witch is directed to a beautiful pond or lake. Here, the Witch encounters the object of the quest. Some activity in this setting should be included, and this can form around a tale or legend.

Once the quest of the guided meditated has been completed, the Witch is directed back in reverse order. Each key must be noted on the return journey, and this includes the water, the entryway, the tree, and finally, the flight back home. With continued journeys, the Witch can receive Inner Planes teachings that will greatly enhance their spiritual and magickal path.

Concerning Magick

The art of magick is essentially one of attracting or raising energy, condensing it, impregnating the energy with a formed thought, and directing it off to achieve the desired goal. It is an occult teaching that a force resides in all things, and the ancients knew this as a presence called *numen*. The "energy feel" of any object is said to be the vibration of its numen vitality. This essence possesses a type of consciousness that is closer to a presence than it is to something's self-awareness.

The Witch's experience in their Craft, along with their personal alignment to nature, allows them to call upon the raw energy of any numen force. This force may reside within a crystal, stone, or any inanimate object. Once tapped, the numen energy can enhance the ritual or magickal work of the Witch.

From an occult perspective, anything that shares the same nature or essence forms like links in a chain. Through one thing, the Witch can influence another. This principle is at work in the poppet or doll image commonly associated with spellcasting. Here, the mind conveys intent through thought and desire, thereby generating the power to contact distance connections through the magickal links.

The energy of magick is effectively controlled and directed through the use of ritual. Ritual attracts power and certain channels of force are formed into links to the goal or target of the rite. As noted earlier, the use of signs, symbols, and gestures helps to empower the process.

The Witch most commonly draws power down from the Moon and nature. Spells, rituals, and works of magick are always timed and performed in harmony with the phases of the Moon and in accordance with the seasons of nature. A Witch's magick is as subtle and active on hidden levels as is the light of the Moon. The powers that are obtained through the knowledge and experience of the Witch's arts are neither good nor evil. It is how a Witch uses such magick that can be viewed as good or evil.

The subconscious mind is directly linked to the Astral Realm through dream gates. A dream gate is an awareness of being in a dream, and the Witch takes conscious control. The conscious mind is directly linked to the physical world and is concerned with the affairs of the material body. It is through the dream mind that the astral levels are easily contacted. There in the astral substance, magickal influences and forms are created. These, in turn, influence the physical world.

It is the purpose and design of symbols to speak to the dreaming mind and to plant the magickal seeds that will manifest in the Material Realm. It is the purpose of rituals (and spells) to establish these patterns of power and initiate the process. Magickal and ritual correspondences are incorporated to take advantage of the numen presence that resides within tools, candles, incense, jewelry, and other objects.

Now that we have explored many of the basic metaphysical concepts, we must now turn to the application of occult principles in the art of Witchcraft. Therefore, let us move to the next chapter where we shall encounter the Ways of the Witch.

CHAPTER NINE

Ways of the Witch

In the course of this book, we have looked at the Mystery Tradition of Witchcraft. We noted the origins rooted in the prehistoric religion and primitive beliefs associated with the natural world. It was in this world that the type of individual arose who later came to be called the Witch. Such individuals were perceived to possess special abilities to communicate with nature and the Otherworld. Magickal powers were also ascribed to the Witch.

In the earliest etymology of words used to indicate a Witch in Western literature, we noted the concepts of the herbalist (*pharmakis*) and seer (*saga*). Here, we found the original concepts of a Witch as something rooted in the plant kingdom and the ability to see into other realms of existence (particularly the spirit world).

Over the course of history, various myths and legends were created around religious ideas and primitive perceptions. These ideas and perceptions are related to both the Physical Realm and the non-physical realm of existence. In these myths and legends, we find the tales of many goddesses, gods, and spirit beings.

In our previous encounter with Medea, the first appearance of a Witch as a priestess is discovered. Here, we also discovered Hecate as the Witches' goddess. Hecate, as we noted, was originally a goddess from a prehistoric era referred to as the Age of the Titans. Hecate appears in Hesiod's ancient tale (*Theogony*) as having reigned over the three realms that comprised the known cosmos.

It is not surprising to find that Hecate, as a prehistoric Goddess, is associated with symbols, concepts, and animals that feature prominently in Paleolithic and Neolithic culture. These include the Moon, hounds, snakes, toads, and owls. It is noteworthy that we continue to find these particulars associated with Witches (in an unbroken chain) from ancient times, to the period of the Inquisition, and on into the modern era.

One interesting feature in Witch trial transcripts is the mention of inheritance. In the Chelmsford trial (1582) of Elizabeth Frauncis, the accused stated that she inherited her familiar (a cat) from her grandmother. In the Chelmsford trials of 1556, the accused stated that familiars are passed down from Witch to Witch. In the trial of Margerie Sammons at St. Osyht (1582), Margerie claimed that she had inherited her familiar. Francesco Guazzo, an Italian Witch Hunter, wrote in his *Compendium Maleficarum* (1608) that children inherit Witchcraft from their parents.

The traditions of folklore, folk magick, and ancient beliefs enrich the totality of modern Witchcraft. The customs and lore of a people speak to the heart and soul. The heart and soul look to the spiritual experience. In modern Witchcraft, some people miss this understanding and tend to view the Craft through a strictly historical filter. This is like the poet being so concerned with proper form that the spirit of the poem becomes buried beneath the formal verse.

Tradition as Preservation of Interface Portals

The English word *tradition* is ultimately derived from the Latin *tradere*, which means "to hand on or entrust." This implies that whatever is handed on or entrusted to another person has value. If this were not so, then it would dishonor both the giver and the receiver. Therefore, the question raised is, what value does tradition have in the Mystery Religion of Witchcraft?

The value resides in the fact that the Mystery Tradition preserves the alignments as well as the methods of achieving altered states of consciousness. It also provides the means through which interfacing with non-material beings and realities. Through such requisites, the Witch can expand their consciousness and advance their understanding of the divine process.

The spiritual evolution of the soul is part of the Mystery Quest. Such knowledge and realization prepare the soul not only for a less stressful death experience but also for the realm to which it passes. In a mundane example, if a person knew they had to move to Japan, wouldn't it make sense to prepare by learning about the culture, lifestyle, and language?

Tradition also provides a sound, practical, and functional structure to guide the initiate in ways that have passed the test of time. By studying a tradition, a person can learn relatively quickly what took generations to test, perfect, and record. This minimizes the time a person may waste with studies that ultimately have no practical benefit. Tradition can steer an initiate away from blind alleys, dead-end roads, and trails that go only in pointless circles.

Long ago, our ancestors created a system of traditional correspondences. These assign various magickal properties, planetary influences, and areas of effectiveness to such things as plants, minerals, and animals. These represent the three kingdoms of alignment for the Witch. Here, we see the classic Witch with an herbal potion, a magickal stone, and a familiar spirit. Each of these fields requires its own in-depth study.

Earlier in the book, we came upon the concept of the momentum of the past. It's useful to note that traditional time-proven techniques behave much like a row of dominos. All that is required is to trip the first one and the rest is automatic. This is similar to the way tradition works, as it supplies the dominos, the way to line them up, and how to trip the first in a connective pattern. What happens then is the process: the occult principle is released and the momentum moves along the chosen path.

The Altar

The Witches' altar is the center and focal point of the microcosmic alignment to the divine process. In the Mystery Tradition, the altar is placed directly center within a ritual or magickal circle. In this way, the elemental forces of the cardinal points intersect at the center of the altar.

Whatever is placed on the center of the altar becomes the point of alignment to the Elemental Realm. It also establishes a portal or gateway between the worlds and the inner planes. In some traditions, a candle or oil lamp is set in the center spot. Fire, as the earliest of divine images, establishes the presence of the fifth element upon the altar. Placing the pentacle beneath the candle or lamp directly establishes an open connection between the material dimension and the non-material dimension. It is a ritual sign indicating "as above, so below."

From this point on, everything performed in the ritual (each vibration and emanation of energy) will be drawn into the center of the altar. From here, it will flow into the elemental portals. Once amplified by the elements, the ritual intent will be drawn into the astral substance, where it will take on a representation in form. This process was examined in Chapter Eight.

The symbolism incorporated into the appearance of the altar is important. In part, it will evoke and invoke certain alignments associated with the symbolism. Therefore, it is important to decorate the altar accordingly. The alignments that you create will affect your ritual and your magick (for better or for worse).

In the Mystery Tradition of Witchcraft, a black altar cloth is laid across the surface. This represents the procreative darkness from which all things issue forth. In the center of the altar is a candle or oil lamp to represent the Great Unmanifest. Two altar candles representing the Goddess and God are set away from the center, and with the middle object, the placement creates a triangle (pointed towards the practitioner). These candles represent the first manifestations that arise from the Source of All Things. The color of the Goddess candle is red and the God candle is black. The meaning of these colors will become evident as we proceed.

Next to the altar candles are placed an image of the Goddess and one of the God. These figures serve as interface points, the space in which an image links to a concept, and a concept to an energy. We will expand upon this later in the chapter.

Between the God and Goddess images is placed a representation of a human skull. This symbolizes the knowledge and wisdom of our ancestors who preserved and passed on the Mysteries. A black candle is set on the head of the skull and is lit for all rituals performed from the autumn equinox until the spring equinox. A red candle is used from the spring equinox until the autumn equinox. Black symbolizes the ancestral knowledge retained within the source, the realm of the Otherworld. Red symbolizes the ancestral knowledge that flows from the Otherworld to the world of mortals.

During the course of the year, the color of the skull's candle will match either the Goddess or God candle. Black represents the secret shadow realm, the deep dark forest, and the mystical journey that leads to the Otherworld. The God is the escort of the dead who aids in transition. Cernunnos is one example of this aspect of the God.

Red represents life's blood, the inner pulse that sustains and empowers. Regarding the Goddess, it runs through the earth beneath the soil, for she is the giver of life. Red symbolizes the place of life and renewal, which is reflected in the menstrual blood cycle. In the context of the skull figure, red symbolizes the ancient knowledge flowing into the world of the living from the source of its wellspring.

In front of the skull, a small cauldron is placed. This represents the Moon Gate, which is the womb of the Goddess. Through the Goddess, all things are birthed from the Otherworld and return to her again. Therefore, the cauldron leads to and from ancestral knowledge. Because of this, it contains the magickal essence of transformation.

The remaining tools of the Craft are now placed on the altar in association with their quarter element. The wand is set in the East portion of the altar. The athame occupies the Southern section, and the chalice is set in the West area. The pentacle has been previously set in the center beneath the candle or lamp. The altar itself is oriented to the East, meaning that the practitioner is facing East as they view the altar.

The Pentacle, Wand, Dagger, and Chalice

In Witchcraft, we find the traditional tools of Western occultism, which are the pentacle, wand, dagger, and chalice. Each of these represents an elemental force and a spiritual nature. Alignment with the symbolism of each tool establishes a deep connection and roots the concept in both the conscious and subconscious mind.

This alignment can be performed through an exercise using the image of each tool. The actual tool can be used or one can utilize tarot cards by selecting the aces from the four suits of the Minor Arcana. In the choice of cards, it is best to use a deck that has clear images of the tools instead of something stylized.

Place the image of the tool on the altar so that it is clearly visible. If using a card, you can prop it up against something. Choose a comfortable position and focus your attention on the image, beginning with the pentacle. Each tool image should stand alone, and you can work with one after the other.

You will also need to have the element present, which you will use with each associated tool. Therefore, you will need a rock, incense smoke, a candle and match, and a small bowl of water. Place these near the altar so you can obtain them without having to leave the area. All that now remains is to perform the following steps.

1. When you are ready, gaze upon the pentacle image and acknowledge its association with the element of Earth. Say something like: *"Here is the pentacle, which represents the element of Earth."*

   Pick up the rock, squeeze it in your hand, and then feel the texture as you hold the rock between both palms. Next, make the alignment to the element, saying: *"Earth is form, strength, foundation, endurance, and fortification."*

   Look back at the pentacle and join the concepts together saying: *"Here is the pentacle, which represents the element of Earth. Earth is form, strength, foundation, endurance, and fortification."*

2. Place the tool or image of the wand on the altar. Gaze upon the wand image and acknowledge its association with the element of Air. Say something like: *"Here is the wand, which represents the element of Air."*

   Place the incense on the altar and light it. Wait until the smoke is clearly billowing before proceeding. When you are ready, lightly blow into the smoke so that it disperses. As you watch the smoke, make the alignment to the element, saying: *"Air is movement, flow, expansion, and liberation."*

Look back at the wand and join the concepts together saying: *"Here is the wand, which represents the element of Air. Air is movement, direction, expansion, and liberation."*

Remove the incense from the altar (or wait until there is no more smoke).

3. Place the tool or image of the dagger on the altar. Gaze upon the dagger image (sword, if using the tarot) and acknowledge its association with the element of Fire. Say something like: *"Here is the athame, which represents the element of Fire."*

Place the candle on the altar and light it with a match. When you are ready, pass the palm of your left hand over the candle flame so that you can feel its heat. Be careful not to have your hand close enough to the flame to get burned, and do not pass your palm too slowly over the flame (for the same reason).

As you feel the flame, make the alignment to the element, saying: *"Fire is vitality, passion, force, and transformation."*

Look back at the dagger and join the concepts together saying: *"Here is the athame, which represents the element of Fire. Fire is vitality, passion, force, and transformation."*

Remove the dagger or image from the altar.

4. Place the tool or image of the chalice on the altar. Gaze upon the chalice image and acknowledge its association with the element of Water. Say something like: *"Here is the chalice, which represents the element of Water."*

Place the bowl (half-filled with water) on the altar. When you are ready, dip your left hand (palm up) into the water. Cup your hand and lift it slowly out of the water. Allow the water to trickle through your fingers and back into the bowl. Repeat this as you listen to the sound of the water and make the alignment to the element, saying: *"Water is flow, adaptation, purification, and magnetism."*

Look at the chalice image or tool and join the concepts together saying:

"Here is the chalice, which represents the element of Water. Water is flow, adaptation, purification, and magnetism."

Remove the chalice image from the altar. Now it is time to associate a sound with each image or tool and its corresponding element. As noted in Chapter Eight, sound is vibration, which carries communication to the other realms. Therefore, we will take each tool image and link it to a vowel sound. The sounds are given in long trailing and tapering tones, repeated three times as follows:

Pentacle/Earth: *Aaaaa...Aaaaa ...Aaaaa*
Wand/Air: *Iiiii...Iiiii...Iiiii*
Athame/Fire: *Eeeee...Eeeee...Eeeee*
Chalice/Water: *Ooooo...Ooooo...Ooooo*

At a later time, the sounds can be blended into a chant when you desire to call forth the four elements for use in a spell or work of magick. The chant is called the Quintessence and consists of two parts. The first part is:

IIIEEEAAAOOO (the tempo is a slow and trailing "one-two-THREE-four" beat. There is an emphasis on the third beat, and the chant is repeated three times).

Once the elements are summoned, the second half of the chant is used to bring them together in equilibrium. To accomplish this, the vowel sound "U" is added:

Uuuuu...Uuuuu...Uuuuu (This is chanted as you trace a pentagram in the air with the index finger of your dominant hand).

This represents the binding of the four elements through the presence and activity of Spirit.

Statues as Interface Portals

In the Mystery Tradition of Witchcraft, a statue serves as the image of the divine concept it represents. The concept is venerated for its connection to the divine essence that resides within the Source. Some people mistake the attention given to statues as a form of idol worship.

In Chapter Eight, we explored the idea that a form connects to a concept that, in turn, connects to the energy behind it. This concept represents the circuitry that serves to establish communication between the physical and non-physical realms. Therefore, the statue becomes the meeting or interface portal wherein human and divine consciousnesses send and receive communication.

In the ancient Mystery Schools, it was the custom to design statues to reflect the symbolism of the concept that the deity reflected. These included animals, tools, weapons, musical instruments, and other items intended to help the initiate learn about the deity concept. Initiates were taught about each symbol and what it represented. Then they were taught about how each applied to the deity who bore the symbols. Next, the overall concept was explained, and the memory chain was thereby passed to the initiate.

The God of the Old Religion, as a Mystery figure, is depicted as a muscular, bearded man in his prime with rough-cut hair to his shoulders. Stag antlers are sported on his head, and he wears a wreath of grape leaves and grapes across his brow.

Across his left shoulder is a strap with a straw basket slung at waist height. It is filled with acorns, nuts, and berries from the forest. A few sheaves of wheat jet out from the collected goods. In his left hand, he carries a hand sickle of a golden hue. Slung over his right shoulder is a wolf pelt, the head and legs of the wolf draped down over the God's right breast.

The God is nude, except for these items and the animal fur boots he wears, which top beneath his knees. His genitals are large and fully displayed, signs of his generative power in nature. The hand of the God rests gently on the head of a stag by his side. The body of the stag is positioned sideways behind the God, with the head of the stag turned to face the viewer. The posture of the God is upright and powerful.

The images that appear with the God figure represent the Mystery Teachings that contain his overall mythos. His antlers represent his primal power as Lord of the Woods. The grapevine wreath around his head reveals that his consciousness extends from the wild into the cultivated. It is also a crown, the sign of kingship. In this case, he is the Divine King, the sacrificial Slain God-to-be.

The basket slung over the left shoulder of the God is a harvest basket. It is a sign of his birth and his death, as noted in Chapter Seven. The acorns, nuts, and berries represent the harvest of the forest, preserving the original figure of the God known to the hunter-gatherer tribes.

The sheaves of wheat represent his transplantation into the cultivated fields of the agrarian culture. The sickle in the left hand of the God signifies his death as the Harvest Lord. The blade is crescent-shaped to represent that his life is drawn back to the Goddess. All the harvest symbols are found on the left side of the God, which indicates a feminine and lunar connection to the theme.

On the right side of the God is found the wolf pelt and the stag. This represents the waning and waxing forces of nature as they appear in connection with the God. The theme represents the covenant between the hunter and the hunted. The wolf pelt also symbolizes the death aspect of the God as Lord of the Underworld. The stag represents the God's role in the protection of the forest, the primal source. His animal fur boots reveal that the God walks in the feral ways of nature and is not domesticated by the society that embraces him.

Like the God of Witchcraft, the Goddess also appears as a Mystery figure with symbolic representations in her imagery. The Goddess wears a silver circlet bearing a crescent Moon with the tips upward. To both sides of the circlet, her hair is adorned with vervain blossoms. On her neck is a necklace of thirteen pearls. From the necklace is suspended a silver triangle with a black sphere set in the center. The tip of the triangle is upright.

The Goddess wears a gown that is unfastened and fully exposes her left breast and shoulder. The gown parts slightly at the genital area and splits open to reveal her right leg. The gown is of dark velvet color. In her left hand, the Goddess holds a distaff of unspun flax. On her left arm, a serpent is coiled three times around it. In her right arm is held a lighted torch.

At her feet on the right side of the Goddess is a cauldron, which rests atop a primitive hearth of stone. Her right foot wears a sandal laced to

the ankle and her left foot is bare. Both feet appear fully beneath her open gown, which touches the ground behind her.

The crown circlet on the head of the Goddess designates her reign as the Moon Goddess. The vervain blossoms in her hair symbolize her connection with the Faery race, of whom she is Queen. Around her neck, the Goddess wears thirteen pearls, which represent the Moons within a year.

The triangle suspended from the necklace symbolizes her triple nature as Maiden, Mother, and Crone. The black sphere in the center is her fourth hidden nature. This is the Enchantress who goes unseen during the three nights in which the Moon is not visible. The triangle points upward indicating that the Goddess is the inward path of enlightenment. The tip points to the inner thread that holds the pearls together, for therein is the hidden work of the divine process.

The untied gown of the Goddess indicates that she can reveal or conceal her nature as she wishes. The bare left shoulder shows that she is not hidden in her own realm. Her covered right shoulder indicates that in the mortal world, the Goddess cannot be fully perceived.

As the gown parts, the genital area of the Goddess is only partially shown. Here, it is like the Moon amidst the clouds at night. The symbolism tells us that the generative power of the Goddess is both in this realm and in the next. It is seen and yet unrevealed at the same time.

In the distaff of unspun flax is the Harvest Lord bound to the Goddess. The serpent wrapped around her arm is the sexual and healing energy of the Goddess that transforms all that she favors. The torch in her right hand is her light in the world of mortals. The light of her torch reveals the path that awaits those who worship the Goddess.

The cauldron of the Goddess points to her as the womb of transformation, the giver and receiver of life. Her essence is the mystical brew within the cauldron. The hearth of stone represents the ancient grotto, the origin of her veneration. The darkness in the opening of the hearth symbolizes the passage to and from the Underworld. This is the Moon Gate that connects the past generation with the present one.

The sandal on the right foot of the Goddess symbolizes the extension of her nature to the walk of mortals through life. Only with the sandal of the Goddess can the initiate enter the Moon Gate into the Otherworld of their choosing. Historian Peter Kingsley

(*Ancient Philosophy, Mystery and Magic*, 1995) notes that a single bronze sandal was the "chief sign or symbol of Hecate" in ancient times. Kingsley also states that Hecate was the "mediator between this world and the next." The bare left foot of the Goddess symbolizes that she is not separable from the nature of the lunar and astral substance that supports the Otherworld.

Each symbol appearing in the imagery of the Goddess and God statues preserves a teaching related to the specific detail. Initiates are trained in each study so that they may pass on the teachings to others when they become priestesses or priests. In this way, the ancient knowledge is preserved for future generations.

When selecting statues for your altar, it is beneficial to consider the symbolism of the icon. Whenever possible, try and match Goddess and God images. In this way, the symbolism complements and works in harmony with the polarity of deity forms expressed within the statues or images.

The Circle as an Energy Field

Within the Mystery view, the circle is perceived as a containment field of energy. The polarity of the field prevents disharmonious energy from penetrating the circle. This is accomplished by the affirmation ·that nothing harmful or disruptive to the rite may enter. The statement alone, of course, is no more effective than saying that you're going to lock the house door but not walking to the door to do so. Energy must accompany intent if one wishes manifestation to take place. Otherwise, it is all fantasy, illusion, or self-deception.

The ritual circle, once properly established, exists in a space between the worlds. This can be pictured as a disk floating within a sphere. The edge of the visible circle (where it has been marked out or traced) borders with the elemental counterpart. The counterpart is evoked in order to establish the circle using the creative elements of Earth, Air, Fire, and Water. Therefore, the ritual circle is actually a circle within a circle.

The outline of the physical circle marks out the barrier, and the ritual participants remain within the interior of the circle. Because the circle is a sphere of energy, some people imagine that standing literally at the circle's edge creates a problem. If the circle were a globe, then the curvature of the sphere would be lowest at the edge and, therefore, the height of the person would extend through that portion of the sphere. However, that is not the reality of the concept, nor is it how the energy of the sphere operates.

The occult nature of the ritual circle reveals that the marked circumference of the circle is a reference point for humans. When we establish an energy sphere as a ritual circle, we actually move into a non-physical realm. Time and space operate differently here, and in this place, we encounter thoughts that become things. For a physical being, the idea that an edge exists becomes a reality, and this helps the consciousness to function within an alien realm.

When viewed as an occult concept, the sphere is larger than the circle. The circle is suspended within the center of the sphere. Between the edge of the ritual circle and the actual edge of the sphere exists elemental energy. At the cardinal points of the physical circle are gateways through the energy field to the edge of the sphere. These are known as the elemental gateways or portals. From here, the way through meets with the Watcher Gates or Portals, which open directly into the Astral Dimension. These points are also known as the *Watchtowers.* Additional information can be found in my previous book, *The Wiccan Mysteries.*

When we examine the occult principle, two things become clear. First, the physical rim of the circle pertains to the Material Realm, and the outer, extended rim pertains to the elemental energy. The second factor that we're talking about is a corridor between two worlds. Here, the physical demarcation is a literal border that refers to a point in time and space between the worlds. It's not the edge of a globe; it's the edge of safety.

For material beings, crossing the barrier can be harmful. This is because passage beyond the barrier forces the aura and the astral body of the Witch into an intense field of energy. The shock can cause harm to the subtle energies of the aura and astral fabric. Damage to either will eventually manifest in some way within the material body to which they are linked ("like attracts like"). On a mundane level, exposure to radiation is not apparent at the time but manifests in or on the body sometime after the event.

The athame is used by the Witch to open a mundane passageway to or from the circle during a ritual. This allows a participant to leave or enter the circle as needed. The athame is a tool of Fire and therefore of transformation. Because of this, the proper use of the athame can establish a safe corridor through the surrounding energy. This corridor leads back to the Material Realm from between the worlds.

In a group ritual, inserting two crossed athames over the edge of the circle can open the doorway. Once inserted, the athames are quickly slid away from each other. This causes an energy disruption in the outer field and a tunnel then forms in the sphere. The athames are then placed on the ground or floor, far away enough from each other to form a walkway between them (usually about two or three feet will work nicely). While the doorway is open and idle, a charged sword or wand can be placed across the opening (on the inside of the circle) to prevent unwelcome energy from flowing inward.

Once opened, the height of the doorway needs to be established. This requires using another tool such as a wand or athame. While standing inside the circle, a Witch touches the opening on the ground or floor between the separated athames with the tool. Next, they will slowly raise the tool above their head and hold the tool out in front, slightly away from the body. The Witch then exits the circle, taking a minimum of three deliberate steps before lowering the tool. At this point, the circle doorway can be safely entered or exited. To close the doorway and reseal the circle, everything is simply done in reverse order.

The opening of a circle by a solitary requires a different method. In such a case, the solitary Witch uses the wand and athame together, crossing them as described when using two athames. The method of opening is the same and the wand and athame are set to mark the width of the walkway. The Witch then pours a line of salt to block the opening (same principle as the sword in the group example). Next, the solitary Witch must lift the wand and athame, holding them outward and away from the body as they stand. The tool is then lifted to just above the head (still away from the body) and the Witch may then exit in the same way described in the group work. To close the doorway and reseal the circle, everything is simply done in reverse order.

The Circle as a Sacred Well

When performing a sabbat or Full Moon ritual, energy is drawn and flows into the circle. There are two schools of thought regarding how this happens. The first holds that the energy enters the circle through the alignment with the divine process that is established at the center of the altar. In other words, it flows through the connection to the inner planes. The triangle comprised of the center candle and two deity candles forms the gateway.

The second school of thought maintains that energy is drawn through the established sphere of energy. In this view, the energy of the sabbat or Full Moon flows directly through the energy sphere and into the ritual or magickal circle. Once inside the circle, the energy is directed from the altar by the priestess or priest of the ritual.

Regardless of how the energy of the seasonal shift or the Full Moon enters the circle, the circle becomes a pool or a well as energy is received. The circle is designed to contain the energy that is raised within or drawn to it. The ritual participants are therefore bathed in the sacred essence of the well.

It is ideal if the Witch can establish a permanent circle area that is outlined in some fashion. The circle can be marked with stones, coarse salt, natural fiber rope, or etched into a floor or pad of some natural material. Stone (or any mineral substance) possesses the nature of remembrance and actually retains some essence of each rite performed within its boundary. Therefore, a presence can be felt in any area where repeated rites have been performed.

In accordance with this principle, a "blessing stone" or "stone of initiation" can be charged for ritual use. This technique requires a small stone and a bowl of water. At the beginning of each seasonal or lunar ritual, the stone is placed on the altar. A bowl of water is set at the West quarter. Once the circle is cast (and before the night's ritual begins), the stone is passed clockwise once around the circle to each member.

When it returns to the altar, it is then carried to the East quarter. Here, it is placed on the circle's edge and left until the close of the circle. Before the circle is dissolved at the close of the rite, the stone is carried to the West and placed in the bowl of water. This symbolizes the rising and setting of the Moon or Sun.

After the night's ritual has been completed, the bowl of water is poured out in libation. The stone is then dried off and passed around to each Witch who attended the rite. After this, it is placed in a pouch for safekeeping. Direct sunlight must never fall upon the stone when it is outside of the pouch. Once the stone has been present in ritual for thirteen Full Moons and a complete cycle of sabbats, it is then fully charged. The stone can now be used in several different ways.

One method of using the stone is to place a drop of oil on it and then use the stone for anointing. A new Witch can be anointed in an initiation rite by gently pressing the stone on the third eye area of the forehead. This helps join the initiate with the group members and aligns the person with the type of rituals performed by the coven. When the stone is returned to the pouch, the new member will join the group as the stone is passed around.

Another method of using the stone is to pour ritual wine over the stone and into the ritual chalice. This charges the wine with the Wheel of the Year energy. It's best not to use a stone that is small enough to simply place in the chalice, as it can accidentally be swallowed. If desired, the stone can be placed in a bowl with the wine and then removed when the wine is ready to pour into the chalice. If the stone has previously been anointed with oil, wash it off thoroughly, as it can taint the taste of the wine.

When using the stone for any type of alignment or joining, an invocation can be performed. Before placing the stone against the forehead or using the wine method, you can say:

"Thirteen Moons have I seen,
From East to West and in between.
Solstice, equinox, and each quarter rite,
Pass I the blessings to you this night."

In the last verse, the word "blessings" can be replaced with the word "vision" or whatever you deem appropriate to the intent.

Offerings and Veneration

The idea of offerings or sacrifices to a Goddess or a God is of extreme antiquity. It is most likely rooted in the idea of appeasement and sharing in order to build an alliance or rapport. Over the course of time, the concept and structure regarding offerings became quite formal.

In the older forms of Witchcraft, it is said that the deities need us as much as we need them. This idea is rooted in the primitive belief that offerings provide sustenance to gods and spirits. From an occult perspective, the numen emanation provides a vital essence that can be drawn upon or absorbed. Therefore, a case can be made for an occult foundation behind the concept.

The Mystery view holds that offerings connect a form to a concept (the intent of the offering) that, in turn, connects to energy and then on to the Source. In this regard, the offering initiates a ripple and triggers a series of reactions across the inner planes. In other words, offerings are catalysts to draw the awareness of deity to something specific. A prayer can be said to fulfill the same function. The difference is that prayer asks to receive without giving something in return. It is an old axiom in the Mystery Tradition that "nothing may be received except that something be given. And nothing may be given except that something be received."

The axiom addresses the teaching that everything is in relationship with everything else. Acknowledgment of this principle and participation in its cycle brings a person into the flow of the divine process. Relationship joins consciousness, and this is the key to offerings made in this context. Offerings draw the Witch and deity together through an agreement of consciousness.

In the context of offerings, an "agreement of consciousness" reflects the occult correspondences associated with specific offerings (i.e., *this* will mean *that*). Also of consideration are the likes and dislikes of deities as reflected in their myths and legends. Such stories contain working examples of the nature and character of any Goddess or God. These have been compiled and passed on by our ancestors.

It is beneficial to learn about what is sacred to a specific deity and what things are associated with its worship. Most deities will have animals, plants, scents, objects, and other things that are favored. Incorporating these things will help establish communication with a specific deity. Communication will help create a relationship.

In modern Witchcraft, there is a tendency to refer to "the Goddess" or "the God" instead of using a specific identifying name. This is not unlike writing to the government and using the salutation of "Dear Government Official." Your communication will be delivered to the building, but will it get to the person in the department you need it to reach? Here again, we must consider the axiom, "as above, so below, and as below, so above."

Using specific names such as Lugh or Diana brings the archetypal consciousness into a specific focus and a resulting emanation. The archetype relates through a name to a finite deity form that is appropriate to the needs of the person calling upon it. This is why our ancestors depicted many goddesses and gods, each having a particular sphere of influence. By analogy, a person would not write to the President of the United States about a matter that is handled by a local city council. Nor would a person call a plumber to deal with a burglar or a police officer to fix a leaky pipe. Instead, we call upon an agreed category and the appropriate associations and correspondences.

Offerings are best placed in a sacred setting and upon a designated plate or in a special bowl. Having a particular offering dish or plate is a sign of veneration and brings energy to the act of offering. Typically, offerings are placed on an altar or in front of a statue or image. This sanctifies the offering because it removes it from the mundane experience.

Classic offerings are fruit, grain, bread, honey, or wine. In various myths, you will find specific things that are sacred to certain deities, and can therefore be used as offerings. Some examples are grapes to Dionysos, spelt grain to Ceres, or pomegranates to Hecate. You can grow herbs as offerings or even plant and grow a tree in honor of a specific deity.

Prayers or requests can be made with an offering, but it is also good to simply give offerings as a gift. From a spiritual perspective, the best request is to ask that one's needs be fulfilled.

In the Mystery Tradition of Witchcraft, ancestral veneration is an important component. Offerings are made at specific times such as at Samhain. They can also be made to observe the anniversary of the crossing of a loved one. The sense of an unbroken connection to loved ones and ancestors can be a meaningful and empowering experience.

Veneration, whether of a deity or the ancestral spirit, is not the same thing as worship. Veneration is a heartfelt deference; an honoring and a reverence towards something or someone. Worship is an ardent devotion that is expressed through rituals and ceremonies. They are similar natures, but veneration is less formal or intense than worship.

The veneration of deity can express itself in the care of an altar or shrine. Keeping it clean and free of debris is an active sign of veneration. The placing of flowers and seasonal decorations on the altar is also a sign. In addition, veneration of deity can be expressed in the dusting and cleaning of deity statues on a weekly basis. Monday, being the day of the Moon, is an excellent time to attend to the Goddess statue. Sunday, the day of the Sun, is a good day to care for the God statue.

Of Time and Season

Our ancestors lived closely in tune with nature in order to survive. The changing of seasons was something of great significance to our ancestors when they were hunter-gatherers as well as an agrarian culture in later times. Today, other than the inconvenience of bad weather and the curtailment of recreation, the changing of the seasons does not impact our lives as seriously as it did our ancestors. It would be more accurate to say that it doesn't affect our awareness to the same degree.

When we look at nature as the Great Teacher, or as the holder of the blueprints or the divine process, we note that there is a specific timing. The cycles of the seasons, the phases of the Moon, and the journey of the Sun all occur in accord with a pre-established pattern. Therefore, time and season are part of the divine process.

It is for this reason that the rites of Witchcraft are performed on specific dates and in accordance with specific phases of the Moon. The ritual or magickal circle serves as a pool into which these energies can flow. Here, the energy is condensed and aligned with the human vibration so that merging can take place.

By participating at the prescribed times, the Witch is bathed in the flow of energy that occurs at these peak levels within nature. The aura of the Witch is then vitalized by the absorption of energy drawn to the circle. When the Witch performs rituals at each sabbat and each Full Moon at the proper time, then the principle of "like attracts like" arises. In this context, the aura of the Witch becomes like the natural pattern of nature, which is the stronger and greater frequency. This means that the Witch becomes more like nature.

When the Witch resonates with the energy of nature, then the inner awareness of balance and purpose arises within their consciousness. Everything within nature is about balance and purpose, even when humans tamper with the natural order. Our ancestors knew and experienced this, but modern humans have collectively removed themselves from the natural flow. The modern Witch works to restore balance and to allow integration.

In ancient tales, Witches are depicted as living away from the cities and among the herb-clad hills. Here, the energy pattern is less contaminated by the auras that cities generate. Creatures that live in the natural order have what we often refer to as "heightened senses."

These senses are actually normal, but because humans have collectively weakened their own senses through the process of "civilization," the senses of wild creatures, therefore, appear to be exceptional.

The human concepts of "wild" and "wilderness" are very revealing. Among the definitions of the word *wild,* you will find a reference to something as being "uncontrolled" or "uncontrollable." Likewise, amidst the definitions of *wilderness,* we find a reference to something that is "perilous." To our distant ancestors, the type of area that was once home is what modern humans now call "wilderness." This view has contributed to a severing of our natural connection to the land and the spirit of the land.

When the Witch opens to the natural flow of "uncivilized" energy, they return to the natural vibration. It is not unlike the benefits of drinking pure clean water as opposed to a soft drink or eating free-range chicken instead of a cage-raised one that is pumped full of hormones and other chemicals. What is absorbed, and the effects of that absorption, is quite a different experience. Ultimately, the matter we consume makes a significant difference in how we feel and function. The same is true of the energy we absorb.

In modern Witchcraft, we find that for some Witches, "close enough" is acceptable. In this view, a sabbat or a full Moon ritual can be performed in accordance with personal convenience. In other words, the ritual takes place on a night when the participants don't have to get up and go to work the next morning. Here, the inconvenience of the natural event does not deter the individual from performing the rite. For example, if the Full Moon or sabbat actually falls on a Wednesday, the individual feels that the rite can be performed as close to that time as their personal schedule permits.

In the Mystery Tradition of Witchcraft, rituals are performed when the energy of a sabbat or Full Moon is actually present and functioning. In this view, appropriate timing is considered necessary in order to align with nature while the process is initiated and put into motion. On a mundane level, it's like catching the bus at the time it arrives and being on it when it moves to the destination.

The value for modern humans regarding the actual timing of a ritual to the date of the event is the alignment with nature. Many Witches live in cities and have no place to perform a ritual beneath the Moon and stars. Cut off from this aspect of Witchcraft, the importance of timing becomes even more significant. This is because each individual thing that separates us from the natural order contributes to our disconnection with its Source.

The Harmony of Spirit

One of the benefits of practicing Witchcraft is the inner peace that it can help bestow. The foundation of this peace is built upon the integration of masculine and feminine polarities within. It also arises from the alignment to nature through the rites of the Wheel of the Year. This directly connects one to the divine process, the inner mechanism that maintains equilibrium throughout the universe.

Earlier in the book, we encountered the concept of balance and its symbolic appearance in the caduceus figure. As a symbol of harmony, it represents opposites held in balance. These polarities are depicted as two serpents, which are representations of magnetic energy.

The two serpents entwine a center staff intersecting at three points, which is a common theme in the Mystery Tradition of Witchcraft. Here, the serpents are named Ob and Od, usually depicted left and right, respectively. The staff around which they coil bears an orb on its top. This orb is called *Aour.*

In occult tradition, Ob is the lunar current and Od is the solar. Their interaction creates a magnetism that is drawing and stabilizing as long as they remain equal. When this is achieved, it creates a state of consciousness known as the *Aour.* Aour is referred to as the perfect equilibrium. As a Mystery symbol, the sphere of Aour is a winged orb.

The practice of Witchcraft brings the Witch into connection with the masculine and feminine polarities of the Source of All Things. This is the Goddess and God consciousness that is reflected in the myths and legends associated with the Wheel of the Year. Through the Mystery Teachings, we learn that this same nature exists within us. This is not surprising when we understand that the Divine created us, and we therefore bear the essential pattern inherent within the divine makeup.

The Wheel of the Year, as a reflection of the divine pattern and intent, teaches us that nothing is caused by chance. Random occurrence is something outside of the pattern, and cannot become part of the divine process. There is comfort and peace in knowing that, as Witches, we actively carry the alignment with the divine process, and are, therefore, not touched by random occurrence. Everything has a reason, a time, and a purpose. From this concept, harmony also arises.

Aradia, the legendary Witch Queen, is said to have taught that the powers of a Witch awaken and are maintained through unbroken participation in the Wheel of the Year. This connection vitalizes the Witch and makes them aware of their personal power. This awareness grants peace and harmony because it bestows self-confidence. The Witch never misuses personal power because they do not act out of fear. All acts of violence are ultimately rooted in fear.

Through participation in the Wheel of the Year, the Witch realizes that they are like everything in nature. The Witch journeys with nature, all its beings, and all it encompasses through the year. Here, the Witch understands that they are never alone or disconnected. The Witch is part of everything that is happening within existence. More importantly, they are a harmonious partner within the Divine process. Here, the Witch finds liberation and identity, a unique individual within a community of souls.

Skyclad Ritual Practice

In Witchcraft, we find the term *skyclad,* which refers to being unclothed and means to be "clad in the sky." References to nudity in Witchcraft are found in ancient tales such as the work titled *Rhizotomoi,* written by Sophocles. In this tale, the Witch Medea appears naked while she uses a bronze sickle to reap herbs.

Ovid, in his work titled *Fasti,* writes of why ritual nudity was commanded in the fertility rites of the god Faunus (one of the deity forms associated with Witchcraft). He also mentions the practice of the Luperci, who annually perform rituals in the nude, and there seems to be a connection between Faunus and the Lupercalia.

Historian Ruth Martin, in her book *Witchcraft and the Inquisition in Venice 1550–1650* (1989) comments that it was a common practice for Witches of this era to be "naked with their hair loose around their shoulders" while reciting conjurations. In several woodcuts from the seventeenth century, we also find Witches dancing naked in a circle.

In the late nineteenth century, folklorist Charles Leland wrote his classic work titled *Aradia: Gospel of the Witches*. The material depicts Witches who gather at the time of the Full Moon. In the text, they are told:

"Whenever you have need of anything, once in the month and when the moon is full, you shall assemble in some desert place. Or in a forest all together join to adore the potent spirit of your Queen, my mother, Diana. She who fain would learn all sorcery yet as not won its deepest secrets, them my mother will teach her, in truth all things as yet unknown. And you shall be freed from slavery, and so you shall be free in everything. And as a sign that you are truly free you shall be naked in your rites, both men and women..." (Leland, *Aradia: Gospel of the Witches*, 1899).

The idea of freedom associated with nudity is nothing new. Many people find it very liberating to experience nudity in a ritual setting with other practitioners. For others, the idea of nudity can be challenging, intimidating, frightening, or even dreaded. The inhibition against nudity is at the very core of what is meant by being free.

The issue for many people who object to practicing nudity is often rooted in shyness, body image, or sexuality. These objections typically have their foundation in the views and limitations that are imposed by society or are self-imposed. People often fear being judged by others and by themselves. In addition, many people come from religious backgrounds that teach shame and guilt associated with open nudity.

Aradia's message is about the freedom to choose, but to do so from a place of liberation and not from captivity. One can be a captive to personal inhibitions and social constraints. The goal is to obtain the freedom of personal choice outside of any attachment to the judgment of individuals or society as a whole. Sometimes the greatest challenge we face in life is the challenge to question whether our beliefs are our own or whether we simply believe what others have led us to accept.

In the reflection upon what our beliefs are, we must also now consider what the Mysteries have spoken to both heart and mind. Let us now recall our journey and what we noted along the way. It is time now to turn to the last chapter and return home from the Mystery Quest.

CHAPTER TEN

Returning from the Mysteries

It was Joseph Campbell who often spoke of the return of the hero. The idea of the hero is that of a quest undertaken to retrieve that which is lost or hidden. In the Mystery Tradition of Witchcraft, we find the *Legend of the Descent of the Goddess*. In this tale, the Goddess descends into the Underworld where she ultimately finds enlightenment and wholeness through the integration of the feminine and masculine polarities within.

For you, the reader, this book has been a journey into the Mysteries. But entering and exploring the Mysteries is of little avail unless one can bring something back from the Otherworld. The journey of the hero is to return with what they have learned, experienced, or retrieved. This is sometimes referred to as "retrieving the cauldron within."

The question now becomes: where have we traveled and what have we gathered for our return from the depths of the Mysteries? Our journey began in an ancient world of primitive beliefs that were expressed in puzzling images and carvings. Here, we noted the evolution of deity forms from bird-like entities to a Great Goddess who transformed into a Mother Goddess. In prehistory, we noted the beginnings of formal burials that included personal effects and we reflected on the dream world and how our ancestors may have linked it to the idea of survival beyond death. We also encountered beliefs related to spirits and discovered the ancient concept of Three Worlds: Overworld, Middleworld, and Underworld.

In the writings of Hesiod, we heard the tale of this half-forgotten prehistoric world. For Hesiod, it was remembered in the fragments of myths and legends that told the tale of the Titans. The Titans, we were told, were an Elder race of deities that belonged to an era before the time of the Olympic gods and goddesses of ancient Greece.

Early in the book, the Witch was depicted in a manner consistent with the etymology of the earliest words used to indicate Witches in Western literature. Here, we found the Witch to be an herbalist and seer. The Witch also appeared as a priestess of a goddess who belonged to a half-forgotten race of the prehistoric period, Hecate of the Titans. We discovered that Hecate was originally a goddess who ruled the Overworld, Middleworld, and Underworld (the ancient worldview of our ancestors). In Roman culture, the Witch is identified with birds, a creature that appears in the earliest iconography used to depict deity during the prehistoric era.

Continuing our journey, we found the Witch associated with the crossroads, a place viewed in ancient times as a portal to the spirit realm. Early tradition also placed the Witch in caves, a theme popular in both Southern and Northern Europe. Caves have also been depicted in ancient lore as doorways to the Underworld. In connection, we encountered the Faeries associated with Witches and the concept of doorways into their mystical realm.

Our quest next turned to explore the Otherworld of myth and legend. Here, we once again encountered the Faery Folk. In addition, we discovered a deep connection in the Otherworld to water, which introduced the fish and the dolphin as mystical beings. In the Otherworld, we came across rivers and mountains that surrounded a hidden realm where the souls of the dead dwell. In this secret place, we encountered the cauldron as a central theme. Here, it served the power of regeneration in the hands of a goddess.

In our Otherworld journey, the theme of the cauldron became linked with fire, stone, and wood. We noted that fire was the earliest formal concept of deity, that stone was used to demarcate ancient gathering sites and erect altars, and that trees were once worshipped as deities. It was here that we first encountered the goddess Brigit, who we found intimately linked with fire. She was also associated with smithwork, and it is the smith who creates cauldrons and hearth tools to tend the fire.

Traveling deeper, we explored the connection between the Women's Mysteries and the hearth tradition of the keepers of the fire. Here again, the cauldron arose as a Mystery symbol. Within the Hearth Mysteries, the broom appeared and we found it connected to Hecate, the Witches' Goddess of the Three Realms. Throughout the book, we noted the preservation of Pagan beliefs and customs, and we encountered the concept of memory-chain associations. These proved to be the keys used by Witches to preserve the Old Religion.

As we passed along the shadow's edge of the Mysteries, the concept that deity dwells within nature arose, which is a core theme within nature religions such as Witchcraft. This brought us to explore the ancient God of Witchcraft. It was noted that he first arises from nature as the Lord of the Forest, the primal god of our ancestors. Here, he is linked with the stag, an animal that supplied food, clothing, and tools to primitive humans. Through this, the God is linked to the idea of the provider.

We next encountered the God as humans left the forest and cultivated the fields for the growing crops. Here, the Lord of the Forest became transformed into the Lord of the Harvest. In this way, the God maintained his role as the provider, changing only in his physical form. But the Stag-Horned God does not vanish; he reappears within pastoral cultures in the form of animals appropriate to this new way of living. Therefore, we find him with the horns of a bull and later with the horns of a goat. Yet, within agrarian culture, the God is popularly disguised as the Green Man.

Traversing the open fields, we were led through the Harvest Lord connections where we discovered the concept of the Sacrificial King or Slain God figure. It was here that the connection between seeds and the God became of paramount importance. Here, the idea of the spirit of the land and the burial of the seed and the God merged within the mythos.

The Sun rising, seemingly from the Earth, as it climbed above the horizon linked the God to the spirit of the land. As night vanished beneath the rays of the Sun, so too did the realm of dreams, and the God became viewed as the banisher of darkness and danger. In time, the care of the dead was given over to the Sun God, who escorted them to and from the Underworld in his setting and rising.

Looking to the sky, we beheld the importance of keeping the Sun God bound to the land. This is reflected in the hard work employed to cut and gather in the harvest each season. The seeds must be cared for and preserved for the next season of planting. The spirit of the land must never escape. In the importance of the God as a fertility symbol, we found the old Lord of Forest appearing in agrarian societies with a large club. Here, we noted such figures as Dagda, Silvanus, and Hercules.

A needed God that meets death is a God that requires rebirth. In Chapter Three, we found the newborn Sun God who is called the *Child of Promise*. This name also befits the seed, which promises to be a new plant for the next harvest. Here, we find the young God bearing such names as Mabon, Hermes, or Dionysos. The idea of a waning or setting Sun brought us to the concept of the Lord of the Underworld. Here, we found him not as something dark or dreaded, but as the Lord of the Riches that are beneath the Earth. The richness of mineral gems was not the only prize of the Underworld God, for it was also from beneath the earth that the harvest rose again from seed. Therefore, the Lord of the Underworld was a deity of life.

As our journey continued, we encountered the Hammer or Smith God, a deity associated with primal fire and transformation. He is the only god who can control the relationship between undomesticated fire and the power of transformation. The Smith God appeared to us under such names as Sucellus, Goibniu, and Hephaestos (or Vulcan). Among his many symbols, we discovered the dog, a frequent companion. The hound is the classic animal form of the Goddess of Witchcraft, which suggests an implied relationship. When we consider that Brigit is a Smith Goddess, we are given more to consider.

In Chapter Four, the Goddess of Witchcraft was introduced in her many forms. She first appeared as a bird-like deity associated with wetlands. In time, she rose to the position of the Great Goddess. This was the giver and taker of all life, who, in time, evolved into the Mother Goddess.

As the Mystery Tradition evolved, we noted a focus on the Moon Goddess and a triformis nature. The phases of the Moon became linked to the phases of human life: youth, maturity, and old age. These became personified as the Maiden, Mother, and Crone. Because the menstrual cycles of women were associated with the phases of the Moon, it was only natural to personify the triformis nature as a female.

As the lunar-based concepts evolved, the Moon Goddess gave birth to a son who eventually became the Sun God, one light birthing another. In the mythos, he is both her son and her consort. This notion may have evolved from prehistoric times when the adolescent son protected the mother during periods when others were away on hunting trips. The taboo against incest came at a later period, and we cannot discount an intimate relationship between mother and son in prehistoric times. For more information on this topic, I refer the reader to my previous book, *The Wiccan Mysteries*.

The idea of a Moon Goddess naturally led to noting that moonlight possesses special qualities. In the context of the Mysteries, these qualities are both magickal and spiritual. In previous chapters, we noted the ancient concept of Drawing Down the Moon and the presence of the cauldron in Witchcraft. The cauldron appears in ancient myths and legends throughout continental Europe and the British Isles. Here, it appears with the power to transform and regenerate.

In Chapter Four, we discovered the Star Goddess and her connection to the constellation known as the *Corona Borealis*. We noted the association of Arianrhod and Ariadne with this star pattern and the legend of Taliesin that links the constellation to the Otherworld Realm. Here, the Goddess becomes linked to the abode of departed souls.

The theme of the Goddess as an Underworld deity is not surprising when we consider the course of the Moon and its setting in the West. The Western quarter has long been associated with the Otherworld and the Underworld. Therefore, a Moon Goddess disappearing beneath the Western horizon, and one who is absent from the night sky for three days, is easily linked to the Hidden Realm.

The concept of a gateway (the West) and a Hidden Realm (Otherworld or Underworld) within a Mystery Tradition naturally evokes the thought of a guardian and a guide. This leads us back to the goddess Hecate, who has long been associated with doorways, crossroads, and spirit realms. In ancient times, she was viewed as a triformis goddess who stood at the three roads, which constituted a crossroad in ancient times. Symbolically, the three roads can be viewed as past, present, and future.

Hecate belongs to the torch-bearing class of goddesses which links her to night and the night realms. In ancient art, she is frequently depicted carrying two torches, one to shed light on where we stand and the other to give light on where we can go.

In Chapter Four, we encountered the Fates, a triformis concept rooted in the ancient belief of the "daughters of the night." We noted that the darkness of night represented that which is hidden or veiled and the potential of all that is yet unseen. The image of the Fates became linked to the spindle and the idea of weaving. Perhaps this arose from the setting in which women spun wool at night when the daily chores of hearth, home, and family were put to rest.

In Chapter Five, we explored the connections of Witchcraft to ancient themes and symbols. Here, we came across the places of Standing Stones and the concept of the Sacred Grove. This led us to explore the ancestral connection and its current of energy that flows from the Underworld. In our exploration, the sacred branch arose as a powerful symbol. Throughout the book, we noted the importance of the Silver Bough or Golden Bough, a magickal branch that allowed the living to journey to and from the Underworld or Otherworld.

The idea of the path or guided journey is well represented in the concept of the memory-chain association, which we encountered in Chapter Five. Here, we explored the idea of ancestral and genetic memory. We also came to understand that the memory-chain association is a bridge to the momentum of the past.

In Chapter Five, we looked at the connection between reincarnation, memory-chain associations, and the momentum of the past. We noted that time is spherical and not linear, which led us to the notion that all time periods exist together at different points along the sphere. It is here that the connection to memory-chain association vitalizes the concept of the momentum of the past. Here, we see it as bridging two places within the sphere, which results in a linear expression of time between the two simultaneous events. In other words, the so-called "past" event becomes available to the consciousness of the person in the "present" through a mental linking of mental concepts ("like attracts like"). The mechanical process is not unlike transferring files on a hard drive to a disk, or vice versa.

In Chapter Six, we turned to the mythos of the Wheel of the Year. Here, we were introduced to the tides of power that flow through and across the Earth at different points in the year. The nature of these energies became personified into various deities that represent aspects of the divine consciousness at work within the process. Participating in these shifting tides through sabbat rituals establishes an alignment with the inner mechanism. This, in turn, links our own nature to the natural flow which keeps order and balance within our spiritual condition. Ritual serves as a means of interfacing with the divine consciousness that is present in the inner mechanism of the seasonal shifts. This helps establish and maintain a line of communication to and from the Source of All Things.

It was through our study of the inner mechanism within nature that the teaching of "seed and sprout, and stem and leaf, and bud and flower" arose. Here, we discovered that our ancestors formed a spiritual and magickal system rooted in this cycle. From this arose the Harvest Lord, the idea that the spirit of the land carries the life cycle. To become one with the Harvest Lord is to align with the very essence of that life cycle, which is ever-renewing. We see the very core of the ceremonial purpose behind cakes and wine in Craft ritual, which is a rite of union. As the popular saying goes, "you are what you eat."

In the Wheel of the Year, we see the journey of the seed (its life cycle) expressed in the myths and legends of various gods and goddesses. This is also the story of our own journey, which is vitalized and held integral through participation in the Wheel of the Year experience. This is one of the reasons why Mystery Traditions exist; they merge the participant with the process so the two become one. It is the same principle of magick where the image becomes the concept.

Just as the seed produces a plant that produces fruit (through the process), our journey also leads to fruit; a fruit of the Mysteries. Previously in the book, we came upon the concept of the Moon Tree and its fruit of enlightenment. This essential theme also presented itself in the faery apple and the sacred bough, which allowed a mortal to freely enter and leave the mystical realm. The fruit also nourished the mortal and sustained them on their quest. It is still what nourishes and sustains those who practice the Mystery Tradition of Witchcraft.

In old lore, the faery apple or sacred bough allowed a mortal to enter the Otherworld. This means that it also allowed them to leave the mortal world (as in not having to remain there). In the Otherworld, the apple or bough allowed the mortal to leave this realm as well, for no mortal could do so of their own will without the sacred object. Here, we can view the fruit as a metaphor that represents spiritual liberation. In this context, the fruit of the Mysteries is the ability to freely sever the unwanted and reach the desired.

In Chapter Six, we noted that the Moon Tree is adorned with either thirteen blossoms or torches. These represent the completed journey of the Moon through the Wheel of the Year. The fruit of the Moon Tree is produced from the completed process, which in Mystery terminology takes "a year and a day." Like the process itself, the fruit bears within it the divine essence. It is initiation and directly experiencing the difference between knowledge and realization.

The concept of the Moon Tree is rooted in the archaic origins of the pillar of wood at the crossroads. This brings us back to Hecate, as do all things that are associated with Witchcraft. The pillar is symbolic of the one sacred tree that stands in the center of the Sacred Grove of the Goddess. The sacred tree is rooted in the past, secured in the present, and extends out to the future. This is also true of the Mysteries of Witchcraft.

In the oral tradition of the Old Religion, it is said that a sacrificial candidate was bound to a tree or wooden pole. As we noted in previous chapters, the tree is the bridge between the worlds. Here, the tree, as the Mother Goddess, received the blood of the Slain God back into herself. In this way, his spirit was tied to the land and bound to the Mother. It is a teaching of great antiquity.

An interesting connection arises between Hercules and the sacred tree. As we noted earlier, Hercules is a Slain God figure in the Mysteries. In one of his tales, he is assisted in obtaining the sacred apples by the daughters of Atlas. Their mother is Hesperis, a personification of the Western region where the Sun dwelled beneath the horizon. Here, the sacred golden apples grew in abundance. In mythology, the seven daughters of Atlas become the constellation known as *the Pleiades*. The Pleiades rise following the spring equinox and set following the autumn equinox. The constellation appears with Taurus the bull, and as we noted, the bull is one of the guises of the Horned God, which is another Slain God figure.

In Chapter Seven, we explored each sabbat, its associated deities, and the lore that surrounds each season. The sabbats reflect an ongoing mythos that tells the story of gods and goddesses who change names and attributes but whose essence remains. In the solar mythos of the

Wheel of the Year, it is possible to construct a cohesive theme that can be expressed throughout the year. Using the Celtic pantheon, we find the god Angus Og born on the winter solstice. He grows into adolescence by Imbolc, and at the spring equinox, he emerges under the name Lugh or Llew.

With the onset of Beltane, the Sun God courts his bride-to-be. He marries at midsummer, enjoys the fullness of his days at Lughnasadh, and then dies at the time of the autumn equinox. In the Underworld, he takes on the name Mabon, which marks his imprisonment in the Otherworld and the separation from the Mother Goddess. This enclosure is a rite of initiation, which we shall see later in the chapter.

At the time of Samhain, the God returns to his primal nature; the seed bearer and the seed. Here, in the Otherworld Realm, the God takes on the name Dagda and reigns as the King of the Faery Race, the Tuatha de Danann. In time, the Great Mother comes to him from the world of mortal kind. Sometime during their sojourn, they mate, and Dagda is drawn into her womb as the seed is drawn into the soil. He is then born on the winter solstice as Angus Og, and so the cycle continues.

A similar construction can be applied to Brigit or Brighid. At the winter solstice, she is Matrona, the Divine Mother who gives birth to the Sun God. She reaches adolescence at Imbolc, where she becomes aware of her power over the primal fire she carried with her from the Underworld or Otherworld. Here, she takes the name Brigit, the exalted one. The word *exalted* is of interest as it has several meanings, including "to increase the effects or intensity of." As a deity of fire and its connection to the smithcraft and forging, the word *exalted* holds much meaning.

With the arrival of the spring equinox, the Goddess emerges from the Underworld or Otherworld. Lakes (and other bodies of water) are classic openings into the Otherworld realms. It is not difficult to view the return of the Goddess from the waters of the lake. Here, we can view her as the Lady of the Lake, and give her the name *Nimue*. In this persona, she binds the sexual drive of the God (as Nimue once bound Merlin in legend) in order to control it until the rites of May.

At Beltane, the Goddess takes on the name Brid, the Flower Bride. During this season, a maiden is often selected to be the May Queen, and the Goddess may also go by this title. With the arrival of midsummer, the Goddess becomes Bride and marries. In this persona, she remains until the autumn equinox. At this time, she takes on the name *Blodeuwedd* and opens the way for the death of the Sun God. With the arrival of Samhain, the Goddess becomes Boand (or Boanna) and flows into the Underworld where she mates with Dagda to produce Angus Og.

In the book *Ladies of the Lake* by Caitlin and John Matthews, the authors note that to enter the "circle of the Goddess" is to undergo three initiations. This befits our Mystery theme in connection with the Sun God, his consort, and his Underworld journey. The Matthews noted that the first "enclosure" is his existence within the womb of his mother. The second is when he penetrates a woman in a sexual union, and the third is his death when he enters the initiatory temple of the Goddess.

In a sense, this book has brought you into the circle of the Goddess. Early in the book, the seed was planted in the cauldron womb of the Goddess, the mystical cauldron that is found deep within your ancestral memory. Throughout the book, you have been nourished with the waters of the womb, the magickal elixir of the cauldron that bubbled up the concepts we have encountered in these pages.

You have also penetrated the Mysteries, peering into the teachings that compel us to go deeper. Because the Mysteries exist in the circle of the Goddess, we must return in order to understand and discern the many teachings. You now know more than you think you know about the Mystery Teachings in this book, but it must be read again in order to realize the truth of this statement.

I have taken you as far as I can now in your quest for the Mystery Teachings, and can accompany you no further at this time into the circle of the Goddess. Therefore, I must leave you before the entrance to the Temple of Initiation which brings our journey together to an end.

In the Mystery Tradition of Witchcraft, it is taught that all endings are beginnings and all beginnings are endings. The word *initiate* is derived from the Latin word *initiare,* which itself is derived from the Latin *initium*. The latter means "beginning" and indicates an action taken towards achieving a goal.

With this book, you have now initiated a process—a beginning— but only you can continue and fulfill the circle of the Goddess. Congratulations on your initiation into the Mystery Tradition of Witchcraft. There is much work for you to do now, so I will leave you to it. In closing, I impart to you the words of the Mystery blessing: *May you come to know that within you, which is of the eternal gods.*

Appendix One

Equivalent Deities

The list of deities and their compilation here is my own pairing based upon a matching of etymologies, mythical themes, natures, characterizations, and symbolism.

Celtic	Aegan/Mediterranean
Aeracura	Hecate
Angus Og	Apollo, Adonis, Eros
Ariadne	Arianrhod
Belenus	Apollo
Brigit	Minerva
Cernunnos	Dis pater
Cerridwen	Ceres
Dagda	Cronus, Dis Pater, Hercules
Dana	Gaia
Donn	Pluto or Hades
Esus	Silvanus or Faunus
Flidais	Artemis, Diana
Goibhniu	Vulcan or Hephaestus
Lugh	Mercury
Mabon	Apollo, Hermes
Manannan	Neptune or Posiedon
Matrona	Juno
Nodons	Neptune
Ogmios	Faunus or Hercules
Sucellus	Silvanus or Vulcan
Taranis	Jupiter
Teutates	Mars

Appendix Two

Baphomet, the Sabbatic Goat

The image of Baphomet is a classic Mystery Teaching figure designed to challenge the sincerity and depth of dedication one must possess when seeking the Mystery Teachings. Seekers who were afraid of the image and turned from proceeding further failed the test and were never again considered for teaching or training. This is because the seeker allowed appearance alone to be the deciding factor for approaching the Mysteries.

Baphomet is sometimes called the *Goat of the Witches' Sabbat*. Upon its forehead appears the sign of the pentagram with one point in the upward position. This denotes the pentagram as a symbol of light, for the upper point signifies the presence of Divine Spirit. The position of the arms, one raised and one lowered, is the sign of the magician (who draws from the heavens and manifests within the world of matter).

On Baphomet's head appears a torch, which symbolizes the presence of active divine intelligence. The torch sits between the horns to denote its equilibrium. Here it shines as "the soul exalted above matter." However, for a soul to fully function in the Material Realm, it must animate a material form. In the symbol of the torch, the divine flame clings to the torch just as the soul clings to the body.

The seemingly monstrous head of the goat upon a human form symbolizes the compromised condition of the soul that resides in a material body. The generative organ on the body of Baphomet is replaced by the symbol of the caduceus and represents eternal life. The area of the belly is scale-covered, which represents the element of Water and characterizes the emotional nature. Above this appears a circle, which represents the element of Air and characterizes the mind. The pair of wings on the body of Baphomet represents the ability to lift oneself above emotions and intellect, rising to the Spiritual Realm. The androgynous body symbolizes the balance between the masculine and feminine polarities, which is essential for enlightenment.

Appendix Three

The View from Colleges & Cauldrons

In this section, we will explore the different and often opposing views offered by scholars and by those Witches who believe in the antiquity of their religion. The disagreement is essentially centered on what constitutes "evidence" and what does not.

Scholars frequently dismiss as invalid the literary and historical documentation that Witches offer as evidence. Even those scholars who are not dismissive tend to feel that Witches misinterpret the data, which itself is accurate but misunderstood by the Witch. In the latter case, the scholar disagrees with the conclusion the Witch draws from reliable data.

In her book *Solitary Witch* (2003), author Silver Ravenwolf mentions a personal correspondence between herself and scholar Ronald Hutton. Hutton remarks about the ancient Greek philosophers and their views regarding the concept of deity. He goes on to note that there is no indication that the vast majority of common people of that era paid attention to the scholarly position, noting instead that they continued believing in their own perceptions.

What Hutton points out is interesting and demonstrates the fundamental difference between those who practice certain beliefs and those who simply investigate and examine them. Here we find a difference in perception between the heartfelt experience and the intellectual discernment. Hippokrates and Plutarch, for example, were well-known skeptical rationalists who frequently ridiculed the "superstitions" of the "less-educated."

Historian Albert Grenier (*The Roman Spirit in Religion, Thought, and Art*) wrote of the College of the Crossroads, a quasiorder of social misfits and outcasts in ancient times. Grenier states that gods of the streets, fields, roads, and crossroads take such people under their protection.

There would be no record of this sect had it not been for the rivalry between two ancient Romans known as Clodius and Cicero and the disputes between Cicero and another figure named Milo. Clodius paid people to form gangs in order to intimidate the city, and these individuals were drawn from the poor street people of the times. Motivated by extreme poverty, some people from the College of the Crossroads accepted payment in exchange for aiding Clodius and his agenda. In response, Milo organized a conservative gang, and Rome was plagued with bloody rioting until Milo's gang killed Clodius.

Without this incidental recognition of the College of the Crossroads, this curious sect would have disappeared without historical record or notice. The scholarly community would then take the position that no evidence exists of such a cult. Therefore, many scholars would accordingly dispute the reality of this sect in ancient times. To many scholars, an absence (or lack) of evidence automatically equates to nonexistence. However, to be fair, some scholars would simply remain highly skeptical of claims that such a cult ever existed. One can only wonder at the volume of various things that once existed in ancient times but are now denied reality by modern scholars due to a lack of notation.

In Chapter Eight of his book *The Pagan Religions of the Ancient British Isles*, Ronald Hutton writes,

"It would have been inconceivable to any ancient European pagan of whose thought we have evidence, that the purpose of religious ritual was to 'raise' a deity and 'work' with her or him. No ancient goddess or god worth the name could be summoned by worshippers, to a particular place, and there employed."

Hutton's statement is difficult to reconcile with ancient writings and customs. Scholar Franz Cumont (*After Life in Roman Paganism*) quotes an ancient invocation text that reads, *"Come into me Hermes as children do into women's wombs"* (Cumont, 20). This, of course, points to a literal invocation of a deity into a human body.

Another concept that doesn't fit Hutton's view is the ancient temple erected to various deities, which did indeed occupy a particular place. The English word *temple* is derived from the Latin word *templum*. *Templum* signified the abode of deity (associated with divine worship).

In *Solitary Witch*, Hutton is quoted as stating that the concept of Drawing Down the Moon refers to a trick mentioned by Aristophanes related to the Witches of Thessaly. Hutton, like Aristophanes before him, appears to be a skeptic of contemporary beliefs, and seemingly joins the ancient writer in dismissing this ancient practice. However, other ancient writers such as Horace, Ovid, Lucan, and Petronius depict Drawing Down the Moon as a belief in the actual magickal ability performed by Witches.

Horace (*Epodes*) attributes the Witch Canidia with the power to call the Moon down from the stars. Ovid (*Metamorphoses*) depicts the Witch Medea giving an incantation that includes the words *"You too, Moon, I draw down."* Lucan writes, *"Lowered by incantations (the moon) suffers greatly, until, almost on the earth, she drops foam upon the green herbs below."*

What Hutton does not mention in his reference to Aristophanes is the widespread popular belief among the common people related to the ability of Witches to "pull the moon down from the sky." However, modern scholar Richard Gordon (*Imagining Greek and Roman Magick*) describes the concept as rooted in known beliefs of the ancient period. Gordon points to the writings of Petronius (*Satyricon*) in which a Witch speaks of the image of the Moon descending. Gordon also notes Lucan's reference to a magickal substance (*lunare virus*) that is produced on the ground by the Moon's descent.

Another area that Hutton dismisses as having ancient origins is the notion of a triformis goddess in Witchcraft. According to Hutton, the concept of such a goddess in Witchcraft did not appear until the nineteenth century or later. However, there are indeed several references in ancient literature.

Lucan writes of a dialogue wherein a Witch proclaims, *"Persephone, who is the third and lowest aspect of our goddess Hecate."* Ovid, in his work *Metamorphoses,* quotes the Witch Medea who says, *"I pray only that the threeformed Goddess will help me and come to give her blessings to our immense enterprise."* Ovid also presents the hero Jason making an oath to Medea in which he says, *"I will be true by the sacred rites of the threefold goddess."* In various writings, Horace, Ovid, and Lucan present three goddesses as a set of deities that are central to the practice of Witchcraft. These are Hecate, Diana, and Proserpina.

One final area of disagreement that is noteworthy relates to the idea of ritual nudity. Hutton states that there is no support for the concept of Witches practicing nude prior to modern times. However, such references are not difficult to discover.

Sophocles, in his work *Rhizotomoi,* depicts the Witch Medea as being naked while she uses a bronze sickle to reap herbs. Ovid, in *Fasti,* writes of why ritual nudity was commanded in the fertility rites of the god Faunus (one of the deity forms associated with Witchcraft). He also mentions the practice of the Luperci who annually perform rituals in the nude, and there seems to be a connection between Faunus and the Lupercalia.

Historian Ruth Martin, in her book *Witchcraft and the Inquisition in Venice 1550–1650,* comments that it was a common practice for Witches of this era to be "naked with their hair loose around their shoulders" while reciting conjurations. In addition, there are several examples of nudity appearing in various seventeenth-century woodcuts that depict Witches dancing naked.

Bibliography

Adkins, Lesley and Roy. *Dictionary of Roman Religion.* Oxford University Press, 1996.

Allen, Richard Hinckley. *Star Names: Their Lore and Meanings.* Dover Publications Ltd., 1963.

Anderson, William. *Green Man: The Archetype of Our Oneness with the Earth.* HarperCollins, 1990.

Ankarloo, Bengt and Stuart Clark, eds. *Witchcraft and Magic in Europe: Ancient Greece and Rome.* University of Pennsylvania State, 1999.

—. *Witchcraft and Magic in Europe: The Eighteenth and Nineteenth Centuries.* University of Pennsylvania State, 1999.

—. *Witchcraft and Magic in Europe: The Middle Ages.* University of Pennsylvania State, 2001.

—. *Witchcraft and Magic in Europe: The Period of the Witch Trials.* University of Pennsylvania State, 2002.

—. *Witchcraft and Magic in Europe: The Twentieth Century.* University of Pennsylvania State, 1999.

Arbiter, Petronius. *The Satyricon.* Oxford University Press, 2009.

Bailey, Cyril. *Phases in the Religion of Ancient Rome.* University of Berkeley Press, 1932.

Baring, Anne, and Jules Cashford. *The Myth of the Goddess: Evolution of an Image.* Arkana, 1991.

Baring-Gould, Sabine. *Myths of the Middle Ages.* Blandford, 1996.

Baroja, Julio Caro. *The World of Witches.* The University of Chicago Press, 1961.

Bergman, Charles. *Orion's Legacy: A Cultural History of Man as Hunter.* Dutton, 1996.

Bonfante, Larissa. *Etruscan Life and Afterlife.* Wayne University Press, 1986.

Bonnefoy, Yves. ed. *Roman and European Mythologies.* University of Chicago Press, 1992.

Bord, Janet and Colin. *Earth Rites: Fertility Practices in Pre-Industrial Britain*. Granada Publishing Ltd., 1982.

—. *The Secret Country: More Mysterious Britain*. Granada Publishing Ltd., 1980.

Boyle, A.J., and R. D. Woodward, eds. *Ovid: Fasti*. Penguin Books, 2000.

Breslaw, Elain G., ed. *Witches of the Atlantic World*. New York University Press, 2000.

Brumfield, Allaire Chandor. *The Attic Festivals of Demeter and Their Relation to the Agricultural Year*. The Ayer Company, 1981.

Burke, John. *Roman England*. Artus Books, 1983.

Burkert, Walter. *Creation of the Sacred: Tracks of Biology in Early Religions*. Harvard University Press, 1996.

Butler, Samuel, ed. *Homer: The Iliad and the Odyssey*. Platinum Press, 1999.

Calasso, Roberto. *The Marriage of Cadmus and Harmony*. Vintage, 1994.

Campbell, Joseph. *The Hero With A Thousand Faces*. Princeton University Press, 1973.

—. *The Masks of God: Primitive Mythology*. Arkana, 1991.

Case, Paul Foster. *The Tarot: A Key to the Wisdom of the Ages*. Macoy Publishing Company, 1947.

Catullus, Gaius Valerius. *The Poems of Valerius Catullus Translated into English*. William P. Nimmo, 1867.

Clark, Stuart. *Thinking with Demons: The Idea of Witchcraft in Early Modern Europe*. Oxford University Press, 1999.

Clark, Thomas. *The Works of Q. Horatius Flaccus*. David McKay, 1884.

Collingwood, R. G. *Roman Britain*. Barnes and Noble, 1994.

Condos, Theony. *Star Myths of the Greeks and Romans: A Source Book*. Phanes Press, 1997.

Cumont, Franz. *After Life in Roman Paganism*. Yale University Press, 1922.

Cryer, Frederick H., and Marie-Louise Thomsen. *Witchcraft and Magick in Europe: Biblical and Pagan Societies*. University of Pennsylvania Press, 2001.

Ellis, Peter Berresford. *A Dictionary of Irish Mythology*. Oxford University Press, 1991.

Farrar, Janet and Stewart. *The Witches' God: Lord of the Dance*. Robert Hale Ltd., 1989.

Fortune, Dion. *The Circuit of Force*. Thoth Publications, 1998.

—. *The Esoteric Orders and Their Work*. The Aquarian Press, 1982.

—. *Principles of Hermetic Philosophy*. Thoth Publications, 1999.

Frazer, James G. *The Golden Bough: A Study in Magick and Religion*. Macmillan Company, 1972 [1890].

Friend, Hilderic. *Flowers and Flower Lore*. Swan Sonnenschein, 1886.

Gimbutas, Marija. *The Goddesses and Gods of Old Europe: Myths and Cult Images*. University of Berkeley Press, 1982.

—. *The Language of the Goddess*. HarperSanFrancisco, 1991.

Ginzburg, Carlo. *Clues, Myths, and the Historical Method*. John Hopkins University Press, 1992.

—. *Ecstasies: Deciphering the Witches' Sabbath*. Pantheon Books, 1991.

—. *The Night Battles; Witchcraft and Agrarian Cults in the Sixteenth and Seventeenth Centuries*. Routledge and Kegan Paul, 1983.

Goodison, Lucy, and Christine Morris. *Ancient Goddesses, The Myths and the Evidence*. University of Wisconsin Press, 1998.

Gordon, Richard. "Imagining Greek and Roman Magick." *Witchcraft and Magic in Europe: Ancient Greece and Rome*, ed. by Ankarloo and Clark. University of Pennsylvania Press, 1999. 159-276.

Graves, Robert. *The White Goddess*. Farrar, Straus and Giroux, 1948.

Gray, William G. *Evoking the Primal Goddess: Discovery of the Eternal Feminine Within*. Llewellyn, 1989.

—. *Inner Traditions of Magic*. Samuel Weiser Inc., 1970.

—. *Western Inner Workings*. Samuel Weiser, Inc., 1983.

Green, Miranda. *Dictionary of Celtic Myth and Legend*. Thames and Hudson Ltd., 1992.

—. *Symbol and Image in Celtic Religious Art*. Routledge, 1989.

Greenwood, Susan. *The Encyclopedia of Magic and Witchcraft*. Lorenz Books, 2001.

Grenier, Albert. *The Roman Spirit in Religion, Thought, and Art*. Alfred A. Knopf, 1926.

Grigsby, John. *Warriors of the Wasteland: A Quest for the Pagan Sacrificial Cult behind the Grail Legend*. Watkins Publishing, 2002.

Grimassi, Raven. *Encyclopedia of Wicca and Witchcraft (2nd edition, revised)*. St. Paul: Llewellyn, 2003.

—. *Spirit of the Witch*. Llewellyn Publications, 2003.

—. *The Witch's Familiar*. Llewellyn Publications, 2003.

—. *The Witches' Craft*. Crossed Crow Books, 2024.

—. *The Wiccan Mysteries*. Crossed Crow Books, 2023.

Guazzo, Francesco. *Compendium Maleficarum*. Dover Publication, 2012.

Harding, M. Esther. *Woman's Mysteries: Ancient and Modern.* Shambala, 1990.

Harris, Mike. *Awen, the Quest of the Celtic Mysteries.* Sun Chalice Books, 1999.

Haynes, Sybille. *Etruscan Civilization.* J. Paul Getty Trust Publication, 2000.

Hesiod. *Theogony, Works and Days, Sheild.* Translated by Apostolos N. Athanassakis. John Hopkins University Press, 2004.

Highet, Gilbert. *The Classical Tradition: Greek and Roman Influences on Western Literature.* Oxford University Press, 1985.

Hole, Christina. *Witchcraft in England.* B.T. Batsford Ltd., 1947.

Homer. *The Homeric Hymn to Demeter.* Edited by Nicholas James Richardson. Clarendon Press, 1974.

Horace. *Epodes.* Cambridge University Press, 1995.

Hutton, Ronald. *The Pagan Religions of the Ancient British Isles.* Blackwell Publishers Ltd., 1991.

—. *The Stations of the Sun: A History of the Ritual Year in Britain.* Oxford University Press, 1996.

—. *Triumph of the Moon: A History of Modern Pagan Witchcraft.* Oxford University Press Inc., 1999.

Jackson, Nigel Aldcroft. *Call of the Horned Piper.* Capall Bann, 1995.

—. *Masks of Misrule: The Horned God and His Cult in Europe.* Capall Bann, 1996.

Johnston, Sarah Iles. *Hekate Soteira: A Study of Hekate's Roles in the Chaldean Oracles and Related Literature.* The Scholars Press, 1990.

—. *Restless Dead: Encounters Between the Living and the Dead in Ancient Greece.* University of California Press, 1999.

Jones, Evan John, with Chas S. Clifton. *Sacred Mask, Sacred Dance.* Llewellyn Publications, 1997.

Jones, Evan John. *The Roebuck in the Thicket: An Anthology of the Robert Cochrane Witchcraft Tradition.* Capall Bann Publishing, 2001.

Jones, W. H. S. *Pausanias: Description of Greece.* William Heinemann Ltd., 1918.

Kingsley, Peter. *Ancient Philosophy, Mystery, and Magic: Empedocles and the Pythagorean Tradition.* Oxford University Press, 1995.

Kligman, Gail. *Calus: Symbolic Transformation in Romanian Ritual.* University of Chicago Press, 1981.

Kondratiev, *Alexei. The Apple Branch, A Path to Celtic Ritual.* Citadel Press Books, 2003.

Knight, W. F. Jackson, ed. *Virgil: The Aeneid.* Penguin Putnam Inc., 1958.

Levi, Eliphas. *Transcendental Magic.* Weiser Books, 2001.

Lindahl, Carl, et al. *Medieval Folklore: A Guide to Myths, Legends, Tales, Beliefs, and Customs.* Oxford University Press, 2002.

MacKillop, James. *Dictionary of Celtic Mythology.* Oxford University Press, 1998.

Mackenzie, Donald A. *Crete and Pre-Hellenic Europe Myths and Legends.* Gresham Publishing Co., 1917.

Martin, Ruth. *Witchcraft and the Inquisition in Venice 1550–1650.* Basil Blackwell Inc., 1989.

Matthews, Caitlin. *Mabon and the Guardians of Celtic Britain.* Inner Traditions International, 2002.

Matthews, Caitlin and John. *Ladies of the Lake.* The Aquarian Press, 1992.

Matthews, John. *The Quest for the Green Man.* Quest Books, 2001.

—. *Taliesin: The Last Celtic Shaman.* Inner Traditions International, 2002.

—. *The Winter Solstice.* Quest Books, 1998.

McCall, Andrew. *The Medieval Underworld.* Barnes and Noble Books, 1993.

McNeill, F. Marian. *Scottish Folklore and Folk Belief Vol. 1.* William Maclellan, 1977.

Merrifield, Ralph. *The Archaeology of Ritual and Magic.* New Amsterdam Books, 1988.

Murray, Alexander. *Who's Who in Mythology.* Crescent Books, 1988.

Narby, Jeremy. *The Cosmic Serpent: DNA and the Origins of Knowledge.* Penguin Putnam Inc., 1998.

Neumann, Erich. *The Great Mother: An Analysis of the Archetype.* Princeton University Press, 1972.

Normand, Lawrence, and Gareth Roberts. *Witchcraft in Early Modern Scotland.* University of Exeter Press, 2000.

Ogden, Daniel. *Magic, Witchcraft, and Ghosts in the Greek and Roman Worlds.* Oxford University Press, 2002.

Otto, Walter F. *Dionysus, Myth and Cult.* Indiana University Press, 1965.

Ovid. *Metamorphoses.* Translated by Frank Justus Miller. Harvard University Press, 1960.

Paine, Lauran. *Witchcraft and the Mysteries.* Taplinger Publishing Company, 1975.

Pennick, Nigel. *The God Year.* Capall Bann Publishing, 1998.

Pocs, Eva. *Between the Living and the Dead: A Perspective on Witches and Seers in the Early Modern Age.* Central European University Press, 1999.

Purkiss, Diane. *The Witch in History: Early Modern and Twentieth-Century Representations*. Routledge, 1996.

Pyle, Howard. *The Merry Adventures of Robin Hood of Great Renown in Nottinghamshire*. Scribner's, 1883.

Ravenwolf, Silver. *Solitary Witch: The Ultimate Book of Shadows for the New Generation*. Llewellyn Publications, 2003.

Rabinowitz, Jacob. *The Rotting Goddess: The Origin of the Witch in Classical Antiquity*. Autonomedia, 1998.

Riley, H. T. *The Pharsalia of Lucan*. George Bell & Sons, 1909.

Rolleston, T. W. *Myths and Legends of the Celtic Race*. George G. Harrap and Company, 1911.

Russell, Jeffrey. *A History of Witchcraft*. Thames and Hudson Ltd., 1980.

Sagan, Carl, and Ann Druyan. *Shadows of Forgotten Ancestors*. Ballantine Books, 1992.

Scullard, H. H. *Roman Britain; Outpost of the Empire*. Thames and Hudson, 1979.

Seznec, Jean. *The Survival of the Pagan Gods: The Mythological Tradition and Its Place in Renaissance Humanism and Art*. Princeton University Press, 1953.

Simpson, D. P. *Cassell's Latin Dictionary*. Macmillan Publishing Compay, 1968.

Simpson, J. and S. Roud. *The Oxford Dictionary of English Folklore*. Oxford University Press, 2000.

Spence, Lewis. *The Magic Arts in Celtic Britain*. Aquarian Press, 1970.

Squire, Charles. *Celtic Myth and Legend*. New Page, 2001.

Stewart, R. J. *Celtic Gods and Celtic Goddesses*. Blandford, 1990.

—. *Power Within the Land: The Roots of Celtic and Underworld Traditions, Awakening the Sleepers and Regenerating the Earth*. Element, Inc., 1992.

—. *The Underworld Initiation: A Journey Towards Psychic Transformation*. The Aquarian Press, 1985.

—. *The Waters of the Gap: Magick, Mythology and the Celtic Heritage*. Ashgrove Press, 1989.

Valiente, Doreen. *Witchcraft for Tomorrow*. St. Martin's Press, 1978.

Valiente, Doreen, and Evan Jones. *Witchcraft, A Tradition Renewed*. Phoenix Publishing, 1990.

Walton, Evangeline. *The Mabinogion Tetralogy*. The Overlook Press, 2002.